VIOLENCE IN THE FORUM

Factional Struggles in Ancient Rome (133–78 BC)

Natale Barca

CASEMATE

Pennsylvania & Yorkshire

Published in the United States of America and Great Britain in 2024 by
CASEMATE PUBLISHERS
1950 Lawrence Road, Havertown, PA 19083
and
47 Church Street, Barnsley, S70 2AS, UK

Hardcover Edition: ISBN 978-1-63624-447-1
Digital Edition: ISBN 978-1-63624-448-8

A CIP record for this book is available from the British Library

Map on page xxxii © Casemate Publishers.

Printed and bound in the United Kingdom by CPI Group (UK) Ltd, Croydon, CR0 4YY

Typeset in India by Lapiz Digital Services, Chennai.

For a complete list of Casemate titles, please contact:

CASEMATE PUBLISHERS (US)
Telephone (610) 853-9131
Fax (610) 853-9146
Email: casemate@casematepublishers.com
www.casematepublishers.com

CASEMATE PUBLISHERS (UK)
Telephone (0)1226 734350
Email: casemate@casemateuk.com
www.casemateuk.com

Contents

Abbreviations and Acronyms   v

Glossary   ix

Preface   xxxiii

Introduction   xxxix

I   A Bloody Reform   1

II   The Politicization of Justice   25

III   The Italic Question   33

IV   A Mysterious Death   41

V   The Massacre on the Aventine   47

VI   Saturninus's Tribuneship   65

VII   An Excellent Crime   93

VIII   The Social War   99

IX   Sulpicius's Tribuneship   109

X   The Outbreak of Civil War   117

XI   Marius and Cinna Capture Rome   127

XII   Marius's Reign of Terror   141

XIII   The Death of Marius   155

XIV   Sulla's Proscriptions   163

Conclusions   177

Chronology   183

References   185

Further Reading   188

Indexes   199

Abbreviations and Acronyms

Primary sources

Aen.	Vergil, *Aeneid*
App. *B. Civ.*	Appian, *Civil War (Bella civilia)*
App. *Mithr.*	Appian, *The Mithridatic Wars*
Asc. *Sc.*	Asconius, *In Defense of Marcus Scaurus*
Aur. Vict.	Aurelius Victor, *Of Illustrious Men*
Cic. *Ac.*	Cicero, *On Academic Skepticism*
Cic. *Amiciis*	Cicero, *Letters to his Friends*
Cic. *Arch.*	Cicero, *In Defense of Aulus Licinius Archias*
Cic. *Balb.*	Cicero, *In Defense of Lucius Cornelius Balbo*
Cic. *Brut.*	Cicero, *Brutus*
Cic. *Cael.*	Cicero, *In Defense of Marcus Caelius Rufus*
Cic. *Cat.*	Cicero, *Cataline Orations*
Cic. *Clu.*	Cicero, *On Behalf of Aulus Cluentius*
Cic. *de Orat.*	Cicero, *On the Orator*
Cic. *Dom.*	Cicero, *On his House*
Cic. *Fin.*	Cicero, *On the Ends of Good and Evil*
Cic. *Leg.*	Cicero, *On the Laws*
Cic. *Luc.*	Cicero, *Lucullus*
Cic. *Mur*	Cicero, *In Defense of Lucius Licinius Murena*
Cic. *Nat. D.*	Cicero, *On the Nature of the Gods*
Cic. *Off.*	Cicero, *On Duties*
Cic. *Pis.*	Cicero, *Against Piso*
Cic. *Planc.*	Cicero, *In Defense of Gnaeus Plancius*
Cic. *Rab. Perd.*	Cicero, *On Behalf of Gaius Rabirius*
Cic. *Rep.*	Cicero, *On the Commonwealth*
Cic. *Rosc. Am.*	Cicero, *In Defense of Sextus Roscius of Ameria*
Cic. *Sest.*	Cicero, *In Defense of Publius Sestio*
Cic. *Sulla*	Cicero, *In Defense of Publius Cornelius Sulla*
Cic. *Verr.*	Cicero, *Against Gaius Verres*

CIL   *Corpus Inscriptionum Latinarum* (1863–)

Comm. Bern. at *Luc.*   *Commentaria Bernensia, Lucan's On the Civil War*

Comm. Pet.   Pierre-Daniel Huet, *Commentarius De Rebus Ad Eum Pertinentibus*

Dig.   *Digest of Justinian*

Dio   Cassius Dio, *Roman History*

Diod. Sic.   Diodorus Siculus, *Library of History*

Dion. Hal.   Dionysius of Halikarnassos, *Roman Antiquities*

Eutr.   Eutropius, *Abridgement of Roman History*

Firm. Mat.   Firmicus Maternus

Flor.   Florus, *Epitome of Roman History*

Gell.   Gellius, *Attic Nights*

Gran. Lic.   Granius Licinianus, *Epitome of Roman History*

ILLRP   *Inscriptiones Latinae Liberae rei publicae*

Liv.   Livy, *History of Rome*

Liv. *Per.*   Livy, *The Periochae*

Luc.   Lucan, *Pharsalia*

Obseq.   Julius Obsequens, *Book of Prodigies*

Od.   Homer, *The Odyssey*

ORF4   H. Malcovati, *Oratorum Romanorum Fragmenta*, 4th ed. (1962)

Oros.   Orosius, *Histories against the Pagans*

Ov. *Am.*   Ovid, *Amores*

Ov. *Fast.*   Ovid, *Fasti*

Ov. *Tr.*   Ovid, *Tristia*

Paus.   Pausanias, *Description of Greece*

Plin.   Pliny the Elder, *Natural History*

Plut. *C. Grac.*   Plutarch, *Life of Caius Gracchus*

Plut. *Caes.*   Plutarch, *Life of Caesar*

Plut. *Comp. Ag. Gracch.*   Plutarch, *Comparison of Agis and Cleomenes and the Gracchi*

Plut. *Luc.*   Plutarch, *Life of Lucullus*

Plut. *Mar.*   Plutarch, *Life of Marius*

Plut. *Pomp.*   Plutarch, *Life of Pompey*

Plut. *Publ.*   Plutarch, *Life of Publicola*

Plut. *Sert.*   Plutarch, *Life of Sertorius*

Plut. *Sulla*   Plutarch, *Life of Sulla*

Plut. *T. Grac.*   Plutarch, *Life of Tiberius Gracchus*

Polyb.   Polybius, *Histories*

Prop.   Propertius, *Elegiae*
Ps. Aur. Vict.   Pseudo Aurelius Victor, *Of Illustrious Men*
Quint. *Inst.*   Quintilian, *Institutes of Oratory*
Rhet. Her.   Unknown, *Rhetoric for Herennius*
Sal.   Sallust, *The War with Cataline*
Sen. *Clem.*   Seneca the Younger, *On Mercy*
Sen. *Ep.*   Seneca the Younger, *Letters*
Sen. *Helv.*   Seneca the Younger, *On Consolation to Helvia*
Sen. *Min.*   Seneca the Elder, *On Consolation to Marcia*
Serv.   Servius, *Commentary on the Aeneid*
Strab.   Strabo, *Geography*
Suet. *Iul.*   Suetonius, *The Life of Julius Caesar*
Tac. *Dial.*   Tacitus, *Dialogue of the Orators*
Ter. *Haut.*   Terence, *The Self-Tormentor*
Tib. *Corpus Tib.*   Tibullus, *Corpus Tibullianum*
Val. Max.   Valerius Maximus, *Memorable Deeds ad Sayings*
Varro, *Ling.*   Varro, *On the Latin Language*
Veg. *Epit.*   Vegetius, *Concerning Military Matters*
Vell. Pat.   Velleius Paterculus, *History of Rome*
Vitr.   Vitruvius, *The Ten Books on Architecture*

Journals

AAN   *Atti dell'Accademia di Scienze Morali e politiche della Società Nazionale di Scienze, Lettere e Arti di Napoli*
AAntHung   *Acta Antiqua Academiae Scientiarum Hungaricae*
AFLN   *Annali della Facoltà di Lettere e Filosofia dell'Università di Napoli*
AHR   *American Historical Review*
AJPh   *American Journal of Philology*
AncSoc   *Ancient Society*
ANRW   *Aufstieg und Niedergang der römischen Welt*
CA   *Classical Antiquity*
CJ   *The Classical Journal*
CPh   *Classical Philology*
CQ   *Classical Quarterly*
CR   *Classical Revue*
CSCA   *California Studies in Classical Antiquity*
CW   *Classical World*

DUJ	*Durham University Journal*
Hant	*Hispania Antiqua; revista de historia antigua*
Historia	*Historia: Zeitschrift für Alte Geschichte*
Hist Z	*Historische Zeitschrift*
HSCPh	*Harvard Studies in Classical Philology*
JRS	*Journal of Roman Studies*
J. Savants	*Journal des Savants*
MDAIR	*Mitteilungen des deutschen archäologischen Instituts, Römische Abteilung*
MEFRA	*Mélanges d'Archéologie et d'Histoire de l'école Française de Rome, Antiquité*
MIL	*Memorie dell'Istituto Lombardo Accademia di Scienze e Lettere, Cl. Di Lettere, Sc. morali e storiche*
PAPHS	*Proceedings of the American Philosophical Society*
PBSR	*Papers of the British School at Rome*
RE	*Realencyclopädie der classichen Altertumswissenschaft*
REA	*Revue des etudes anciennes*
RFIC	*Rivista di filologia e di istruzione classica*
RIL	*Rendiconti dell'Istituto Lombardo, Classe di Lettere, Scienze morali e storiche*
RSCI	*Rivista di studi classici*
RSS	*Rassegna storica salernitana*
RUB	*Rèvue de l'Université de Bruxelles*
SCI	*Scripta Classica Israelica: year of the Israeli Soc. for the promotion of classical studies*
SLLRH	*Studies in Latin Literature and Roman History*
Studi. stor.	*Studi storici per l'antichità classica*

Glossary

Note: Almost all the dates referred to in this book are BC, and therefore all dates are to be understood as BC unless otherwise indicated. Numbers indicated in parentheses refer to calendar years; for example, (88) means 88 BC.

aedilis (pl. aediles) A magistrate, elected by the people. There are two plebeian aediles and two patrician aediles. The latter are named *curulis* (curule aediles) because they sit on a folding chair called a *sella curulis*. The curule aedileship is open to plebeians every other year. The aediles are responsible for maintaining public buildings and the road, water, and sewage networks; regulating commercial activities to prevent speculation and abuse, as well as public festivals; protecting the public peace; and supplying the city. They control the weights and measures, prices, and the quality of foodstuffs sold on the market. In times of crisis, they make grain available for sale. They also take care of the public archives and monitor vehicular traffic and grain handouts to the people, with the power to issue fines. The patrician aediles also organize public games and act as secretaries for tribunes of the plebs when the latter issue sentences. Like praetors, they are required to issue an edict at the start of their mandate to establish the rules they will abide by while fulfilling their duties.

aerarium The public treasury.

ager publicus populi Romanorum Public land; the collective property of the Roman people.

amicitia

A bond of friendship or pact of alliance established between equals. It is closely related to *fides* ("loyalty, dependability") and implies the individuals' mutual commitment to help each other reach common political goals, for example, in elections.

aristocrats, aristocracy

Members of senatorial and consular families. They may be patricians or enriched plebeians.

augur

A specialist in divination.

auspicium (pl. auspicia)

Augury, divination, prediction, omen, portent. *Auspicia* are the divine signs that must be consulted before performing any public activity to ensure that it has been blessed by the gods. If the convening magistrate is a consul, his remit may be limited by a tribune vetoing the undertaking or completion of proceedings.

basilica

A large, two-story building, almost twice as long as it is wide, for administering justice and handling business affairs. The interior is split into one central nave and two side naves, separated by rows of columns, while a colonnaded portico runs along the sides of the exterior.

censor (pl. censores)

A magistrate, elected by the people, responsible for updating the census lists, conducting a census of the population every five years, and safeguarding the homogeneity and cohesion of the senatorial structure regarding the entry of unwanted persons and senators who have become undesirable. In other words, those eligible for senatorial rank (those elected to the praetorship) must pass the filter of the censors to be elected to the Senate. After being admitted, they can be expelled for moral reasons or because they have been sentenced to a punishment that includes the loss of Roman citizenship and the confiscation of their possessions. The censors also contract out commissions for public works and the supply of goods and services to the state administration, including the tax office (collecting taxes from the provinces), particularly coveted by the *publicani*.

civitas	Roman citizenship, to which a series of rights and duties were connected. The level of citizenship could be full (*c. optimo iure*) or without the right to vote (*c. sine suffragio*).
cliens (**pl.** *clientes*)	Those Roman citizens who, as free men, place themselves at the disposal of a patron, generally a nobleman, and therefore a senator, and maintain a very close relationship with him in fulfillment of a sacred bond based on loyalty and fidelity. Every day, early in the morning, the client visits his patron in his house to say good morning, take an interest in his and his family's health, and express or renew his willingness to take responsibility for his every need: as an armed escort, to intervene with economic aid, to vote in elections according to his instructions, to work in the fields, to carry out all types of errands, or to follow the patron to public events. The patron receives clients individually in his study. He shows that he appreciates their respect, takes care of them (if necessary, he defends them in court, helps them financially, and recommends them for various purposes), and pays them a modest daily sum, not as compensation but as a display of generosity.
cognomen (**pl.** *cognomina*)	The family name of ancient Romans.
cognomen *ex virtute*	An adjective added to the family name of a victorious general derived from the name of the region that was the scene of his military exploits.
colonia (**pl.** *coloniae*)	A self-governing city founded outside the Roman state in accordance with the will or a law of the Senate of Rome.
comitium	An open-air meeting space in the Roman Forum, close to the official seat of the Senate, reserved for meetings of senators and the *comitia curiata*.

commentarius

A written personal memoir or historical narrative in which the author is the protagonist (or one of the protagonists). It is based either on a notebook on disparate subjects, gradually compiled by the author, or on a personal diary, and is not very elaborate from a stylistic perspective.

commission of inquiry

Organ of the Senate of Rome that carries out fact-finding investigations and interrogations with the same powers and limitations as the judicial authority and precedes and prepares the authority's intervention on the same issues.

consilium

A council of advisors or legionary staff, depending on context.

consul (pl. *consules*)

The most powerful and authoritative elected magistrates. There are two. Usually, one is a patrician, while the other is a plebeian (an enriched plebeian). Each of them serves for a one-year term and has the power to veto the decisions of the other, commands an army (usually of two legions), and proposes laws. He is hierarchically superior to all other magistrates. Due to all the powers, roles, and prerogatives tied to the office and the glory surrounding them, they are considered gods on earth. They alternate in the administration of their powers based on a mutual agreement made at the beginning of their mandate. It is up to them to convene and preside over all the meetings of the Senate, the *comitia centuriata*, and the *comitia curiata*. They also have the power of legislative initiative. Their bills are called *rogationes* (sing. *rogatio*) and are voted on by the *comitia centuriata*; if approved, the bills become comitial legislation.

contio (pl. *contiones*)

A public reunion at which the consuls or the tribunes of the plebs, as the case may be, inform the Roman citizens of their bills.

cooptatio

A method for choosing new members of a collegiate institution. It consists in the election of a candidate by those who are already part of the institution.

corona obsidionalis **(blockade crown), also known as the** *corona graminea* **(grass crown)**	A crown formed of intertwined grasses from the battlefield. A highly prestigious and rare military decoration, its recipient is honored by his soldiers.
coup d'état	The illegal seizure of power of the state by a magistrate or the army.
crimen	An illegal act detrimental to the public or private interest, different from the *delictus* (pl. *delicti*). For example, murder was a *crimen*, while theft was a *delictus*.
crimen maiestatis	The abuse of power by a civic magistrate that damaged the dignity of the Roman people.
curia (pl. *curiae*)	A primitive subdivision of the Roman people, previous to the introduction of the Servian constitution.
Curia Hostilia	The Senate House from the beginning of the Republic to Sulla's dictatorship for life, when it was replaced by another *curia*. Sulla's *curia* was destroyed in a fire in 52. It was rebuilt (though in a slightly different position from the original) by Caius Julius Caesar, who inaugurated it in 46.
duumviri	Annually elected magistrates tasked with local public administration in a *colonia* or *municipium*.
edictum (pl. *edicti*)	The act by which a magistrate *cum imperio* publicly declares the criteria that will inform the exercise of his duties.
emancipatio	The legal phenomenon of Roman private law according to which parental authority ceases and a legitimate child becomes an autonomous subject in law, separated from the father of the family, and, as such, from the holder of all the rights and duties connected with the possession of full Roman citizenship (*civitas optimo iure*) and the individual capable of acting in the world of law. Not to be confused with *mancipatio*.

eques (pl. equites) A member of a social group hierarchically positioned between the senators and the plebs, mainly composed of entrepreneurs and landowners.

Etruscans A pre-Roman people who settled in Tuscany and, originally, in other parts of central and northern Italy.

evocatio The religious rite by which a Roman consul "invites" the tutelary deity of a besieged city to join the Roman pantheon, thus depriving the city of divine protection.

flamen dialis The priest of Jupiter, god of the civilized community and guarantor of its destiny. He is the most important of the numerous *flamines*, who, unlike the *pontifices*, don't form a college.

Gallaecia The northwestern part of the Iberian Peninsula, north of the River Douro.

Gauls A pre-Roman people who settled in northern Italy.

gens (pl. gentes) A clan, that is, a group of families with a common ancestor.

gladius A short sword, the typical weapon of Roman legionaries.

Hispania Ulterior A Roman province in the southwest of the Iberian Peninsula.

homo novus A self-made man who has risen due to his own merits; without an established power group backing him, he has had to rely on his own talents. In the eyes of the patriciate, he is a *parvenu*.

imperium Depending on the context, *imperium* may refer to the power to command an army or the power of life and death.

interrex A magistrate appointed by the Senate with the specific task of bringing together the *comitia centuriata* to elect the consuls in a period in which it is difficult for this to happen regularly.

Italia propria	Everything on the Italian peninsula lying to the south of the hypothetical line that connects the mouth of the Magra River in Tuscany to the mouth of the Esino in the Marche region; in effect, the whole of central and southern Italy.
Italics	A pre-Roman people who settled in central and southern Italy.
Italiotes	A pre-Roman, Greek-speaking people who descended from the Greeks who founded colonies in Italy well before the Roman conquest of *Magna Graecia*.
iudicia populi	Illegal acts detrimental to the public interest (called *crimina* to distinguish them from other illicit acts called *delicti*) were punished through public trials. In the Monarchical Age, the public prosecutors were supported in trials by the *duumviri* and quaestors. The condemned could appeal to the people, who would definitively condemn or acquit them. The Republican Age established the concept of a criminal trial before a permanent tribunal (*quaestio perpetua*), in which the accuser was a private citizen, and the jury was presided over by a praetor.
iugerum (pl. *iugera*)	A Roman measurement of surface area. One *iugerum* corresponds to about 2,500m² (= ¼ hectare), and 1,000 *iugera* to approximately 2,500,000m² (= 250 hectares).
lares compitales	Divinities, perhaps of Etruscan origin, responsible for watching over and protecting the crossroads inside and outside cities. Not to be confused with the *lares*, the tutelary geniuses of the house and its inhabitants.
latinitas	A reduced form of Roman citizenship that could be granted to non-Roman citizens. It allowed the owner to exercise only some of the rights belonging to owners of *civitas*.

lex (pl. *leges*)	Law/laws.
lex Acilia de repetundis (or *lex Acilia repetundarum*)	Introduced in 123, probably on the initiative of Caius Gracchus, by a tribune of the plebs to prevent provincial magistrates' corruption. This law provided for members of the equestrian group (*equites*) being jurors in courts.
lex Appuleia de maiestate minuta	Introduced either in 103 or 100 on the initiative of Lucius Appuleius Saturninus, tribune of the plebs. This law established *maiestas* as a separate form of treason from *perduellio*.
lex Appuleia de quaestio extraordinaria istituenda	Introduced either in 103 or 100 on the initiative of Lucius Appuleius Saturninus, tribune of the plebs. This law established a permanent criminal court in Rome called the *quaestio maiestas*, whose juries consisted of *equites*.
lex Caecilia Didia de modo legum promulgandarum	Introduced in 98 on the initiative of the consuls Quintus Caecilius Metellus Nepos and Titus Didius. This law established a minimum period between proposing a law and voting on it, and a ban on miscellaneous provisions in a single law.
lex curiata de imperio	A law passed by the *comitia curiata* confirming the rights of higher magistrates to hold *imperium*.
lex Domitia de sacerdotiis	Introduced in 103 on the initiative of the *pontifex maximus*, Cnaeus Domitius. This law provided for the *comitia tributa* as the popular assembly responsible for electing all the main priests (pontiffs, augurs, *flamens*, etc.). It was repealed by Sulla (*lex Cornelia de sacerdotiis*), who reinstated the right of *cooptatio*. Before the *lex Domitia de sacerdotiis* was approved, the procedure was different: new priests were brought into a college by the *cooptatio* of the priests themselves, while the *pontifex maximus* was appointed by the *comitia tributa*.

lex Genucia de magistratibus	Introduced in 342 by Lucius Genucius, tribune of the plebs. This law banned lending that carried interest, forbade holding two magistracies at the same time or a second magistracy within 10 years of the first, and required at least one consul to be a plebeian.
lex Julia de civitate latinis et sociis danda	Introduced in 90, i.e., during the Social War (91–88), on the initiative of the consul Lucius Julius Caesar. This law extended Roman citizenship to the Latins and the remaining Italic *socii* who had remained faithful or laid down their arms.
lex Licinia Mucia de civibus redigundis	Introduced in 95 on the initiative of the consuls Lucius Licinius Crassus and Quintus Mucius Scaevola Pontifex. This law set up a *quaestio* to investigate Latin and Italic allies registered as Romans on the citizen rolls.
lex Livia iudiciaria	Introduced in 91 on the initiative of Marcus Livius Drusus, tribune of the plebs. This law ruled that the *equites* should leave the positions in the courts provided for them by the *lex Sempronia iudiciaria* and that 300 of them should become part of the Senate.
lex Maria de suffragiis ferendis	Introduced in 119 on the initiative of Caius Marius, tribune of the plebs. This law reduced the width of the *pontes* ("bridges") through which voters passed during elections to improve voting secrecy and reduce the chances of fraud.
lex Plautia-Papiria de civitate sociis danda	Introduced in 89 on the initiative of the tribunes of the plebs Marcus Plautius Silvanus and Caius Papirius Carbo. This law established that people registered as citizens of federate cities and domiciled in *Italia Propria* and in *Gallia Cisalpina* south of the River Po at the time of the law's approval would have Roman citizenship if they requested it within 60 days.

lex Pompeia de Transpadanis

Introduced in 89 on the initiative of the consul Cnaeus Pompeius Strabo. This law granted Latin rights to local communities in *Gallia Cisalpina* north of the River Po (and possibly some Ligurian communities south of the river) as a reward for remaining faithful to Rome during the Social War.

lex provinciae Asiae

Not a law approved by the people gathered in assembly, but a consular decree endorsed by the Senate. It was modified in 89 or 88 to allow the governor of the province of Asia to be a proconsul appointed by the Senate *intuitu personae*, that is, due to his personal qualities.

lex Sempronia (C. Gracchi) de provincia Asia a censoribus locanda

Introduced in 123 on the initiative of Caius Sempronius Gracchus, tribune of the plebs. This law removed the collection of taxes in the province of Asia from the Senate's purview and contracted it to the *publicani*.

lex Rubria de colonia Carthaginem deducenda

Introduced in 123 on the initiative of Rubrius, a tribune of the plebs elected alongside Caius Sempronius Gracchus. This law established that a colony should be founded on the soil of the former city of *Carthago*.

lex Sempronia agraria

Introduced in 133 on the initiative of Tiberius Sempronius Gracchus, tribune of the plebs. This law ordered the assignment of lands in Italy to indigent Roman citizens (*ager publicus* and lands owned by private individuals above a certain surface area).

lex Sempronia de potestate tribunicia M. Octavio abroganda

Introduced in 133 on the initiative of Tiberius Sempronius Gracchus, tribune of the plebs. This law removed the tribune of the plebs Marcus Octavius from his office for having acted against the plebeians' interests (because he had vetoed the agrarian reform bill).

lex Sempronia frumentaria	Introduced in either 123 or 122 on the initiative of Caius Sempronius Gracchus, tribune of the plebs. This law established that the Roman state should purchase grain in Sicily and transport it to Rome, where the cereal would then be sold at a regulated price.
lex Sempronia Ti. Gracchi agraria secunda	Introduced in 133 on the initiative of Tiberius Sempronius Gracchus, tribune of the plebs. This law established that a triumviral commission should be charged with assigning lands to indigent Roman citizens and have jurisdiction in disputes over the public or private nature of the lands exceeding the surface area limit imposed.
lex Servilia Caepio de repetundis	Introduced in 106 on the initiative of the consul Quintus Servilius Caepio. This law provided for the reintroduction of senators into the *quaestio perpetua de repetundis* (see below).
lex Servilia Glaucia de repetundis	Introduced in 101 on the initiative of Caius Servilius Glaucia, tribune of the plebs. This law provided for the reintroduction of *equites* into the *quaestio perpetua de repetundis* (see below).
lex Sulpicia de bello mithridatico C. Mario decernendo	Introduced in 88 on the initiative of Publius Sulpicius Rufus, tribune of the plebs. This law established that the office of governor of the Roman province of Asia, including the direction of the war against Mithridates VI, should be assigned to Caius Marius (instead of the consul Lucius Cornelius Sulla).
lex Valeria de sacrando cum bonis capite eius qui regni occupandi consilium inisset	Introduced in 509 on the initiative of the consul Publius Valerius Publicola. This law abolished the monarchy, dedicating to the infernal gods and condemning to death any individual who aspires to tyranny or supports its re-establishment. Anyone thus condemned to death may be killed with impunity.

lex Varia de maiestate   Introduced in 90 on the initiative of Quintus Varius Hybrida Sucronensis, tribune of the plebs. This law punished those who had induced one or more of Rome's allies to go to war against it and established a special court of justice to judge the accused.

lex Villia annalis   Introduced in 180 on the initiative of Lucius Villius, tribune of the plebs. This law regulated access to ordinary magistracies, prescribing that candidates must fulfill certain subjective and objective requirements.

lictor (pl. lictores)   Civil servants attending a magistrate who holds *imperium*. They escort the magistrate and clear the way for him. They can be recognized by their bundle of rods, with or without an axe blade, symbolizing the magistrate's power of life or death, which can only be exercised outside the city and against non-citizens.

Ludi Apollinares   Solemn games held annually in honor of the god Apollo.

magistrates, extraordinary   The proconsul, the *interrex*, and the dictator are the extraordinary magistracies and are appointed by the Senate *intuitu personae* ("by virtue of personality"). The proconsul is appointed to undertake a specific task, the nature of which can vary. The *interrex* is appointed in the absence of both consuls for the sole purpose of convening the popular assemblies for elections. The dictator is appointed to replace the consuls. They remain in office for a predetermined period: the proconsul, for the time required to carry out his duties; the *interrex* for five days, which can be extended; and the dictator for a maximum of six months.

magistrates, ordinary Ordinary magistrates are elected by the people gathered in assembly and are Roman citizens with the prescribed prerequisites, among which is that of age. (The *comitia centuriata* elect censors, consuls, and praetors; the *comitia tributa* elect the quaestors and aediles; and the *concilia plebis* elect the tribunes of the plebs.) They are elected in October, take office on 1 January the year following their election, and remain in office for one year. The tribunes of the plebs (see below) are an exception. The elected civil magistracies mark stages in one's career in the sense that someone cannot be elected to one of them if he hasn't held the previous magistracy. The order, from beginning to end, is: quaestor, *tribunus plebis*, aedile, praetor, consul, censor. It follows a hierarchy—each magistracy is hierarchically superior to those preceding it—with some exceptions: the tribune of the plebs (who can be elected even if he hasn't previously been a praetor and isn't subject to any other magistrate), the praetor (someone can be elected to the praetorship without ever being an aedile), and the consul (who isn't hierarchically subject to the censor). Ordinary magistracies are further divided into whether they are major or minor. The major magistrates (praetor, consul) are invested with *imperium*, hence the term "magistrates *cum imperio*," and have the right to use the *sella curulis* and an escort of lictors, 12 in the case of the consul and six in the case of the praetor.

Magna Graecia The geographical area that the Greeks defined as *Megàle Hellàs* and understood as the set of territories they colonized in Italy. For the Romans, the term "*Magna Graecia*" does not include Sicily.

maiestas The dignity of the Roman people. See *crimen maiestatis*.

mancipatio

A solemn contract with very ancient origins relating to the transfer of people and things and requiring the presence of witnesses and a public official; the transfer of ownership took place in exchange for the payment of a price in the form of metal, which could be a merely symbolic sum, e.g., a coin.

military tribune (in Latin: *tribunus militum*)

A senior officer. There are 24 in the army, and they change every year. Invariably, one tribune in each legion is of senatorial extraction and is particularly proficient. He is called the *tribunus laticlavius*. In the legionary chain of command, the *tribunus laticlavius* is immediately beneath the legate; in effect, he is the second-in-command. All the other military tribunes are of equestrian extraction and are called *tribuni angusticlavii*. Some military tribunes are elected by the people gathered in assembly; others are appointed by the consul in command *intuitu personae*. The tribunes are divided into pairs, and each pair holds office for two months out of six. Thus, two tribunes are constantly on duty in each legion. The tribunes are responsible for overseeing any activity in the fortified encampment or the over-wintering camp, including those of the centurions, and for providing for all the legion's needs during military campaigns.

mos maiorum

The "way of the ancestors": the unwritten code from which the ancient Romans derived their social norms. This expression identifies the set of rites and ceremonies that were already typical of the Latins before the foundation of Rome, and which formed the essence of Roman traditions. It also identifies the set of values that inspire and guide the Roman citizen from birth: *auctoritas* (prestige and trust), *dignitas* (reputation, honor, esteem), *fides* (loyalty, good faith), *gloria* (recognition and praise from the community), *gravitas* (imperturbability in the face of adversity), *integritas* (consistency, honesty), *maiestas* (the pride of belonging to the Roman people), *pietas* (religious devotion and the feeling of patriotic love and respect toward the family and the hierarchical order), and *virtus* (personal value, courage, fortitude, firmness of character).

municipia   Local administrations in the Roman state.

naturalization   The extension of Roman citizenship to individuals, groups of people, communities, or an entire *civitas* through the adoption of a specific administrative act relating to the advantage that Rome may derive from the recipient's ability to control their community, their courage and valor in battle, or their long service among the *auxilia*. If the recipient is a soldier, the act can only be legitimately passed by a magistrate *cum imperio* who has heard the advice of his *consilium*.

nobilis (pl. nobiles)   A member of a senatorial family.

nonae   Originally, the Roman calendar was based on the phases of the moon: the *calendae* were the day of the new moon, the *nonae* the day of the first quarter (half-moon), and the *idi* the day of the full moon. The *calendae* always fell on the first of the month. The *nonae* and *idi* fell on the seventh and fifteenth day of the month, respectively, in March, May, August, and October. In other months, the *nonae* fell on the fifth day, while the *idi* fell on the 13th.

optimas (pl. optimates)   The ultra-conservatives, constituting almost the entirety of the Roman ruling class (*senatores, possessores, equites*) and the majority in the Senate.

ovatio   A less ostentatious but no less solemn form of celebration than a proper triumph. The procession takes place along the same route, but the victorious general doesn't ride through on a chariot, nor does he paint his face cinnabar-red or wear the triumphal robes. The musical accompaniment is the sound of flutes instead of trumpets, and a sheep is sacrificed instead of a bull.

patricians (in Latin: *patricii,* **sing.** *patricius*) The upper class, usually wealthy, as opposed to the plebeians. They descend from the family clans that settled early in the city founded by Romulus and are represented in the Senate.

pax deorum The state of harmony between the Roman people and its gods.

perduellio A form of high treason, referring to a crime committed by a soldier.

plebeians (in Latin: *plebes,* **sing.** *plebs*) The commoners, free Romans who aren't patricians or *equites,* ranging from enriched plebeians to the very poor.

plebiscite (in Latin: *plebiscitum,* **pl.** *plebiscita*) A bill initiated by a tribune of the plebs; laws deriving from the bills' approval are given the same name.

pomerium The religious boundary of any Roman city.

pontifex **(pl.** *pontifices*) A high-ranking priest of the state religion and a member of one of the major priestly colleges, composed of five members and presided over by the *pontifex maximus.* Their duties involve advising the Senate on issues pertaining to the gods, supervising the exercise of public and private worship, and guarding the *libri pontificales.* As the custodians of legal science and the forms of law, they are also the only authorized interpreters of the legal system. Supervision of the Vestal Virgins is a task specifically reserved for the *pontifex maximus.*

popular assemblies There are four assemblies of the people: *comitia centuriata, comitia tributa, concilia plebis,* and *comitia curiata.* Each of these has its own composition and meets in an electoral, legislative, juridical, or jurisdictional forum, as the case may be, with the exception of the *comitia curiata.*

popularis **(pl.** *populares*) Roman political leaders on the side of "the people." The *populares* protect (or claim to protect) the interests of the lower social classes (*proletarii, humiliores, capite censi*). Their political opponents are the leaders of the *optimates*.

porticus
A porch, often colonnaded.

praetor (pl. *praetores*)
A magistrate elected by the people. There are six, and, except for the two who are based in Rome, they oversee the government of a province for two years or more. The praetors based in Rome are called the *praetor urbanus* and the *praetor peregrinus*, and they are the praetors who received the most votes during the elections. The praetors are many things but principally comprise a judicial body responsible for implementing rules that aim to safeguard individual rights or provide for and punish criminal offenses. Among other things, they also have limited functions as substitutes for the consuls. They can convene the Senate and the *comitia centuriata* and, as magistrates *cum imperio*, can lead armies to war. Like the consuls, they can also convene the *comitia curiata*. They are required to issue an edict at the beginning of their mandate to establish the rules they will adhere to when carrying out their jurisdictional functions, with reference, for example, to the sale of slaves and livestock in the market.

praetor pellegrinus
The praetor elected by the people with the second-most votes. He deals with disputes between Roman citizens and foreigners, those among foreigners, and administers justice in the countryside. When the *praetor peregrinus* leads the army, the *praetor urbanus* performs the duties of his colleague in Rome.

praetor urbanus
The praetor elected by the people with the highest number of votes. He governs the city of Rome and also acts as a judge, dealing with disputes between Roman citizens, and Roman citizens charged with crimes, as well as legal acts specific to his own magistracy. In addition, he oversees the organization of the *Ludi Apollinares*. He cannot leave Rome for more than 10 days at a time.

princeps

First in time or order, e.g., *princeps senatus*, "first senator," the spokesman and general secretary of the Senate.

proscriptus
(pl. *proscripti*)

An outlaw, one under a ban, who can be killed with impunity.

propraetor
(pl. *propraetores*)

A former praetor appointed by the Senate to govern a province.

publicanus
(pl. *publicani*)

A public contractor who erects or maintains public buildings, supplies armies overseas, or collects sums due to the state, such as taxes, tithes, and customs.

quaestor
(pl. *quaestores*)

A magistrate elected by the people who supervises the state treasury and the mint and exercises other public functions. Quaestors must be at least 30 years old (or at least 28 if they are patricians). They carry out administrative functions in financial and accounting matters. There are eight: two remain in Rome and administer the *aerarium* (the public treasury); two supervise the maritime grain supply, one in *Ostia* (a town near Rome at the mouth of the Tiber) and the other in *Puteolis* (Pozzuoli, in Campania); and the others are posted to the provinces. If the consuls and provincial governors undertake a military campaign, the quaestors seconded to them manage the military budget, the most important part of which concerns the payment of wages.

quaestio
(pl. *quaestiones*)

A court of justice, either permanent or provisional, which deals with a specific category of crimes. The *quaestiones* were initially established to conduct investigations into certain types of crimes, all with a public (i.e., political) significance, to compensate for the inadequacies of the primitive judicial system called the *iudicia populi*.

quaestio perpetua
de repetundis

A permanent court that specifically tries defendants of crimes against the state's administration, such as bribery, extortion, embezzlement, etc.

quaestio perpetua de maiestate	A permanent court for contempt of *maiestas*, understood as the authority and dignity of the state.
quindecimvir (**pl.** *quindecimviri*)	A member of a 15-member college with priestly duties.
res publica	A political organization *sui generis*, without precedents or parallels, resulting from a mixture of monarchy, oligarchy, and democracy, the first of which is represented by the consuls, the second by the Senate, and the third by the popular assemblies. This form of government has been in force since 509 when Tarquinius Superbus, the last king of the Etruscan dynasty, was driven out and the monarchy was abolished. The latter had been in force since 753, when *Roma Quadrata* was founded by Romulus.
rex	King.
rex sacrorum	The priest who, during the *res publica*, exercises the same religious functions that once belonged to the king. In theory, the *rex sacrorum* is the highest-ranking priest of the traditional Roman religion. In practice, he is above the senior *flamines* but inferior to the *pontifex maximus*, who confers the office upon him, choosing him from among three candidates put forward by the College of Pontiffs.
rogatio (**pl.** *rogationes*)	A bill proposed on consular initiative.
romanitas	The sum and synthesis of the political and cultural concepts and practices defining what it is to be a Roman and what makes the Romans different from other peoples. This concept is based on being part of a political and religious community with common values, customs, morality, and way of life.

Salii	The *Salii*, Salians, or Salian priests are a college of the traditional Roman religion composed of 12 priests of Mars, the Roman god of war, supposedly introduced by Numa Pompilius (r. 715–672).
sella curulis	A foldable chair with legs in the shape of an "x." It was a symbol of public authority.
Senate of Rome	A college of current and former civil magistrates responsible for advising magistrates, deciding foreign policy and declaring war, administering the state (in the sense that it appointed extraordinary magistrates, provincial governors, and legionary commanders, decided when troops were to be levied, and declared states of national emergency), and exercising jurisdiction when it comes to trying one or more people accused of political crimes or sacrilege.
senatus consultus (pl. *senatus consulta*)	A decree of the Senate of Rome that, while not juridically binding, is, due to the authority of the body expressing it, *de facto* prescriptive.
senatus consultus ultimum	A special decree of the Senate of Rome that declares a state of national emergency and gives special powers to the consuls, or a consul, to face a particular situation, authorizing them/him to use any means necessary so that the state does not suffer damage.
socius (pl. *socii*)	A people who became friends and allies of the Roman people by virtue of a contract of association with the *imperium* of Rome called a *foedus* (pl. *foedera*). This should not be confused with the act establishing a federation or confederation, even though the *socii* are sometimes called *foederati* (from the fact that they have contracted a *foedus*). In this case, the word *imperium* is not to be understood as the authority of the highest magistrates of Rome but as the complex of the Roman state and its satellite states.

suberate coin	A coin with a low-value metal core covered with a light patina of silver (or sometimes gold), thus devaluing the coinage.
toga	A distinctive garment of ancient Rome, a toga is a roughly semicircular cloth draped over the shoulders and around the body. It is usually woven from white wool and worn over a tunic. They come in different colors. For example, candidates running in elections for the renewal of the magistracies wear a white toga called a *toga candida*.
tresviri capitales,* or *tresviri nocturni	Minor magistrates who walk through the city's most notorious areas at night, escorted by public slaves armed with clubs, with the power to arrest drunken revelers, thieves, and cutthroats, on whose guilt the competent magistrate will rule the following day.
tribune of the plebs (in Latin: *tribunus plebis*)	A magistrate elected by the *concilium* (or *concilia*) *plebis* to defend the plebeians' interests. He can promote laws, convene and preside over the *concilium plebis*, and veto anyone, even a consul. He is sacrosanct, immune from coercion, and personally inviolable while in office. There are 10 tribunes of the plebs at any one time. They take office on 10 December of the year of their election and remain in office until 9 December the following year.
triumviri coloniae deducendae	The three magistrates responsible for assigning colonial lands and dealing with the complex work of founding and organizing a colony.
ius migrandi	Latins' right to choose to settle in Rome and acquire Roman citizenship after renouncing their former citizenship.

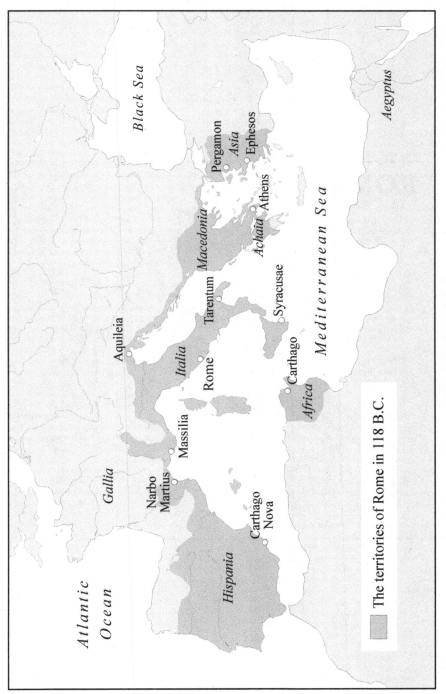

The territories of Rome in 118 B.C.

(Credit to Studio Aguilar)

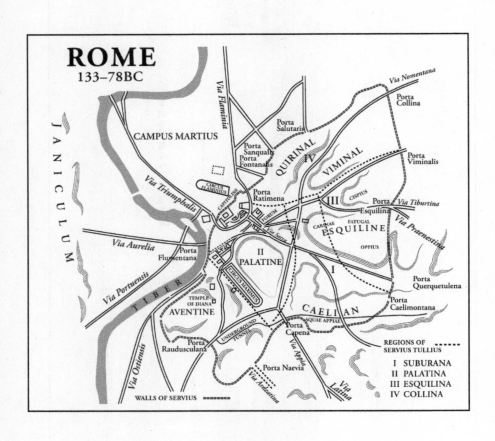

ROME
133–78BC

JANICULUM

CAMPUS MARTIUS

Via Flaminia

Via Triumphalis

Via Aurelia

Via Portuensis

TIBER

CIRCUS FLAMINIUS

CAPITOLINE

FORUM

Via Sacra

Porta Ratimena

Porta Flumentana

II PALATINE

CIRCUS MAXIMUS

TEMPLE OF DIANA

AVENTINE

Via Ostiensis

Porta Raudusculana

UNDERGROUND TUNNEL

Porta Naevia

Via Ardeatina

WALLS OF SERVIUS

Porta Sanqualis
Porta Fontanalis

Porta Salutaris

QUIRINAL

IV

VIMINAL

Porta Collina

Via Nomentana

Porta Viminalis

Porta Tiburtina

CISPIUS

III

Esquilina

CARINAE

FATUGAL

ESQUILINE

OPPIUS

I

Via Praenestina

Via Tiburtina

Porta Querquetulena

Porta Caelimontana

CAELIAN

AQUAE APPIAE

Porta Capena

Via Appia

Via Latina

REGIONS OF SERVIUS TULLIUS

I SUBURANA
II PALATINA
III ESQUILINA
IV COLLINA

Preface

This book deals with the internal politics of Rome in the Late Republic, with particular reference to the period between the Gracchi and Sulla (133–78). It discusses:

- the agrarian reforms of Tiberius Sempronius Gracchus, the plots of the Senate of Rome against this tribune of the plebs, and his violent death;
- the mysterious death of Publius Cornelius Scipio Aemilianus, the destroyer of *Carthago* and *Numantia*, which some commentators ascribe to murder—the result of a conspiracy by friends of the Gracchi, his wife Sempronia, and the victim's mother-in-law and aunt, Cornelia Africana Minor—and others to suicide;
- the massacre on the Aventine, which framed the killing of Caius Sempronius Gracchus;
- the ferocious lynching of Lucius Apuleius Saturninus, the seditious tribune of the plebs;
- the civil war between Marius and Sulla, which was fought in two stages and saw, among other things, the siege and capitulation of Rome and Marius's reign of terror; and
- the definitive victory and proscriptions of Sulla.

The introduction aims to help non-specialist readers better orient themselves in the complex world of the Romans as it was in the historical period considered in this book, with particular reference to the places of political power, the form of government of the Roman state, the political institutions, and the political game. For the same reason, some entries in the Glossary are more in-depth than others, and the Chronology summarizes the salient events that occurred each year.

Personal and place names are given in Latin. Places are indicated by their ancient name, with their modern correspondent reported in parentheses. Exceptions are made for those that have disappeared into the archaeological record or never changed their name.

The references lists the works of contemporary authors mentioned in the book. The subsequent list of suggested further reading is a selection of books on the main characters mentioned in this volume. It aims to provide appropriate documentation, stimulate in-depth analysis of the topics covered, and orient readers toward relevant literature and publications. Obviously, it makes no claim to be exhaustive in this respect.

***

The Roman world only recognized the civil and political rights of those who held full Roman citizenship and, to a lesser extent, those who held Latin rights, with the consequence that whoever found themselves outside the cities and was not a Roman citizen, or who didn't enjoy Latin rights, was without rights and had to bend the knee if he wanted to save his life. Furthermore, the Roman world was well-acquainted with the most brutal forms of violence, the savage exploitation of man by man, the tendency toward territorial expansion (imperialism), the massacre of entire populations, the plundering of natural resources, the inhuman slave trade, and cultural colonization. Its positive aspects, however, were no less numerous than its negative ones, nor did they carry less weight. Rome's expansion didn't just consist of massacres and robberies but also of civilization, of economic, cultural, technological, and scientific progress. Where there was a state of barbarism, it brought cities, written laws, political stability, roads, aqueducts, baths, theaters, etc. The Roman state also transformed the vanquished into friends and allies, then into Roman citizens, with all that this entailed in terms of social integration. The Romans also had a moral code—*mos maiorum*—and let themselves be guided by a series of principles (*fides, pietas, maiestas, virtus, gravitas, dignitas, auctoritas, gloria, clementia, humanitas, pax, amicitia*, etc.). Those who didn't have to work hard for a living cultivated beauty in all its forms, such as through the collection of works of art, and they used the time when they were free from the business of political life to look after their houses and farms, to attend to studies, philosophical reflections, and literary activity.

In the Republican Age (509–27), dealing with politics was an activity inherent to the condition of a citizen (later, in the Imperial Age, everything changed). This was commonly considered no less important than war, with which it sometimes ended up coinciding. There were no political parties; instead, the political game was a factional struggle that could degenerate into civil war, as indeed happened several times.

This book goes deep into the political dynamics of the time, politicians' private and public lives, and their family and social environment. There is, therefore, an emphasis on the leading characters' relationships with family and friends to highlight the ties and frequently competitive interactions between the individuals, families, and clans on which the political process depended. Ultimately, this book prioritizes the political aspects of the historical processes and events narrated, and the human, family, and social aspects of the political process. In addition, it proposes a broader reading of the political process by putting emphasis on more minor characters.

This book leaves a slightly bitter taste in the mouth because it describes the negative, violent, dark, and cruel aspects of politics, however, this is an attempt to reconstruct the truth of the facts, which, to be judged objectively, are considered from the perspective of people at the time.

***

I have been writing ancient history books for many years now. Most recently, these have focused on the political and military history of Republican Rome and the life and death of ancient cities. The tone is lively; the text makes use of the "historical present" (see below), but with scientific solidity throughout.

Otherwise, the general approach in all my works on the political and military history of Ancient Rome is similar. As I highlighted in *Before Augustus*, published by Casemate in 2023, these books set the characters in the complex social and political system of the time, give a thorough account of major historical events, offer detailed portraits of key figures, whether famous or less well-known, and provide analyses of epic battles. The narrative contained in them forms a chronologically ordered continuum. It doesn't aim to be exhaustive but rather to provide a broad and evolutionary picture. I refer to what is deducible from the accounts of ancient authors, in which these statements and their connections find their place in their consequentiality.

I write my books to help the reader understand the complexity of the social interactions of the time and to guide them to discover the political process in a state which, in the so-called Republican period, from the point of view of the form of government, was not a monarchy, nor an oligarchy, nor a democracy, but the sum and synthesis of all these things. Ultimately, my approach seeks to clarify the complexity of the Roman world from the point of view of social interactions and transport the reader to the environments and atmospheres of antiquity, illuminating both the background and the key events themselves. Details are explained clearly, providing the non-specialist reader with all the information behind the facts and situations to help them understand the reasons for historical events and people's behaviors and follow the processes as they unfold. I start from the premise that I'm also addressing an audience of non-specialists and that if the reader doesn't understand what I'm saying, I'm the idiot.

Another characterizing element of my works is the extensive use of the historical present to represent events and construct the text. The historical present is a verbal form that is used to refer to events that belong to the past yet are presented as contemporary, or close to the moment of enunciation, thus obtaining the effect of a perspective approach and an actualization of the events narrated. This also sets the book apart from many other works that adopt a more detached viewpoint—the aim is to immerse the reader not only in the world of Ancient Rome but also in the attitudes that defined it, rather than to review ancient behaviors by modern standards. This isn't common. Unlike in the books in which historical events are always told in the remote past tense, the historical present used in my books reduces the reader's distance from the narrated events, transforms history into a chronicle, and facilitates a non-specialist reader's approach to the subject matter.

***

Violence in the Forum was written in 2023, 10 years after what was a fundamental stage in my training as an essayist writer: my research at the Graduate Group in Ancient History and Mediterranean Archaeology at the University of California, Berkeley, where I was a Visiting Scholar Researcher. I would like to celebrate this anniversary.

Berkeley, located in the Bay Area, 13km from San Francisco, is home to the central nucleus of the University of California (UC), the state's oldest and most important university, founded in 1869. UC Berkeley's campus is divided into institutes, libraries, scientific laboratories, gyms, and playgrounds, spread across a beautiful park with large trees, neatly cut lawns, small streams, little bridges, and many friendly squirrels, accustomed to human presence and therefore easily approachable. It is attended by tens of thousands of students and is firmly placed at the top of the rankings of the best universities in the world. With its many teaching and research centers, including colleges and schools, divided into departments, and with its offer of hundreds of semester-long degree courses, including online, it is one of the main cultural centers on the planet.

UC Berkeley is widely regarded as one of the most democratic universities in the United States. Some major cultural processes originated there before spreading to many parts of the world, such as the so-called Student Revolution of 1968. It was also the site of the strongest student protests in 2017 during the first year of Donald Trump's presidency.

The intellectual heart of UC Berkeley is the College of Letters and Science, the largest and most prestigious of its colleges and schools. It encompasses half the campus, three-quarters of its students, and half of its undergraduates. Its students engage in dialogue with highly esteemed teachers and illustrious researchers and scholars. The college's divisions consist of dozens of departments, one of which is the Department of Ancient History and Mediterranean Archeology (AHMA).

The AHMA offers a PhD program for students studying the history and civilizations of the ancient peoples of the Mediterranean area (*circa* 3000 BC–500 AD), from the Iberian Peninsula to Mesopotamia, from Thrace to Upper Egypt. Those who attend AHMA courses have access, among other things, to numerous libraries, among the best equipped in the world.

UC Berkeley is a magnificent place for study, reflection, and writing. I was lucky enough to be able to benefit greatly from that environment and that climate. One of my most wonderful memories is of the many hours spent reading, studying, and writing at the tables of the Bancroft Library and the Doe Library. Nor can I forget the welcome breaks after studying that I took in a café overlooking Bancroft Way, very popular with students, professors, researchers, post-docs, and other visiting scholars. Sitting at a table among the plants outdoors, I enjoyed the intense, warm light that fell from a clear blue sky.

My first printed book on the political and military history of Ancient Rome was born at UC Berkeley. There began my journey that was later punctuated by numerous other publications on the same subject. I am very grateful to UC Berkeley for this, especially to my formal sponsor, Carlos F. Noreña, Full Professor of Ancient History and Mediterranean Archaeology at UC Berkeley's Department of History.

However, I cannot fail to mention my visits to the Hellenic and Roman Library in Senate House, London, when I was an Academic Visitor at the University of London's Institute of Classical Studies (ICS). I also owe much from this other fundamental stage in my training as a researcher to the then director of the ICS, Prof. Gregory D. Woolf, now Ronald J. Mellor Chair of Ancient History at the University of California, Los Angeles, for which I say many thanks!

***

I would like to thank Ruth Sheppard at Casemate Publishers and her staff for publishing this book, the second of mine published by Casemate. I am also indebted to Anthony Wright, an editor, translator, and writer based in northern England, for his assistance, attention, helpful comments, and suggestions during the linguistic editing and proofreading of the text. Of course, where any inconsistencies or errors remain, they are of my own making.

Natale Barca
Trieste, January 2024

Introduction

Places of political power

Rome, in the Republican Period (509–27),[1] is made up of an urban area and a single suburb, which takes its name of *Transtiberim* (Trastevere) from the fact that it is located on the other side of the River Tiber at the foot of the Janiculum. The urban area extends for 426 hectares, and embraces the seven hills (Aventine, Capitoline, Caelian, Esquiline, Palatine, Quirinal, and Viminal) and the valleys that separate them. It is enclosed within a ring of fortification walls, 11km long.

These are the Servian Walls, built by Servius Tullius (r. 578–535), the sixth of the seven kings who governed the city in the Monarchical Age (753–509). They consist of an embankment 10m high and 4m thick, with parts in tufa masonry (square blocks). The walls stretch from *Porta Collina* to *Porta Esquilina*, approximately 1,300m, have a 15m high defensive embankment in front of them, are covered with tufa blocks on the outside, cement work on the inside, and a wide moat, 13m deep.

There are 17 city gates, but only three major ones. The latter have the shape of a vaulted passage characterized by an effort to combine architectural decoration with monumentality. Despite this, they are not large; even a cart can barely fit through them. They have a solid wooden door on street level and a gallery above, crenelated on the external side and open on the internal side. The guardhouse, stationed under the vault, has staff who open the gate at dawn and close it at sunset.

The urban area is a set of densely populated clusters of houses separated by large uninhabited spaces and served by a network of internal streets. The roads are not wide (6–7m at most) and have an irregular layout, with many narrow, dark alleys and staircases off them.

The city itself is a chaotic mix of houses, places of worship, public buildings and facilities, shops, warehouses, factories, workshops, taverns, inns, gambling

---

1   The description of the city of Rome provided in these pages refers to the Late Republican city as it appeared before the building interventions of Sulla and Pompey the Great.

dens, and guilds. The inhabitants mingle with each other, living cheek by jowl, whether patricians, knights, or plebeians; rich or poor; citizens, foreigners, freedmen, or slaves. Every district follows this pattern, except one: the Palatine. This is where the cream of the city's ruling class lives.

A district's level of sanitation largely depends on whether it is located high up on the hills, lower down in the valleys, or near the Tiber, which flows between the slopes of the Aventine and Capitoline hills. Poor sanitation is mainly due to the proximity of the river—which causes foul odors and fevers in the summer, and floods in winter—but also to the fact that the population density close to the river is higher, the buildings packed more closely together, and the problems of hygiene, overcrowding, and congestion are more serious.[2]

Among the "lower" neighborhoods, the most populous are *Velabrum*, *Subura*, and *Transtiberim*. *Velabrum* is a flat area between the Tiber and the Forum, i.e., between the Capitoline and Palatine. It is contiguous to the *Forum Boarium*, the livestock market, and to the *Vicus Tuscus*, the street of the fabric and clothing merchants, which, starting from the Forum, runs along the slopes of the Palatine up to the *Circus Maximus*. The vast *Subura* extends over the slopes of the Quirinal and Viminal up to the spurs of the Esquiline (Oppian, Cispian, and *Fagutal*). It can be reached from the Forum via the *Argiletum*, the booksellers' street. Its upper part is home to senators and *equites*, while the lower part is a concentration of blocks of *insulae*, a dark and infamous area, the scene of crimes and immorality.

The Romans bury their dead outside the city because it is forbidden to do so within the *pomerium* (with exceptions). Their cemeteries are therefore located along or near the main consular roads. A true city of the dead can be found on the *Campus Esquilinus*, an area of burials and undertakers' shops that extends beyond the city gate of the same name. It is full of tombs of all types, from humble to monumental. The Temple of *Venus Libitina*, the goddess of death and the departed, is in a cypress grove.

Rome is a city of small houses, large blocks of flats (*insulae*), which stand out with their height and contain numerous apartments, and domus-type houses, which are characterized by their large entrance halls, so much so that they are also called atrium houses. *Insulae* are large square buildings, made of wood and mud brick, with several floors connected by stairs. Reaching up to 30m in height, they are used for both residential and commercial purposes. Usually all, or almost all, the real estate units enclosed in the *insulae* are rented out, with prices varying depending on the apartment's size, intended use, state

---

2   For a description of the phenomenon: Cic. *Leg. agr.* II.96.

of conservation, etc. The lower floors are inhabited by wealthy, but not very rich, families; the apartments on the upper floors are occupied by proletarian families; and the attic by sub-proletarians, freedmen, and foreigners, many of whom live in precarious conditions.

The Forum

At the foot of the Capitoline Hill, which dominates Rome from the north, is a slight depression that has the Palatine to the west, the Velian to the south, and the Viminal, Quirinal, and Esquiline to the east. This is the Forum, an aggregation of open or covered contiguous buildings (squares, temples, courts, council rooms, porticoes, streets, and alleys) and the fulcrum of the city's socio-economic and political-institutional life. It is the site for the most important political meetings, eulogies and speeches given to the electors, civil and criminal trials, and solemn sacrifices. Trade of all kinds takes place there, both licit and otherwise. Death sentences are carried out at the Tarpeian Rock. Various political buildings are in the northeastern part of the Forum, with the *Basilica Porcia* a little to the west (beyond which is the *carcer*, the city's infamous prison) and the Column of Phocas to the south. Among others, the *Curia Hostilia*, the *comitium*, the *rostra*, and the *senaculum* are worth mentioning.

The *comitium* is a 30x40m space with steps arranged in a horseshoe shape, and a grandstand for speeches toward the south. This was initially the principal place of political life in Rome because two popular assemblies met there: the *comitia curiata* and the *comitia tributa*. But due to the confined space—no more than 5,000–6,000 people could gather there—the *comitia tributa* were moved to the Forum in 145. Subsequently, the *comitia tributa* also began to meet elsewhere, particularly in the *Area Capitolina*, and they limit their electoral assemblies to the *Campus Martius*. However, the *comitium* remains a meeting place.

The *senaculum* (or *Grecostasis*) and the *rostra* are located near the *comitium*. The *senaculum* is a meeting point and also where the ambassadors of friendly and allied states are received. Sometimes, the Senate meets there. Near the *comitium* is the Orators' Tribune. The platform's eastern side, overlooking the square, is concave, while the western side, overlooking the *comitium*, is convex and stepped. This structure is called the rostra (named after a warship's metal ram) because its eastern side is adorned with the rostra of ships captured by the Romans in the Battle of *Antium* (383).

On the east and west of the Forum are several sacred buildings and various *basilicae*. For the Romans, a *basilica* is a building where public meetings take place, business is transacted, and justice is administered. There are four in the Forum: the *Basilica Fulvia* (incorporated into the *Basilica Aemilia* in 78), the *Basilica Opimia*, the *Basilica Porcia*, and the *Basilica Sempronia*, named after their respective builders. They are all large buildings with numerous columns, marble floors and statues, and mosaics.

The *Curia Hostilia* is in the northwestern part of the Forum, close to the *comitium* and the rostra. The brick building has a gabled façade, high and austere, and is accessed by climbing a staircase and entering through a large bronze door with stone jambs and an architrave. The door opens under a portico and leads directly into a room more than 20m long and approximately 15m wide, its trussed ceiling more than 15m high, with relief decorations and large paintings on the walls. In the hall, the senators' seats are arranged next to each other on two staggered levels, set longitudinally and face to face, and separated by an aisle. Toward the back wall, opposite the entrance, is a sacrificial altar. The building, which takes its name from the fact that it was built during the reign of Tullius Hostilius, is the official seat of the Senate. Its appearance hasn't changed in more than five centuries, except for the placement of two sculptural works in full relief on the access staircase, the addition of paintings inside, and the expansion carried out by Sulla in 82–79.

Traditional religion is polytheistic, and Romans worship both their own divinities and others, usually assimilated from the Greeks. The foreign communities living in the city, mainly Greeks, Anatolians, Syriacs, Jews, and Egyptians, practice different religions. Therefore, Rome contains numerous temples, and *aedicules* (shrines) belonging to various religions. Roman temples' architecture resembles that of the Greek temples of the Archaic Period (roughly 700–500), although it also reflects an Etruscan influence, which dominated *Latium* toward the end of the VI century. These temples consist of a building that stands on a high podium, accessible via a staircase between two foreparts that precede the façade, and are surrounded by columns of the Tuscan order.

Unlike the religious architecture of the Greeks, the building is never made of marble but uses stone for the podium and columns, raw bricks for the walls, and wood for all the upper parts (entablature, pediment, roof). Not even the statues of the deities are made of marble but instead they are of terracotta or sometimes bronze. The columns are always rather squat and rigid. The building also has only one façade; consequently, the colonnade only runs around three sides rather than four. Finally, the side columns are often half columns or pilasters.

The Temple of the Dioscuri and the Temple of Saturn are the oldest sacred places in Rome belonging to the Greco-Roman religion (apart from the

Sanctuary of Vesta and the Temple of Jupiter Optimus Maximus, which will be discussed later). These buildings are simultaneously places of worship and public offices. The Temple of the Dioscuri houses an important court and the official weights and measures. Other areas of the temple are used as "banks" or warehouses. Sometimes, the Senate meets there. The space in front of the temple is used for holding public meetings, with speeches and the traditional *equites* parade. The Temple of Saturn is also the seat of the public office that safeguards and administers the treasury of the Roman people and the state archives. Not only does the treasury contain all the state's financial revenues, but it also houses the insignia of the Roman state and a scale for the official weighing of metal. Laws and public documents are posted outside the temple.

The Acropolis

The Capitoline is the highest hill enclosed within the Servian Walls. It has two peaks, the *Arx* and the *Capitolium*, both surrounded by fortification walls. The hill can be reached from the Forum via two steep routes: *Sacra Via*, which climbs up to the *Arx*, and the *clivius Capitolinus*, which climbs up to the *Capitolium*. On the *Arx* is the Temple of *Juno Moneta* ("She who reminds and warns"), a Temple of Concordia, a mint, and the *auguraculum*, a space where the augurs observe the flight of birds to interpret the will of the gods.

The *Area Capitolina* forms the summit of the *Capitolium*. It is surrounded by a wall and a portico, built in 159 on the internal side of the wall. This 1.5–2-hectare esplanade, located in front of the Temple of Jupiter Optimus Maximus, is characterized by a spectacular concentration of statues, trophies, and temples. The main entrance is on the southeast side, opposite the Temple of Jupiter Optimus Maximus. The temples located in the *Area Capitolina* have imposing architecture and are full of symbolic meanings. The four largest are dedicated to Jupiter Optimus Maximus, Jupiter Feretrius, Mars Ultor, and Fides.

It is worth focusing on the Temple of Jupiter Optimus Maximus, also called the Temple of Capitoline Jupiter or the Temple of the Capitoline Triad. It is at once the oldest place of worship in Rome (inaugurated in 509), the largest (occupying an area of $15,000m^2$), and the most sumptuous. Its effect is similar to that of the Parthenon on Athens because it stands in a dominant position and is visible from many points of the lower city. The cell is divided into three, and houses the simulacra of the Capitoline Triad: the central chamber contains a terracotta statue of Jupiter and is larger than the other two chambers, which contain a statue of Juno, Jupiter's consort, and a statue of Minerva, the daughter of Jupiter and Juno. The temple contains many priceless treasures, including the archives concerning foreign relations and the Sibylline Books, a collection of prophecies written in Greek regarding the future of Rome.

The *Area Capitolina* is one of the most important places in Rome's public life. Victorious generals' triumphal processions finish there with the ritual sacrifices that conclude the celebration. The *comitia tributa* meet there to elect magistrates, make laws, and hold appeal trials, and the inaugural auspices of the new consuls take place by the altar in front of the Temple of Jupiter Optimus Maximus. This is also where the Senate holds its session on 1 January, the date on which magistrates *cum imperio* take office. Furthermore, it meets there whenever it is necessary to decide on issues of particular importance, such as the organization of the *imperium* and wars. The steps in front of the temple façade also act as a speaker's platform during meetings of the *comitia tributa*.

The form of government of the Roman state

In the II and I Centuries, Rome is the capital of a state whose form of government is the *res publica* (literally "public affairs"). This has been in force since 509 when the king of Rome, Tarquinius Superbus, the last of the Etruscan dynasty, was driven out of Rome and the monarchy was abolished. The latter had been in force for more than 250 years since 753, the year *Roma Quadrata* was founded by Romulus.

The Latin phrase *res publica* is often translated as "republic," but this is misleading. The *res publica* isn't, in fact, a republic because in the Roman state, sovereignty doesn't belong to the people, there is no parliament elected by the people, and there is no head of state. The political institutions are the Senate of Rome, the popular assemblies (*comitia centuriata, comitia tributa, concilia plebis, comitia curiata*), and the magistracies. They form the central administration. The devolved administration is formed by the *municipia* and the *coloniae*, which have their own senates and magistrates.

The *res publica* is a political organization *sui generis*, without precedents or parallels, resulting from a mixture of monarchy, oligarchy, and democracy, the first of which is represented by the consuls, the second by the Senate, and the third by the popular assemblies. Although there is no constitution,[3] these institutional bodies nevertheless balance each other.

---

3   "Republican Rome lacked a written constitution and, indeed, a 'rigid' constitution, that is, one that could not be modified except through special constitutional reform procedures. This certainly doesn't mean that the *res publica* lacked a constitution, but it does mean that the Roman constitution resulted from the effectiveness of the system and was therefore extremely

The political institutions

The Senate of Rome is a college of current and former civil magistrates responsible for advising magistrates, deciding foreign policy and declaring war, administering the state (in the sense that it appoints extraordinary magistrates, provincial governors, and legionary commanders, decides when troops are to be levied, and declares states of national emergency), and exercising jurisdiction when it comes to trying one or more people accused of political crimes or sacrilege. At the beginning of the *res publica*, it was such an authoritative institution that it seemed like an "assembly of kings" and remained above the political game. Later, it lost some of its authority because it too became part of the political game.

There are two types of magistrates: ordinary and extraordinary. The ordinary ones—quaestors, aediles, tribunes of the plebs, praetors, consuls, censors—are elected by the people gathered in assembly, and are Roman citizens with the prescribed prerequisites, among which is that of age (the *comitia centuriata* elect censors, consuls, and praetors, the *comitia tributa* elect the quaestors and aediles, and the *concilia plebis* elect the tribunes of the plebs). They are elected in October, take office on 1 January the year following their election, and remain in office for one year. The tribunes of the plebs are an exception. They take office on 10 December of the year of their election and remain in office until 9 October the following year.

The elected civil magistracies mark the stages in one's career in the sense that someone cannot be elected to one of them if he hasn't held the previous magistracy. The order, from beginning to end, is: quaestor, tribune of the plebeians, aedile, praetor, consul, censor. It follows a hierarchy—each magistracy is hierarchically superior to those preceding it—with some exceptions: the tribune of the plebs (who can be elected even if he has not previously been a praetor and doesn't depend on any other magistrate), the praetor (who can be elected even if he has never been an aedile), and the consul (who doesn't depend hierarchically on the censor). Furthermore, ordinary magistracies are divided into whether they are major or minor. The difference is in the fact that the major magistrates (praetor, consul) are invested with *imperium*, "military command, power over life and death," hence the term "*magistrati cum imperio.*" The major magistrates have the right to use both the *sella curulis*, a foldable

---

flexible, that is, it could be integrated with or modified by ordinary laws and in other ways, even if the dominant tendency was not to modify it except in extreme circumstances." A. Guarino, *La coerenza di Publico Mucio* (Naples: Jovene, 1981), 111.

chair with legs in the shape of an "x," and an escort of lictors, 12 in the case of the consul and six in the case of the praetor.

The most powerful and authoritative elected magistrate is the consul. There are two. Usually, one is a patrician, while the other is a plebeian (an enriched plebeian). Each of them serves for a one-year term and has the power to veto the decisions of the other; commands an army, usually of two legions; and proposes laws. He is hierarchically superior to all the other magistrates. Due to all the powers, roles, and prerogatives tied to the office and the glory that surrounds them, they are considered gods on earth. They alternate in the administration of their powers based on a mutual agreement made at the beginning of their mandate. It is up to them to convene and preside over all the meetings of the Senate, the *comitia centuriata*, and the *comitia curiata*. Their bills are called *rogationes* (sing. *rogatio*) and are voted on by the *comitia centuriata*. Another magistracy—the tribuneship of the plebs—is, in some respects, placed on the same level as the consul, if not higher. But we'll talk about this later.

The extraordinary magistrates (propraetors, proconsuls, interrex, dictators) are appointed by the Senate of Rome *intuitu personae* ("by virtue of personality"). The proconsul is appointed to undertake a specific task, the nature of which can vary. The interrex is appointed in the absence of both consuls for the sole purpose of convening the popular assemblies for elections. The dictator is appointed to replace the consuls. They remain in office for a predetermined period: the proconsul, for the time required to carry out his duties; the interrex for five days, which can be extended; and the dictator for a maximum of six months. However, individuals (such as Sulla and Caesar) can also be appointed dictator by law and for life.

There are four popular assemblies: *comitia centuriata, comitia tributa, concilia plebis,* and *comitia curiata.* Each of these has its own composition and meets in an electoral, legislative, juridical, or jurisdictional forum, as the case may be, except for the *comitia curiata.*

The *comitia centuriata* took its name from the centuries, which initially reflected military status. Each has 100 members. It is the only one of the four assemblies that brings together both patricians and plebeians. It meets just outside the city to decree war and peace, approve laws, elect consuls, praetors, and censors, and decide appeals.

The *comitia curiata* is an assembly based on the *curiae*, the 30 political units into which Romulus divided the Roman people, which, since 218, have been represented by as many lictors, elected by the *comitia centuriata*, one for each of the original patrician *gentes* (a group of aristocratic families, having a common name and claiming descent from a common ancestor in the male line). It is therefore the oldest popular assembly. In the Late Republic, it performs only symbolic functions, such as ratifying the elections of magistrates *cum imperio* or conferring *imperium* through the approval of the *lex curiata de imperio*, proposed by the *comitia centuriata*.

The *comitia tributa* is a popular assembly that brings together the tribes, understood as electoral districts. It elects magistrates who do not exercise *imperium* (tribunes of the plebs, plebeian aediles, and quaestors).

The *concilium plebis*, or *concilia plebis*, is a popular assembly reserved for plebeians. Like the *comitia centuriata*, it is able to make laws.

The political game

The arrival of "daggers in the Forum" is a literary expression that identifies a precise historical moment: the one that saw two tribunes of the plebs—the brothers Tiberius and Caius Sempronius Gracchus—die a violent death in Rome in 133 and 122 amidst bloody riots. Later, the Gracchi were subjected to *damnatio memoriae* (the damnation of memory) so that they would be forgotten. Their friends were targeted by legal prosecutions that reflected the desire to make political use of justice, pursued sufficiently tenaciously to extract forced confessions from the accused, i.e., forcing them to admit to offenses they hadn't committed, thereby obtaining convictions at any cost. These events marked the rupture of the constitutional order and the beginning of a political crisis. Thus began a political process that would lead, over the span of three generations, to the end of the *res publica* and its replacement with a different system in which the function of majority political orientation was exercised among various constitutional bodies, today called the Principate. The transition saw endless violence, ransacking, and destruction, including three bitter and bloody civil wars. The third civil war was intertwined with a war against the Pharaonic state of Ptolemaic Egypt, which was decided by the Battle of Alexandria (30). It saw the consolidation of power of Caius Julius Caesar Octavianus, adopted nephew and almost universal heir of the dictator Caius Julius Caesar (who fell victim to a senatorial conspiracy in 44). A little later (27), Octavian became *princeps senatus*, "senior senator," and was called *augustus*, meaning "he who increases the wealth, wellbeing, and prosperity of the state, thanks to the power he holds," but also "revered," "respectable," and, above all, "protected by the gods."

In those days, internal politics in Rome were fueled by social conflict (the constant struggle of the lower-class plebeians against the nobles and aristocrats).

This was the confrontation between the *optimates* and the *populares*, each of which was headed by an eminent figure and was characterized by sectarianism and (factional) intolerance. It played out with speeches delivered in the Senate, in the streets, and in the courts with solemnity and intensity, sometimes underlined by gestures, by orators accustomed to speaking with emphasis and charged intonation. However, it was also marked by the daggers that flashed in the hands of conspirators and assassins; by street riots, with thousands of victims; by real or alleged *coups d'état*, with ferocious mass repressions; by summary executions of people found guilty by popular consensus at the hands of private individuals in the absence of a judicial conviction; by victims abandoned to the fury of the mob; of widespread civil wars whose battles interweaved with those against enemies abroad; manhunts; horrendous crimes; the system of legalized killings that aimed at the annihilation of political opponents known as proscriptions; corruption; and brutal and mass killings.

The *optimates* included a thousand magistrates, ex-magistrates, high-ranking clergy (*pontifices, flamines, rex sacrorum*), successful entrepreneurs, and military commanders from the patriciate or the *equites*. Compared to the rest of society, they were a minority, but they had the majority in the Senate and, through the consuls, controlled the *comitia centuriata*. Furthermore, they were present on the juries of the courts and could count on the best judicial speakers, those who could make trials lean one way or the other. Furthermore, through censors, they could expel senators deemed unworthy of the position and control the private lives of individual citizens. It was, therefore, a small circle, but nevertheless a very rich and powerful one.

They gave themselves the name *optimates*, "the best," because they considered themselves the most authentic and genuine part of society and set themselves up as guardians and defenders of the *mos maiorum*, the complex set of beliefs, opinions, representations, and values that orient the Romans, bind them to each other, justify their common feeling regarding public affairs, and make them feel like a community of citizens. They understand the *mos maiorum* as a set of mandatory principles and norms and demand that it be observed by anyone, not even being able to conceive of a Roman citizen deviating from it. Therefore, they are ultra-conservative (all Romans are conservative in politics, but the *optimates* are more conservative than others), fundamentalists in their way of thinking, and intransigent, extremist, and irreducible in their way of acting.

But all that glitters is not gold. The *optimates*' all-out defense of the *mos maiorum* is not a political doctrine. It is an ideological screen, supported by emotional and fideistic attitudes and used as an instrument of persuasion and propaganda. What is most important to the *optimates* is that the nobility, each noble family, and *gens* (family clan) maintains their own supremacy over the rest of society, the rest of the nobility, and the other *gentes* and grow increasingly rich in wealth, power, and glory. Rather than serving the general interest of the State, they aim to preserve and protect the interest of the ruling class as a whole and that of its individual parts.

The counterparts of the *optimates* on the political scene are the *populares*, those Roman citizens—usually magistrates or ex-magistrates—who feel or try to appear popular in the sense of "friends of the people, by whom they are loved" and who consider themselves as an instrument serving the "interests of the plebs." But the vagueness of this formula leaves room for interpretation. In fact, the word "people" has a different meaning depending on whether those who pronounce it are those *populares* who work in good faith in favor of the weak and oppressed or those who do not. For the former, it indicates all of the lower social classes (*proletarii, humiliores,* and *capite censi*), i.e., the *plebicola* (lower-class *plebs*, lower-class people, populace), that is to say, the largest part of the Roman people, including the most disadvantaged and mistreated. For the latter, it means all the Roman people, comprising the patriciate, the enriched plebeians, and the lower-class *plebs*, as if the interests of the rich and those of the poor were not incompatible. The *populares* demonstrated a tendency toward demagogy and populism and often called on the streets to support their initiatives. They are not always driven by commendable intentions. Sometimes, their "altruism" hides their desire to pursue concrete personal interests.

The *optimates* and the *populares* are the *partes* (sides) into which the Roman people are divided politically and the mirror of the decline of Roman public life, which began in the Gracchan Age (133–121) with the entry of daggers into the Forum. They were relatively balanced in terms of their ability to influence the choices of the state. The *optimates* had the majority in the Senate and always had at least one consul on their side, with a few exceptions. Therefore, they could profoundly influence state policies and control much of public life. The *populares*, however, through the plebeian tribunes on their side, controlled two out of three popular assemblies: the *comitia tributa* and the *concilia plebis*, both of which also had legislative powers. Both often weaponized complaints and criminal trials. In this case, the political dialectic moved into a courtroom and became a big show, attracting a large audience.

It should be noted that these *partes* are not political parties. That is, they are not associations of people sharing the same vision on fundamental issues pertaining to the state and society—or, if they did, only on specific and particular themes—whose organization is divided into committees and councils and whose activity was carried out in the public sphere and mainly aimed at organizing and directing consensus. Instead, they are factions, political sects. Each party is made up of one or more leading exponents and their followers and intolerantly and aggressively pursues excessively particularistic goals, devoid of any sense of the general interest, clashing with other groupings in radical, possibly violent ways. However, no one within it pulls the strings or acts as a spokesperson for all the other members.

The *optimates* and *populares* confront each other continuously and everywhere: in the Senate, in the courts of justice, and in the streets and squares. Sometimes, when the conflict becomes more bitter, and the delicacy of the moment requires it, some senators—Marcus Tullius Cicero, Lucius Marcius Philippus, Marcus Claudius Marcellus, and Lucius Aemilius Paulus, to name only a few—mediated between the contenders. However, when it comes to siding with one or the other, they abstain in view of reaping future advantages that could derive from the indulgent attitude of each *pars* toward them. These senators are not with any *pars* but juggle incompatible situations and interests, paying attention only to immediate benefits. Calling them moderates is not inappropriate, but it is perhaps more accurate to call them opportunists.

CHAPTER I

A Bloody Reform

The tribuneship of the plebs was born to protect the plebeians from the abuses of the patriciate, to understand the plebians' needs, and to promote their interests. Therefore, it can only be held by a plebeian (however, a Roman citizen who was born as a patrician can hold it if he becomes a plebeian through a process called the *transitio ad plebem*). There are 10 tribunes of the plebs at any one time. They take office on 10 December of the year of their election and remain in office until 9 December the following year.

The distinctiveness of this magistracy relates to the personal guarantees and the powers divested in it. The tribunes of the plebs are sheltered from intimidation and reprisals due because the law endows them with various immunities. They are inviolable (no one can offend or harm them), sacrosanct (any offense or harm done to them is sacrilege because it infringes the *pax deorum*), and immune from coercion (they are independent of any political conditioning).

Regarding their powers, tribunes of the plebs can promote laws and exclusively convene the *comitia tributa* and the *concilia plebis* (only the consuls can convene the *comitia centuriata*). They also have the power of veto, which no other civil magistrate in Rome has, except the consuls. However, a consul can only exercise the power of veto against his colleague, whereas each tribune of the plebs can veto any initiative they believe to be detrimental to the plebs' interests, no matter who it was initiated by (even a consul or another tribune). Furthermore, a tribune of the plebs can have anyone who interferes with the exercise of their duties arrested and imprisoned, even if that person is a consul or another tribune. In certain respects, they thus are placed on the same level as the consuls, if not above them.

The tribunes' remit to convene a popular assembly and the power of legislative initiative are crucial because the convening magistrate has the power to decide when, and if, to call the meeting, what topics to discuss, and how it should proceed (suspending it, if necessary); the only limitation is if the *auspicia* are possibly unfavorable.

If, in addition, we consider that a popular assembly is convened to vote on a bill, which it can only approve or reject, without being able to discuss it or amend it, it clearly emerges that the consuls and the tribunes of the plebs are in control of the legislative function. In reality, the tribunes of the plebs have greater control over this than the consuls because the *comitia tributa* and *concilia plebis* pass more laws than the *comitia centuriata* as a result of the activism of particular tribunes. The data bear this out. Until the end of the III century, the ratio between *rogationes* and *plebiscita* favored the former: 47 to 40. In the II century, the ratio reversed to such an extent that, by the end of the century, there had been 113 *plebiscita* and 58 *rogationes* (these figures also reflect an intensification of legislative activity).[1] This prevalence of new *plebiscita* continued through the second half of the II century. However, this doesn't mean the Romans' legislative output became more populist or democratic. In fact, many *plebiscita* were prompted by opinions expressed by the Senate, i.e., they were initiatives of tribunes of the plebs loyal to the Senate.

To say that a tribune is "loyal to the Senate" is a delicate way of saying that he has sacrificed his electoral mandate to promote, pursue, and protect the interests of the plebeians, primarily the lower-class plebeians, to the interests of the noble and aristocratic families. However, the tribuneship was only steered by the Senate until the mid-II century. Beyond this point, it became autonomous, at least to an extent. Few *plebiscita* are now submitted to the Senate before the tribunes explain them at public meetings (*contio*, pl. *contiones*) before the people gathered in assembly vote on them.

Tiberius Sempronius Gracchus was tribune in 133, while his brother Caius was tribune in 123 and 122. In all, they contributed 35 *plebiscita* to the total legislative production. In both this chapter and the next, we will look at these magistrates' personal affairs and political activities, so it's best to start by getting to know them. First of all, for the sake of brevity, we will refer to them from now on as the Gracchi, while we will call their personal and political friends the Gracchans.

The Gracchi were born from the marriage of Tiberius Sempronius Gracchus (220–154) and Cornelia Africana Minor (189–110). In 187 (or 184), Tiberius (the father) was tribune of the plebs. In 178, he was praetor and governor of

---

1 *Rogationes* once more became prevalent over *plebiscita* in the period from 100–44, during which there were 126 of the former and 111 of the latter. T. Lanfranchi, *In nome del popolo romano? Storia del tribunato della plebe* (Rome: Salerno, 2022), 120–121, esp. 120, n. 2.

Hispania Citerior (one of the two Roman provinces on the Iberian Peninsula, the other being *Hispania Ulterior*). After defeating the Celtiberians, he bound them to a robust peace agreement, destined to last for a quarter of a century. He was consul in 177, a strict censor in 169, and consul again in 163.

In 169, he contributed to the process of developing Rome's urban decoration, having the *Basilica Sempronia* built in the Forum (it's tradition that victorious commanders, on the occasion of the celebration of their triumph, donate a glorious public work to the city).[2] When the *Basilica Sempronia* was built, there was only one other *basilica* in the Forum, erected in 184 by Marcus Porcius Cato (nicknamed "the Censor" to distinguish him from his descendant Marcus Porcius Cato Uticensis).[3]

When Gracchus was tribune of the plebs, he vetoed the continuation of criminal proceedings against Publius Cornelius Scipio Africanus Maior and Lucius Cornelius Scipio Asiaticus,[4] two eminent public figures from a family that had contributed significantly to Rome's territorial expansion and to the diffusion of Greco-Hellenistic culture in the city.

Gracchus's gesture earned him the eternal gratitude of the Scipiones, which they expressed by granting him their *amicitia*. This pact was sealed by Gracchus's marriage to Scipio Africanus's daughter, Cornelia Africana Minor. This was followed by Gracchus's election to the consulship (an accomplishment that he would have found difficult to achieve without the friendship of the Scipiones).

Cornelia is a sophisticated, strong-minded woman. Most of her 12 children die in infancy. After the death of her husband in 154, she refuses numerous marriage proposals, including one from a king: Ptolemy VIII Euergetes II Tryphon (nicknamed "Physcon," "potbelly," because of his obesity). She maintains her widowhood and devotes herself to the education of her surviving children. Tiberius, Caius, and Sempronia are the couple's children who live to adulthood. It is said that, in response to a matron who flaunted her wealth,

---

2   E. La Rocca and S. Sortorella, eds., "La processione trionfale come spettacolo per il popolo romano," in *Trionfi romani. Catalogo della mostra (Roma, 5 marzo—14 settembre 2008)* (Milan: Mondadori Electa, 2008), 34–35.

3   Cato the Censor was a formidable judicial orator and writer and was consul in 195 and censor in 184. It was he who convinced the Senate that *Carthago* was about to become rich and powerful again and, therefore, "must be destroyed" as a preventative measure.

4   Scipio Africanus was consul in 205 and 194 and proconsul from 204 to 202. The victory he won at the Battle of Zama put an end to the Second Punic War. He was censor in 199 and *princeps senatus* from 199 before dying in 183. Scipio Asiaticus was elected to the consulship in 190 and, at the end of this year or the start of the next, led the Roman army to victory at the Battle of Magnesia (Syrian War, 192–188).

Cornelia showed her children to her and said, "Here are my jewels." This is why she is lauded as "the mother of the Gracchi."

In 133, Tiberius is 30 years old and has inherited the role and responsibilities of the father of the family, as well as the family's rich patrimony and the patronage of very important clients,[5] both in the city and in several provinces, predominantly in *Hispania*. He is an educated, cultured person with refined manners and is tied to other illustrious families, forming part of the Roman *gotha* (highest level). Specifically, he is linked to the *Cornelii Scipiones* through his mother and sister (he is the cousin and brother-in-law of the twice-consul and triumphator Publius Cornelius Scipio Aemilianus) and the *Claudii Pulchri* through his wife, Claudia.

Scipio Aemilianus played a major part in the public life and military history of Late Republican Rome; his name was known, whether venerated or cursed, from Italy to the Roman provinces of *Hispania* and Africa. He is the biological son of Lucius Aemilius Paullus Macedonicus and the adopted son of Publius Cornelius Scipio, who was, in turn, the son of Scipio Africanus Maior and the brother of Cornelia Africana, the mother of the Gracchi. He belongs, therefore, to two of the most prominent families in Rome, both senatorial and consular, and thus is an aristocrat. He owns considerable amounts of land, advanced through the *cursus honorum* to the very top. He is also one of the most gifted military commanders of recent decades. He was consul twice (147, 134), proconsul of Africa (147–146), and governor of both Iberian provinces (134–132). In 146, as proconsul, he conquered and razed the city of *Carthago*, a city-state in North Africa, capital of a maritime empire, and historically Rome's enemy.

Rome had already successfully fought against it twice (in the First Punic War, 264–241, and the Second Punic War, 218–202) when it attacked it for a third time, sieging it for three years, with immense bloodshed, before razing it to its foundations (Third Punic War, 149–146). When Scipio Aemilianus celebrated his triumph, he was the subject of extraordinary praise, exaltation, and glorification and was awarded the cognomen *ex-virtute* of *Africanus Minor* (not to be confused with Publius Cornelius Scipio Africanus Major, the victor at the Battle of Zama that ended the Second Punic War). Over the next decade, he was Rome's most respected and feared citizen. In 142, as censor, he attempted to curb Rome's growing luxury and immorality. Aemilianus thus notched up another success. As sole consul for *Hispania* (the Iberian Peninsula, i.e., Spain and Portugal), he put an end to the Celtiberian Wars, a series of

---

5   On the provincial clients Tiberius Sempronius Gracchus left to his children, see E. Badian, *Foreign Clientelae, 264–70 B.C.* (Oxford: Clarendon, 1958) 166; 169; 180–181.

conflicts fought from 181 to 133 between Rome and some of the *Hispani* (Iberians), definitively affirming and consolidating Roman dominion in central northern *Hispania*. The war ended with *Numantia*—an Arevaci fortress (near modern Soria in Spain, at the confluence of the Duoro and Tera) and the last stronghold of the revolting Celtiberians—being razed to the ground. After remaining in office for 132, he returned to Rome.

Scipio Aemilianus isn't only a very successful military commander but also a Hellenophile and an intellectual. Being an attentive connoisseur and custodian of the *mos maiorum* and a faithful follower of the true Roman tradition in which he was educated doesn't prevent Scipio Aemilianus from enthusiastically welcoming cultural innovations originating from outside the Roman tradition, especially from Greece. Like both his biological and adoptive parents, he admires and loves the Greco-Hellenistic civilization, recognizes the Greeks' intellectual superiority over the Romans, and advocates integration between the Hellenistic world and the Roman *imperium*.

An educated and cultured man, Scipio Aemilianus is the pivot around which the Scipionic Circle—the largest circle of intellectuals in the city—revolves. The Scipionic Circle formed around Scipio Africanus; after his death, it found new points of reference: first in Lucius Paullus Aemilius Macedonicus, then, after he passed away in 160, now in Scipio Aemilianus. The ideas and ideological convictions that mature in that environment, if carried into the outside world, influence the formation of public opinion, public life, the domestic and foreign policies of the Roman state, and the development process of Greco-Roman civilization.

Probably the main contribution offered by the Scipionic Circle to the Hellenization of Latin culture is having reshaped the set of values and notions tied to the concept of *humanitas*, the Latin equivalent of the Greeks' *philanthropia*, into a form more closely adhering to Roman sensibilities. *Humanitas* is the concept according to which human beings are worthy of the name, provided they aren't barbaric, inhuman, and uncultured. This emerges in a passage of a work by Publius Terentius Afer (190/185–159), a writer of comedies of Berber ethnicity: *"Homo sum, humani nihil a me alienum puto"* (I am human, I regard nothing human as alien to me).[6]

Moreover, the theory according to which Rome's foreign policy has the value and significance of a historic mission aimed at protecting all peoples and assuring them of peace and justice was also born from the Scipionic Circle's ideology of intertwining relations between Rome and the peoples

---

6   Ter. *Haut.* 77.

subject to it with *humanitas*. This understanding shaped the mentality of the more perceptive Romans in the sense that it convinced them that Rome's previous territorial conquests were not final but significant stages of a long-term strategy through which Rome will assume control over an ever more extensive *imperium* and become *caput mundi* (capital of the world) and *patria totius orbis* (government of the habitable world). It has a corollary: since the Romans have the task of civilizing all of humanity, to make it a single *gens*, a single nation, they have the right/duty to govern all the peoples of the Earth.

Tiberius Sempronius Gracchus was elected as tribune of the plebs in 134 for 133, and he presented a bill on agrarian reform. To prepare for this, he took advice from some Roman citizens renowned for their virtue and reputation: his father-in-law Appius Claudius Pulcher, Publius Licinius Crassus Dives Mucianus, and Publius Mucius Scaevola Augur. It cannot be ruled out that he also considered the teachings and advice of the Stoic philosopher Caius Blossius of *Cumae*, who was his tutor and is now a friend.

In 133, the *princeps senatus* is Appius Claudius Pulcher. He is one of the Salii, an augur, a tenacious and skillful judicial orator, and the brother of a Vestal Virgin. He was consul in 143 and censor in 136. He defeated the Salassi, a Celtic tribe from the western Alps, in battle before requesting a triumph from the Senate. Despite being refused, he celebrated a triumph anyway at his own expense. Later, he was censor (from 136 to 132). He is part of a family belonging to the *gens Claudia*, a clan that has lived in Rome for a couple of centuries but originates from Caere, around 40 km north of Rome in *Etruria*. Although they belong to an aristocratic family (three of its members served as consul in 212, 185, and 143), the *Claudii Pulchri* live in hardship, evidence that one's coat of arms and cash don't always go hand in hand. But they haven't lost their predilection for feeling superior. They are known for being hard-hearted and looking down on the lower-class plebeians. Appius Claudius Pulcher, Gracchus's father-in-law, is known among his fellow citizens for being a haughty, conceited man.

Crassus Dives Mucianus has served as praetor and is a jurisconsult. He is a very wealthy, educated, and cultured man and is fluent in Greek.[7] Scaevola Augur, born in 169, is the son of Quintus Mucius Scaevola and cousin of both Publius Licinius Crassus Dives Mucianus and Quintus Mucius Scaevola Pontifex. He was consul in 117. He married Laelia, daughter of Caius Laelius, with whom he has a son and two daughters. He is an augur, a distinguished jurist, renowned as a jurisconsult, and a famed legal scholar. He is considered

---

7   Val. Max. VIII.7.6; Quint. *Inst.* XI.2.50.

one of the founders of civil law, together with Manius Manilius Nepos and Marcus Junius Brutus. He is a person of absolute honesty and moral rectitude. In 141, when he was tribune of the plebs, he put forward and obtained approval for a plebiscite that sought the death penalty for a magistrate who had been bribed while carrying out his judicial functions.[8] It's worth noting that Scaevola was less open about his participation in the preparation of Gracchus's reform project than his brother,[9] being outwardly more reserved and less conspicuous in the eyes of third parties.[10]

The agrarian law reforms developed by Gracchus and his friends are fundamentally aimed at relieving demographic pressure, a problem that Rome has long faced. In fact, the city has been familiar with the issue of immigration since its foundation and has always accepted it, reconciling everyone's needs and integrating immigrants, giving them space to establish themselves.

Since the period of the Roman monarchy (753–509), multitudes of men and women have emigrated to Rome, driven by wars, hunger, famines, and natural disasters, by better job opportunities and living standards, the simple desire to embrace the Roman way of life, or due to propaganda, which described Rome as a promised land and issued an invitation from the Roman authorities to seek "the joy of Rome." Often, it wasn't a question of single individuals who decided to emigrate, perhaps with their families, but of large groups or even entire communities of citizens. They came from wider *Latium* (Latins) or elsewhere in Italy (Italics, *Italiotes*, Etruscans, Gauls), as well as the Roman provinces or even areas beyond these, primarily the Eastern Mediterranean and the Near East. We should mention, for example, the refugees from *Alba Longa*, who settled on the *Caelian* Hill during the reign of Tullus Hostilius (672–641);[11] the refugees from *Politorium*, who settled on the Aventine during the reign of Ancus Marcius (641–616);[12] and the migration of the *gens Claudia* in 504, when the Sabine noble Attius Clausus led a retinue of relatives, friends, and as many as 5,000 clients to Rome from *Inregillum*, or *Regillum*, in Sabinum.

Within a generation or two, immigrants were fully integrated into the urban context through various forms of assimilation and social advancement, including serving in the army and undertaking military careers. They thus became part of a society marked by inequalities and imbalances but where

8   Plut. *T. Grac.* IX*; Cic. *Luc.* XIII.

9   Cic. *Acad. pr.* II.5.13*.

10   A. Guarino, *La coerenza di Publio Mucio* (Napoli: Iovene, 1981), 86.

11   Liv. I.30.1–2.

12   Liv. I.32–33; Dion. Hal. III.43.2.

social mobility was guaranteed and a state whose strengths were in its stable administration, significant military potential, and an integrated economy.

Proof of the foregoing is found in the fact that some major figures of monarchic Rome were not natives: the kings Numa Pompilius (r. 715–672) and Ancus Marcius (r. 641–616) were Sabines, Tarquinius Priscus was born in Tarquinia to a Greek merchant and a local noble, founding an Etruscan dynasty, while other consuls were of Italic or Etruscan origin. Some immigrants became rich after receiving their shares of spoils of war or benefiting from fortune in business, and others made their names in the judiciary and became part of the Senate. Consider, for example, the *Livii*: members of this family became consul, censor, and dictator.[13]

After the Sack of Rome by the Gauls (390/386), many people who worked the land, artisans, and laborers from Rome's suburbs, the rest of *Latium*, and other regions of Italy settled in Rome with their families, attracted by the numerous job opportunities presented by the great rebuilding work. Fifty years later, that is by the end of the Latin War (340–338), Rome had recovered and was one of the largest cities in Europe (426 hectares). On the eve of the First Punic War, it seems it had a population of around 187,000. With its rise to the rank of a great Mediterranean power, marked by the wars of the previous century—Punic (264–241, 218–201, 149–146), Macedonian (215–205, 200–196, 171–168, 149–148), Syrian (192–188), Celtiberian (181–179, 154–152, 143–133), Lusitanian (155–139), and Achaean (146)—it has become the fulcrum of the Mediterranean world and, above all, a vast magnet that draws wealth and people.

In the first half of the II century, its population increased, though by exactly how much is unknown. Another considerable increase occurred in the second half of the century. This was accompanied by rampant property speculation, which made use of an abundant quantity of slave labor for the construction of *insulae*, houses, and entire neighborhoods.

The increase in merchant traffic has led not only to a growth in the comings and goings of sailors through the river ports of the urban area of Rome, but also to the establishment of "colonies" of foreigners from overseas and transalpine regions. The accumulation of spoils of war resulted in the influx of enormous numbers of slaves into the city. In 225, there were already 250,000 of them, and this only increased as time went on. The arrival of so much slave labor in the city prompted senatorial families to use it for any sort of work that needed doing in their residential houses, businesses, or extra-urban agricultural

---

13 The family name *Livius* turns up repeatedly in the *Fasti Capitolini*.

estates. This led to reductions in land workers' wages, if not to them being deprived of work altogether, and to the collapse of small- and medium-level agricultural enterprises, bankrupted by the irrepressible competition from the landowners, capable of producing more and at lower prices. All those who lived in the countryside and had been disadvantaged by this recourse to servile labor saw no other solution to guarantee their survival than to emigrate to the city.

It's worth noting that economic migration is interlinked with another migratory phenomenon—the movement of wealthy migrants who sought opportunities in the capital for social advancement—that, over time, played an increasingly important role, with the result that Italic immigrants were joined by those who came from territories that were gradually being conquered by Roman armies and the consequent creation of networks of high-ranking immigrants.

However, it has always been—and still is —very difficult for the unemployed who have relocated to Rome to settle down there because there are also a vast number of slaves in the city, and some work is managed by slaves or freedmen. Therefore, while there are many opportunities for work in Rome (one only needs to think of those relating to the daily transport of goods and public building works), there are no guarantees. Sometimes, the only option for immigrants is the small itinerant trade. The less fortunate migrants can only add to the poorest ranks of the urban proletariat, living on the margins of legality, using every trick in the book, and increasing the levels of crime and prostitution.

Immigration isn't prosecuted as a crime, but the authorities fear the "social bomb" constituted by the have-nots and do-nothings. From the city authorities' point of view, it's vital to prosecute vagabonds and anyone who leaves their area of origin for no reason and, more generally, to monitor migratory movements and allow only the regular ones, from which less trouble is expected. This result can be achieved by maintaining constant vigilance over the registration mechanisms, enabling population movements to be tracked and more intense consideration being given to mobility by the legislator. The irregular immigrant can be expelled, as has already been done numerous times to restore balance with the Latin cities and regulate grants of citizenship. In 187 and 177, measures were taken to curb indiscriminate immigration with the expulsion of 12,000 people. Later, however, immigration resumed, recreating a scenario of demographic congestion, social tensions, and health, public order, and safety issues.

The project to reform the agrarian law put forward by Gracchus and his friends aims to reduce the demographic pressure in the city by attracting some of the poorest urban proletariat to the countryside through the assignment of portions of arable land. It is foreseen that, in this way, it will also be possible to revitalize small rural enterprises, decimated by continuous military levies and wars, and the irrepressible competition of the landowners, as well as to reconstitute a pool from which to draw for military recruitment.

The lands to be redistributed will be derived from the acquisition by the state, possibly forcibly, of lands that exceed the permitted allowance, the provisions of which have already been established; in the absence of such a transfer, the excess will be confiscated. The allowance is set at 500 *iugera* unless the owner has one or more children, in which case it is raised by 250 *iugera* per child, up to a maximum of 1,000 *iugera*. In exchange for this necessary sacrifice, the landholders will become owners of portions of *ager publicus populi romanorum* ("soil owned by the Roman people") if they rent them, hold them under concession, or occupy them illegally. The lands acquired by the state will be subdivided into lots of a predetermined size (30 *iugera?*); these lots will then be assigned to poor Roman citizens living in the city. A three-member commission, elected by the *comitia tributa*, will oversee the implementation of the reform.

The money needed to compensate the owners who will have to cede to the State the lands exceeding the limit indicated above will be found by accepting and then auctioning the patrimony that King Attalus III, on his deathbed, bequeathed to the Roman people and which consists in the Kingdom of *Pergamum*, the royal treasury, and most of the Crown's assets. It should be understood that the Senate of Rome has not yet accepted the bequest, not out of indolence or carelessness, but because acceptance would imply Rome expanding territorially into Anatolia, and it is reluctant to make this political choice. It must also be said that the province's administration (and, therefore, the choice of what to do with the legacy of Attalus, if accepted) is, by inveterate practice, the competence of the Senate, while Gracchus's planned reform transfers it to the legislator—in practice, the popular assembly that will vote on the relevant bill, presided over by Gracchus himself.

Since it supports the poor and penalizes the rich, Gracchus's legislative initiative isn't looked upon favorably by senatorial (i.e., noble) and senatorial and consular (i.e., aristocratic) families. One of its staunchest opponents is the group of families with the cognomen *Metellus*, of whom the most prominent member is the senator Quintus Caecilius Metellus Macedonicus.

In 133, Metellus Macedonicus is 55 years old (he will die in 116 at the age of 62). He was praetor in 148, consul in 143, and proconsul and governor of *Hispania Citerior* in 142. When he celebrated his triumph (146), he was awarded the cognomen *ex-virtute Macedonicus* for his valor as a general in the Third Macedonian War (171–168), for definitively defeating Andriscus, self-styled son of King Perseus and pretender to the throne of Macedon (Fourth Macedonian War, 150–148), and for having organized the territories of the suppressed republics of Macedon into a new province called Macedonia (later, Achaea was incorporated into the province as well). This completed the Roman conquest of the Balkan peninsula (Epirus, Macedon, and mainland Greece).

Metellus Macedonicus must also be remembered for having participated in the process of adding to the urban architecture of the capital through the construction of the *Porticus Metelli*, one of the most beautiful monuments in Rome. Located in the southern part of the *Campus Martius*, near the *Circus Flaminius*, this complex consists of a long portico with two naves in the Ionic style that encloses an almost perfect square containing two temples rising side by side.

Metellus Macedonicus's children are: Quintus (Balearicus, 170–after 120), Lucius (Diadematus, II century–early I century), Marcus (fl. 115), Caius (Caprarius, 160–after 113), and two girls, both called Caecilia Metella. In addition to Metellus Macedonicus, the group of families that bear the cognomen *Metellus* currently contains his brother Lucius Caecilius Metellus Calvus (200, or at least before 178–after 136),[14] who was consul in 142, as well as their relatives, grandchildren, and great-grandchildren.[15] Metellus Calvus is the father of Lucius (Dalmaticus, 164–after 99), Quintus (Numidicus, ?–91), and Caecilia Metella.

The Metelli are aristocrats of plebeian extraction. Male members of the family are all called Caius, Lucius, Marcus or Quintus, while women are invariably called Caecilia. Many of the men were or will be senators, consuls, censors, provincial governors, augurs, and pontiffs. Metellus Macedonicus's sons will be consul in 123, 117, 115, and 113. Marcus will also be censor. Metellus Calvus's sons will be consul in 119 and 109, and Dalmaticus will be censor in 115 and then *pontifex maximus*.

The women are married into high-ranking families or become Vestal Virgins. Metellus Macedonicus's daughters will be married to Publius Cornelius Scipio Nasica Serapio and Caius Servilius Vatia, Caecilia Metella Calva will be married

---

14 Metellus dies after 136, but exactly when is unknown.

15 On the Metelli during the Republic: D. W. Simmons, "From Obscurity to Fame and Back Again: The Caecilii Metelli in the Roman Republic" (Masters thesis, Brigham Young University, 2011); J. Ooteghem (Van), "Les Caecilii Metelli de la Règublique," *Mémoires de l'Académie Royale Belgique* 59 (Brussels: Palais des Académies, 1967); M. G. Morgan, "The Rise and Fall of the Caecilii Metelli, 284–46 B.C." (Ph.D. dissertation, University of Exeter, 1961).

to Lucius Licinius Lucullus, while Metellus Balearicus's daughter will become a Vestal Virgin and a priestess of the goddess Juno Sospita.

The Metelli are very wealthy. Their patrimony is made up primarily of large tracts of land, with a composite and diversified makeup comprising villas, vineyards, gardens, and estates. In addition, they hold portions of the *ager publicus* either on lease or in concession. In short, the Metelli are significant landowners.

They belong to the *gens Caecilia*, a plebeian family clan that came to Rome after the Sack of Rome (390–386) from the area of *Praeneste* (Palestrina), a city lying on the Monte Ginestro, in southern *Latium*, about 30km southeast of Rome; and are closely linked, by bonds of friendship or marriage, to other families of the ruling class who are themselves leading figures of Roman public life.

Shortly after Gracchus presented his plebiscite, the tribune of plebs Marcus Octavius, loyal to the Senate, exercises his veto during a *contio*, blocking the process of forming the law. In a subsequent *contio*, which is attended by a large crowd, Gracchus tries in vain to persuade Octavius to retract his veto. He speaks to him affectionately, clasping his hands in his.[16] He begs him in front of everyone to back down from his position out of love for the people, who are only asking for justice and who, with the reform's approval, would only receive modest compensation after so much suffering and danger. But Octavius remains unmoved.

During a third *contio*,[17] since he couldn't overcome Octavius's opposition, Gracchus turns to the crowd and asks them rhetorically, "If Octavius assumed an attitude clearly contrary to the interests of the people, can he remain in office?" He doesn't wait for a response, giving it himself: "The tribunes of the plebs answer to the people, who elected them; if the latter recognize the termination of the bond, they can remove him." Gracchus thus sums up the theory of popular sovereignty, which is based on populism, that is, a positive evaluation of the people, understood as the only source of legitimization of power and the repository of all collective energy and intelligence.

Before long, Gracchus presents a bill that aims to have Octavius removed from office and put it to the earliest possible vote[18] of the *comitia tributa* without observing the prescribed interval of three *nundinae* (market days),

---

16 Plut. *T. Grac.* XI*.

17 App. *B. Civ.* I.12 speaks of three public meetings (*contiones* and/or assemblies): in the first, Octavius used his veto; in the second, Octavius confirmed his veto; and in the third, Gracchus proposed Octavius's removal.

18 App. *B. Civ.* I.12*.

equal to 21 consecutive calendar days, following the date of its presentation.[19] Gracchus's nine colleagues, including Octavius, and the consul, Scaevola, sits motionless, waiting for the people to pronounce their verdict.[20]

On the day of the vote, when the first of the 35 tribes voted in favor of approving the plebiscite, Gracchus turns to Octavius and invites him to withdraw his veto. Octavius refuses to give way, so the voting resumes. By the time the first 17 tribes had spoken out against Octavius, Gracchus tries one last time to convince his colleague to drop his convictions, but Octavius is adamant. Voting resumes, and the vote of the 18th tribe against Octavius means the vote reaches a majority.

At this point, since the bill has been passed, it is no longer necessary to get the remaining tribes to vote. Thus, the *lex Sempronia de potestate tribunicia M. Octavio abroganda* is approved and immediately enters into force. Octavius contests the "constitutional legitimacy" of his dismissal, but the pressure from the crowd, which is inveighing against him, forces him to leave the scene. Later, as a simple citizen, he continues to protest that he was the victim of an abuse of power. He refuses to admit that the institutional conflict had erupted because of him. The now-vacant position of tribune is filled by the first of the unelected, Quintus Mummius, a client of Gracchus's.[21]

After Octavius's dismissal, nothing further prevents the land reform bill from being put to the vote. Gracchus, therefore, reconvenes the assembly. On the day of the assembly, it approves Gracchus's plebiscite without hesitation.[22] Thus the *lex Sempronia Ti. Gracchi agrarian secunda* comes into force. All this takes place in the context of highly polarized emotions. Some demonstrations reflect the anger and despair of the landed aristocracy. Others reflect joy, enthusiasm, and admiration, expressing intense, deeply held emotions that reflect the feeling of impassioned participation of the lower-class plebeians, or rather, in the effect that the latter produced on the tribune's supporters.

---

19 Dion. Hal. VII.58.3, X.35.4. It's uncertain whether the *trinundinum* (the interval between three *nundinae*) required 16 days to pass from the proposal or 24. The ban on putting bills to the vote within three weeks of their presentation had been imposed during the reign of Romulus, during the reign of Servius Tullius, or after the expulsion of the kings in honor of Servius Tullius.

20 A. Guarino, *La coerenza di Publio Mucio* (Napoli: Iovene, 1981), 111.

21 The sources disagree on the name of the tribune elected to replace Octavius. According to App. 1.12*, he was called Quintus Mummius, but according to Plut. *T. Grac.* XIII.2* and Oros. 5.8.3*, he was called Minucius. D. C. Earl, "Octavius, trib. pleb. 133 B.C. and his successor," *Latomus* 19, no. 4 (1963): 657–669.

22 Plut. *T. Grac.* XIII.1*; App. *B. Civ.* I.13.50.

Shortly thereafter, Gracchus has himself, his father-in-law Appius Claudius, and his brother Caius elected as commissioners to oversee the division and assignment of lands. We've already met Appius Claudius Pulcher. In 133, Caius Sempronius Gracchus is a young man in his early 20s. He has just returned to his homeland after fighting against the Celtiberians in *Hispania* as a military tribune in the army of his cousin Scipio Aemilianus.

The most significant aspect of what happened isn't the fact that Gracchus is politically very powerful but rather that, before him, no magistrate had ever even dreamed of preventing a tribune of the plebs from exercising his veto, let alone publicly stating that the people gathered in assembly could revoke the mandate of a tribune who hadn't acted in the interests of the plebs. The implication is that when it came to identifying the interests of the plebs, the last word didn't belong to an individual tribune but to the people gathered in assembly (and, ultimately, to the one who oversaw their choices). From this perspective, Octavius's removal from office was an unprecedented and explosive political act.

Previously, the opposition of most of the Senate, dominated by the *optimates*, to Gracchus's policy had remained hidden because the tribune was an aristocrat and was supported politically by some very prominent senators. After Octavius's dismissal, this transforms into open intolerance, voiced with strenuous criticisms of Gracchus's work and even personal attacks. It is claimed in harsh, bitter tones that Gracchus should have waited for Octavius's term to end before taking legal action against him; that, by having acted differently, he has profoundly altered the traditional way of doing politics; and that, therefore, there is now a danger of instability to the socio-political system, which is based on the primacy of the patricians and enriched plebeians and on the secondary role of the low-class plebeians. Gracchus is accused of being a provocateur and a saboteur and is showered with insults.

However, the true reason for the *optimates'* opposition to Gracchus's bill lies elsewhere. They are defending their personal profits, since senatorial families have a quasi-monopoly over access to the economic exploitation of the *ager publicus*, and it is thus in their interests to prevent new beneficiaries from gaining access.

With the discourse's deterioration, the political dialectic becomes harsh, impetuous, and, at times, fiery. An altercation breaks out between Gracchus and Metellus Macedonicus. On another occasion, Gracchus can't find the words to stand up to his interlocutor, Titus Annius Luscus Rufus, consul in 153.[23]

---

23 Plut. *T. Grac.* XIV.

Gracchus has won the land reform game, but he fears losing control of the environment surrounding him and being unable to escape the severity of his circumstances. In other words, he worries he'll be subject to violence and recriminations when his mandate expires, and he no longer enjoys the legal protection associated with his office. Indeed, it's already rumored that the tribune loyal to the Senate, Marcus Minucius Rufus, intends to accuse him publicly of high treason.

The presentiment of coming to a bad end torments Gracchus. He knows danger can manifest in various ways, suddenly and unexpectedly, and this thought makes him feel helpless. He's afraid his enemies will break into his house at night to assassinate him.[24] He's even convinced people are coming after him when they aren't.

After a long period of brooding, Gracchus perceives a possibility for salvation: he will be a candidate in the elections for the magistracies that will take place in October and be re-elected to office; if he is, he will be protected by legal immunity for another year (10 December 133–9 December 132), and he can then re-evaluate things from there.

But he's wrong. Re-election to office will protect him from prosecution—but not from physical violence.

Furthermore, Gracchus plans to have his brother Caius nominated for the tribuneship of the plebs and his father-in-law Appius Claudius Pulcher for the consulship.[25] If they too are elected, they will strengthen his position of power.

Access to the Roman magistracies is regulated by the *lex Villia annalis*, approved in 180. Regarding access specifically to the tribuneship of the plebs, this law states that one must be at least 30 years old. But Tiberius claims to be able to demonstrate that Caius isn't too young to be a candidate and the fact he hasn't been quaestor doesn't render him ineligible. To this end, he invokes a well-known precedent: in 148, Scipio Aemilianus was elected to the consulship for 147 even though he wasn't yet 40 years old (as prescribed by the *lex Villia*), nor had he been praetor. This was possible—he recalls—because the Senate, the consuls, and the *comitia centuriata* had agreed that, in exceptional circumstances, it was possible to contravene the law.

---

24 Plut. *T. Grac.* XVI.7*. Appian also hints at the imminent threat of death.

25 Plut. *T. Grac.* XVI.1*. Dio *Framm. Fr.* 83.7–8 (=EV 72) also reports that Gracchus "attempted to secure the tribuneship for the following year also, in company with his brother, and to appoint his father-in-law consul; and to obtain this end he did not hesitate to make any statement or promise anything whatsoever to people." However, references to the candidatures of Caius and Pulcher aren't found in the other sources.

Gracchus reasons that Pulcher might be enticed by the idea of emulating him. If so, no legal impediment would stand in the way of Pulcher's candidacy for the consulship since the *lex Villia* reduced the minimum interval between magistracies from 10 years (established by the *lex Genucia de magistratibus* in 342) to two years, and Pulcher's tenure as censor ended more than two years ago.

It's legitimate to ask whether Gracchus's determination to run again is due to his irrational fears, or his mistrust of the *comitia centuriata*'s judgment, should he be indicted for high treason. But it isn't obvious that Gracchus, if accused, will be brought to trial, nor that he would be sentenced (to death, which can be commuted to permanent exile), because not all patricians and enriched plebeians are hostile towards him. It shouldn't be forgotten that the *Sempronii Gracchi* are bound by ties of friendship and marriage to the *Cornelii Scipiones*. Moreover, if things go badly for Gracchus, it wouldn't be hard for one of his colleagues to impose a veto to prevent him from being convicted.

The fact remains, however, that running again for the tribuneship of the plebs while already holding this magistracy arouses uncertainty and confusion. During the struggles between patricians and plebeians, a tribune was often confirmed in the office on a continuous basis,[26] but this hasn't happened for two centuries. The *optimates* refuse to allow this to happen again, referencing the fact that the *lex Villia* prescribes a specific interval between two electoral mandates. Gracchus replies that this constraint only applies to the curule magistracies (curule aedile, praetor, consul), not to the tribuneship of the plebs, proof of which is in the fact that more than one tribune has been re-elected before the stipulated two-year period is up. The *optimates* reply that if Gracchus's re-nomination, if it isn't in contradiction with the law, contravenes the custom, understood as an action or behavior repeated by a social group in a uniform and constant way over time in the conviction that it's proper and necessary. Gracchus confirms that his candidacy is legitimate because the early re-election of magistrates shouldn't only be seen from a legal perspective but also from a political perspective, both because it concerns a constitutional practice subordinate to the general interest (which varies according to circumstances) and because the people gathered in assembly have the right to choose their preferred magistrates, above and beyond laws and praxis.[27]

---

26 Caius Licinius Stolo and Lucius Sextius Lateranus were elected as tribunes of the plebs for 10 consecutive years (377–367) until the approval of the *Leges Liciniae Sextiae*.

27 See H. H. Scullard, *Storia del mondo romano: Dalle riforme dei Gracchi alla morte di Nerone* (Milan: Super BUR Rizzoli, 1992), 44–45, n. 14.

Gracchus hesitates to promote a bill that expressly excludes the repetition of the tribuneship of the plebs from the scope of the *lex Villia*. He fears he no longer has a majority in the popular assembly that will have to vote for him (*comitia tributa*). His fears are well-founded. Before long, the bloc of supporters that Gracchus enjoyed, especially among the low-class plebeians, crumbles.[28] Many of his political allies have sensed his political decline and abandoned him. The tribune Cnaeus Papirius Carbo intervenes to help his struggling colleague, promoting a bill to legalize Gracchus's candidacy.[29] Carbo is a member of a senatorial and consular family, so he's an aristocrat like Gracchus, a Roman citizen with a significant amount of noble blood. Like all others of its kind, his proposal will have to be discussed in the Senate and/ or explained in a *contio* before being submitted to the vote of the appropriate popular assembly.

In turn, Gracchus puts forward three bills, two of which are designed to win back some of his lost support: one gives a nod to the low-class plebeians, another to the enriched plebeians. The third aims to secure a measure to protect Gracchus against the threat of prosecution once he has left office.[30] The first bill proposes shortening the duration of compulsory military service, presenting it as a suitable measure to counteract draft dodging, which will also benefit those already in the army and even those assigned lands under the agrarian reforms. The second seeks to obtain a change in the composition of the judicial body of the *question perpetua de repetundis* (the "tribunal of the corrupt") by adding an equal number of *equites* to the senatorial jurors.[31] The third aims to extend the right to appeal to high-ranking individuals convicted of political crimes.

As Rufus has not yet completed his plebiscite, Gracchus is permitted—with reservations—to stand for election. When the election campaign begins, Gracchus seeks votes among the low-class plebeians of Rome's rural districts, who are mostly small landowners and land workers. As the date of the election approaches, however, the more Gracchus is convinced that the number of

---

28 For an in-depth discussion: E. Badian, "Tiberius Gracchus and the beginning of the Roman revolution," Aufstieg und Niedergang der romischen Welt, v. I.1, 1972, pp. 668–732.

29 This bill isn't identified more specifically in the sources.

30 Plut. *T. Grac.* XVI.1–2*. Dio *Framm. Fr.* 83.7–8 (=EV 72) mentions a series of bills proposed by Gracchus to win the people's favor, specifically "certain laws for the benefit of those of the populace serving in the army" and of "transferring the courts from the senate to the knights." Moreover, according to Vell. Pat. II.3.2*, Gracchus promised to extend Roman citizenship to the Italics.

31 Or to transfer control of the court from the Senate to a group of *equites*.

votes he will gain from the rural plebs will be few. Therefore, he intensifies his search for approval. He knocks on every door, canvassing votes, but meets with little success. There's no doubt that the political climate has changed. Something significant has happened. The lower-class plebeians, even those who have benefited from Gracchus's land reforms, are no longer willing to support their benefactor.

The day comes when the *comitia tributa* convenes to vote for Carbo's plebiscite.[32] Rubrius, a tribune of the plebs, is selected by lot to preside over the meeting. He doubts the legitimacy of Gracchus's candidacy, resigns, and is about to be replaced by Quintus Mummius. However, some other tribunes of the plebs, loyal to the Senate, argue that Rubrius's replacement must be chosen, as the law requires, by lot. The debate quickly becomes animated, and a scuffle nearly breaks out. To calm things down, Rubrius adjourns the meeting.

Gracchus is in despair. He is terrified by the thought of what might happen to him if he isn't re-elected. The day before the *comitia tributa* is reconvened to vote on the bill concerning him, he takes advantage of a friend's funeral to make his fear public knowledge.[33] He points to his family and begs the Roman people to take care of them if he were to die. Gracchus's remarks have made him more sincere, and the support that the people give him is more spontaneous. The evening shadows are lengthening when a procession of people accompany Gracchus and his family home and, when parting from the tribune, they encourage him for the following day.

Early in the morning, Gracchus is about to leave his house to go to the *Area Capitolina* to participate in the assembly. While he's thinking about the meeting's agenda—it consists of a single point: a vote on Carbo's plebiscite on Gracchus's re-election—and the fact that his future—and not just his political one—depends on the outcome of that vote,[34] an augur tells him that the day doesn't bode well; the gods are ill-disposed. This comes after some unusual events, which have been interpreted as bad omens (a pair of snakes, as well as

32 On this issue, see App. *B. Civ.* I.14. The incident is unclear. It isn't known whether Carbo's bill sought the legalization of Gracchus's candidacy (because it wasn't legal) or, more generally, to dispel doubts and uncertainties regarding the re-election of a tribune of the plebs who still held office.

33 Plut. *T. Grac.* XIII.3. Both Plutarch (*T. Grac.* XIII.4) and Dio (*Framm. Fr.* 83.8) speak of multiple children (cf. App. *B. Civ.* I.14). Both, however, refer to Sempronius Asellio (Gell. II.13.5), who speaks ambiguously of a single son. Of Gracchus's three children, one died in Sardinia while he was a military tribune, the second died in *Praeneste* at an early age, and the third disappeared in Rome shortly after his father's death. As such, the son whom Gracchus entrusted to the people's protection was probably the one who died in Sardinia.

34 D. C. Earl, "Tiberius Gracchus' Last Assembly," *Athenaeum* 43 (1965): 95–105.

some broken eggs, freshly hatched, from which little snakes were peering out, appeared in a helmet, and when a coop was opened to let some cockerels out, the birds refused to move, except for one, which wouldn't touch the corn).[35]

Gracchus is unsure what to do, but then he's distracted by the arrival of some companions, one of whom is Caius Blossius, and he ignores the warning. This is something that doesn't often happen. As he's leaving the house, he trips on the threshold of the front door, stubbing his toe so violently that he breaks the nail, which starts bleeding. Then, as he walks briskly to reach the meeting place, followed by a disorderly and noisy procession of people, he barely dodges a stone that accidentally fell from a roof. As the oddities add up, they start arranging themselves as harbingers of misfortune. Gracchus is deeply troubled, and, frowning and looking around him warily, he hesitates. To encourage him, Blossius draws on his pride and his role as a political leader: "It would be a shame and a great disgrace,"—he tells him—"if Tiberius, a son of Gracchus, a grandson of Scipio Africanus, and a champion of the Roman people, for fear of a raven should refuse to obey the summons of his fellow citizens; such shameful conduct, moreover, would not be made a mere matter of ridicule by his enemies, but they would decry him to the people as one who was at last giving himself the airs of a tyrant."[36] Gracchus regains his resolve and carries on.

He is awaited by a huge crowd, a multitude that fills every corner of the *Area Capitolina* to the extent that it's difficult to move through the midst of the throng. Gracchus's appearance on the podium of the Temple of Jupiter Optimus Maximus arouses a loud clamor. Gracchus welcomes such enthusiasm for a few moments, then gestures for quiet. After the ritual sacrifice confirms the absence of any impediments, Mummius, presiding over the meeting, begins to call the tribes to vote.[37] But just then, before even a single vote has been cast, a louder clamor arises from the edges of the *Area Capitolina*. A large group of Gracchus's political opponents are pushing through against the Gracchans, who are resisting and reacting to the shoves.

People get scared as the crowd compresses. Some, pushed by those behind them, push back in turn. Bodies are pressed against each other, pushed this way and that. Minor scuffles break out, then the whole square erupts in uproar. Caught in the fray, some people flee for their homes. Others react with speed

---

35   Val. Max. 1.4.2. Plut. *T. Grac.* 17.1–5. See also App. *B. Civ.* 1–2; Diod. Sic. 34–35.7.2.; Obseq. 27; Oros. 5.9.2; Vell. Pat. 2.3.2.

36   Plut. *T. Grac.* XVII.4. The same incident is narrated in the *Prodigiorum liber* by Julius Obsequens.

37   Plut. *T. Grac.* 18.1.

and vigor, allowing themselves to get involved in the fracas, even though they've been caught off guard. Still others fall to the ground and disappear under the mob. Some manage to get up and start running again or climb an altar, a statue, a quadriga, or a rostral column to avoid being sucked into the vortex.

The chaos grows and grows. Gracchus, from his position at the top of the steps leading to the temple, shouts and waves his arms to calm the situation. Meanwhile, the tribune's bodyguards closed ranks at the first signs of danger. Each has drawn a spear, which they use now to hold back the crowd. As the calls for calm have no effect and the turmoil threatens to spread still further, Mummius adjourns the meeting for the second time in two days.

The following day, the *Area Capitolina* is again filled with people from the early morning. Once the voting has begun, history repeats itself. A horde of nobles, clients, freedmen, and slaves, bursts into the square amid the temples, altars, and monuments and begins to cause a crush. In the noise and confusion, people are shouting and jostling, pushing while complaining that others are pushing. Marcus Fulvius Flaccus, one of the leading Gracchans, suddenly arrives at a run. He has come from the nearby Temple of Fides, where the Senate is meeting under the presidency of the consul Publius Mucius Scaevola Augur. The unity of the time and place of the two meetings is worth noting.[38]

Flaccus, prevented from approaching Gracchus by the wall of people, puts himself in full view and, from afar, signals to him. The tribune sees him, points him out to his bodyguards, and orders the people to make room for him. A gap opens up. Flaccus climbs the steps, panting. The confusion is at its peak. The noise is so loud that you cannot hear anyone speak except by shouting words into the ear of the person next to you. Highly animated, Flaccus warns Gracchus that some senators are plotting to get rid of him.

Gracchus makes a sudden gesture. Addressing those closest to him, he places a palm atop his head, meaning that serious danger is hanging over him.[39] The incident doesn't go unnoticed by the tribune's political opponents, who confuse the issue (they imply that Gracchus, by making that gesture, wanted to signify that he wanted to put a crown on his head), and a malicious rumor immediately starts to circulate among the crowd: "Gracchus has deposed the other tribunes of the plebs, proclaimed himself tribune, and is leading a *coup d'état*: he wants to be crowned king."

The agitators' far-fetched rumor soon reaches the senators' ears. The *pontifex maximus* Publius Cornelius Scipio Nasica Serapio, with a thundering voice and

---

38 See A. Guarino, *La coerenza di Publio Mucio* (Napoli: Iovene, 1981), 66.

39 Plut. *T. Grac.* 19.3*.

an imperious tone, asks the consul Scaevola if he's aware that, in the meeting taking place nearby, Gracchus is using violence to force the hand of the people gathered in assembly to be re-elected. Interpreting the situation in his own way, Nasica urges Scaevola to intervene to restore law and order. Scaevola is aware Gracchus is averse to taking initiatives that go against the law but must avoid exposing himself to the accusation of partiality. It should be highlighted that the confrontation is between two high priests of Roman religion, members of that college of pontiffs whose primary task is to indicate the most appropriate way to fulfill religious obligations to the Senate, magistrates, and individual Roman citizens so that the *pax deorum* isn't broken.

Scaevola points out that Gracchus hasn't yet been (re-)elected; if he had been, the correct way to contest his election would be the judicial one. In any case, he, as magistrate, will not take any forceful action and will not put any Roman citizen to death if he hasn't been tried, with all the appropriate safeguards; only if the plebs, by persuasion or force, rise up against the *res publica* will he intervene in its defense. From someone like him, a celebrated jurist and jurisconsult, a master of law, and a loyal and honest person, one wouldn't expect anything else.

Nasica doesn't agree with what Scaevola is saying at all. He is convinced that Gracchus joined the wrong side when he had Octavius dismissed and later ran for the tribuneship of the plebs again, and he strongly suspects that he's posing as a would-be tyrant in front of the people gathered in assembly. As such, he accuses Scaevola of betraying the city, causing a loud outcry. This is followed by interventions in support of Nasica's narrative and others that aim to discredit it, with a prevalence of the former. But no decision is made by the Senate to authorize or encourage the use of force against Gracchus.[40]

We thus reach a turning point from which enormous consequences will arise. It must be underlined that this is the moment from which there is no turning back. What follows will condition not only the internal politics of Rome in this phase but the history of Rome for a century to come.

Nasica takes the initiative. He wraps a fold of his toga over his left forearm, covers his head with another fold—as the priests of traditional Roman religion do when they are about to perform a religious act or ritual sacrifices—and calls Gracchus *nefas* (literally, "illegal, unjust, disastrous") in the sense of one who, by his heinous acts, has offended the gods, drawing their wrath on the citizenry. Then he pronounces the formula *sacer esto* (*sacer*, "accursed"; *esto*, imperative of the verb "to be").

---

40 App. B. Civ. 1.16.67. For the tone of the conversation: Plut. *T. Gracc.* 19.

Thus, the *pontifex maximus*, in the exercise of his functions, acting in accordance with the juridical-religious precepts that have governed Roman society since the beginning of its history, and with all the trappings of officiality, offers the *nefas* to the infernal gods so that they can take revenge, their anger can subside, and the *pax deorum* can be restored. This ritual is called the *consecratio capitis* and constitutes the legal basis of the subsequent declaration of *publicus hostis* (public enemy). It is the Senate's prerogative to make such a pronunciation, which has the juridical effect of stripping the recipient of all rights and privileges, depriving him of his patrimony, making the execution of the death penalty to which he was sentenced compulsory, and giving anyone the license to kill him with impunity, as one would do with a foreign enemy.

But Nasica bypasses the ruling of the Senate and shouts: "Whoever wants to come to the aid of the law, follow me!" Then he sets off at a brisk pace toward the Temple of Jupiter Optimus Maximus.[41] Blinded by fury, many senators tear their chairs to pieces, arm themselves with their curved legs, and, holding them like cudgels, queue up behind Nasica. The group is bolstered by the addition of the same senator's clients, freedmen, and slaves, armed with clubs and sticks. In a state of out-of-control agitation, a frenzied mob sprints the short distance that separates the Temple of Fides from the Temple of Jupiter Optimus Maximus and pounces on the crowd gathered in the open spaces around the latter.

In the meantime, as a precautionary measure, Gracchus's bodyguards have broken their spear shafts into pieces and distributed them to other Gracchans, who have gathered around the tribune with the intention of protecting him, while the priests and orderlies have forced the temple doors closed.[42] Panic quickly spreads through the crowd, and violence breaks out. A fierce hand-to-hand fight ensues, resulting in deaths and injuries. A rapidly growing number of people lose their lives, whether under the blows of the attackers or because they are suffocated and trampled in the crowd. Gracchus doesn't resist but tries to escape—though not out of cowardice but to avoid fueling the fight. Having reached the statues of the seven kings of Rome, he trips over some bodies and falls to the ground. He's getting up again when he's hit on the head, forcefully, with a chair leg by another tribune of the plebs, Publius Satyreius. He lets out a deafening cry and staggers, dazed, but receives another blow on the head, this time from a certain Lucius Rufus, who will later boast

---

41 Val. Max. III.2.17*; Vell. Pat. II.3*; A. J. Clark, Nasica and Fides, *Classical Quarterly* 57 (2007): 125–131.

42 Plut. *T. Grac.* 19.1*.

of his action, reveling in it.[43] Gracchus stays on his feet for a few moments, then goes limp and dies, eyes open and staring into space.

Thus, following the news that the *pontifex maximus* had declared Gracchus *nefas* and *sacer* was soon added the news that Gracchus has been killed. Gracchus's supporters, busy defending themselves from Nasica and his acolytes, fall into a state of shock and give in to despondency. Some extricate themselves from the fray and flee, abandoning the field in silence, stepping over inanimate bodies and wounded men, slumped and groaning, while others, covered in blood, howl and curse. Others continue to fight, though no longer with the impetus and determination of before. Gradually, the turmoil subsides.

The collective drama that has just unfolded ends with a terrifying death toll: 300 dead and an unknown number of injured, many of whom are seriously or mortally wounded. But it isn't over. What follows is an episode of beastly ferocity in which the winners of the battle just concluded are the protagonists. The bodies of the victims are grabbed with hooks and dragged through the streets of the city as far as the banks of the Tiber, where they are thrown into the river. All this is done not only to degrade and humiliate them but also to deny them the possibility of being buried and consequently to prevent them from entering the underworld. Caius Sempronius Gracchus wants to fish out his brother's body but is prevented from doing so.[44]

The massacre and violation of the victims' bodies are horrific and profoundly affect the citizenry. There have never been as many deaths in street riots as this; a tribune of the plebs had never been assassinated, nor had his murder been premeditated by the Senate, or at least by some of the senators. Nor had such a heinous murder been perpetrated for political reasons due to the laws introduced into the system by the magistrate himself in observance of the rules that regulate the legislative process and the functions of the constitutional bodies. The incident is of unprecedented gravity and causes dismay.

A somber sensation spreads that Gracchus's assassination may be a turning point in Rome's history, heralding the crisis of the *res publica*.[45] Effectively,

---

43 Unlike other sources, the unknown author of the *Rhetorica ad Herennium* (IV.55) reports that Nasica Serapio struck Gracchus on the head with a chair leg, killing him. For the suggestion that Scaevola defended Nasica's act: Cic. *Planc.* 36.88*.

44 For the events from Nasica's appeal to Scaevola to Caius being prevented from recovering his brother's body: Plut. *T. Grac.* 19.8–10. Vell. Pat., II.3.2. Ps. Aur. Vict., *De Vir. ill.*, 64.6. Val. Max. II 8,7*. Liv. *per.*, LVIII.7*. For the total of 300 deaths and the fact that all victims were killed with wooden weapons or stones: Plut. *T. Grac.* XX.3–5; Val. Max. IV.6.3, IV.7.1; Vell. Pat. II.6.7–8; App. I.16; Liv. *per.* LVIII; Oros. 5.9.

45 See App. *B. Civ.* I.1–2; Plut. *T. Grac.* 20.1.

from the killing of Gracchus onward, political life—previously based on the strength of ideas and the confrontation of opinions—will be increasingly marked by factional struggles and an inexorable spiral of violence until the outbreak of civil war.

CHAPTER II

The Politicization of Justice

Nasica publicly boasts of having led the movement against Gracchus, so a tribune of the plebs, Marcus Fulvius Flaccus, attacks him in the Senate, vehemently accusing him of instigating or being morally responsible for a collective crime and sacrilege. In the absence of any mandate from the Senate and Roman people, Nasica, in an abuse of office, caused the death of a magistrate elected legitimately by the Roman people, protected by sacrosanctity and immunity, with the false accusation of having broken the *pax deorum* when it was, in fact, he himself who shattered it. Then he looks toward the consul, Scaevola, as if to ask him to confirm the justness of his words.

But Nasica jumps to his feet and points his finger at the consul, saying: "I object! He is unjust!!" This arouses a murmur of reproach, so Nasica explains: "I object to him, senators, not because he is unjust to me but to everyone."[1] By this, he means that Scaevola is a political enemy in that he stands against most of the Senate. In fact, he was a friend of Gracchus, shared his political project, and collaborated with him to prepare the land reforms.

Yet this isn't what complicates the matter; rather, it's because the assassination of a tribune is a matter of national interest.[2] Many senators are opposed to Nasica being put on trial, claiming that if he, as the *pontifex maximus,* were found guilty of murder and sacrilege, there would be a scandal.[3] In that case, the Roman people, already feeling deeply wounded and driven by religious fanaticism, would turn against the established order in what is even now an explosive situation. The political system, the mean or status quo, must not be destabilized, even at the cost of going against the law.

---

1   Cic. *de Or.* 2.285.

2   Cf. Diod. Sic. XXXIV.33.6–7.

3   On the *pontifices* and the *pax deorum*: F. Santangelo, "*Pax deorum* and Pontiffs," in *Priests and State in the Roman World*, eds. J. H. Richardson and F. Santangelo (Stuttgart, 2011), 161–186.

The subject of discussion doesn't veer far from the theme of Nasica's speech. Nasica and others say that Gracchus was an immoderately ambitious man. In indulging his zealous and egocentric desire to establish and distinguish himself, he tried to overthrow the *res publica*, with the complicity of many friends, to restore the monarchy and make himself king. This can clearly be seen by the "procedural ruptures" that punctuated the process of the land reform law's formation and the final developments of the general situation before its tragic epilogue: Octavius's dismissal, the blocking of the magistrates' activity, the attempt to expropriate the Senate of its powers in matters of foreign policy and the administration of the state (particularly regarding the legacy of Attalus), and Gracchus's renomination for the tribuneship.[4] Further proof of the seditious nature of Gracchus's political action, they add, is this: the night before the second meeting of the people's assembly, he gathered his friends around him to agree on a plan of action and the signal that should be made if their attempts continued to be stalled.[5]

There has been continuous chattering in the background as each senator has spoken, an indistinct, subdued noise, often heard when many people are fidgeting and speaking quietly, similar to the rustle of leaves in the wind. But when Scaevola stands up to speak in his turn, a reverent silence descends on the large room. The consul starts by saying that Nasica and the senators, clients, freedmen, and slaves who accompanied him only entered the scene after the brawl had begun at the instigation of Gracchus and his friends, at which point some already lay dead and wounded and the tribunes of the plebs were fighting among themselves. Their intervention was exemplary. They acted in defense of the *res publica*, pitting violence against violence that was proportionate to the perilousness of the situation and in conformity with a general principle introduced by the *lex Valeria de sacrando cum bonis capite eius qui regni occupandi consilium inisset*, according to which, in the event of an attack on the person, property, or security of the state, any citizen can (and, in a sense, must) take personal action against the violence of others. This law is the one that, in 509, abolished the monarchy and established that anyone

---

4   "[...] it becomes clear that with [the land reforms], Tiberius was undertaking a precise and systematic realignment of the tribune's functions; his opponents' criticisms focus on this aspect, almost to the point of obscuring the very contents of the *lex Sempronia*." M. Balbo, *Riformare al res publica. Retroterra sociale e significato politico del tribunato di Tiberio Gracco* (Bari: Edipuglia, 2013), 49.

5   This detail is reported by Appian but isn't mentioned by Plutarch. See N. Barrandon, *Les massacres de la République Romaine* (Paris: Fayard, 2018), 107–108.

who wishes to make themselves a tyrant must be killed with freedom from bloodguilt for the killer.[6]

Thus, by trying to violently overthrow the *res publica* to make himself king, Gracchus would have forced the citizens who most closely adhered to Roman tradition to engage in "lawful" violence in defense of freedom.[7] The obvious conclusion is that Gracchus is to blame for the massacre on the Capitoline, as well as for his own murder. Gracchus fell victim to the violence that he introduced into the system, exercised in response to the laws he pushed through. Nasica and those who followed him into the fray aren't legally prosecutable because they acted in defense of the state, because tyrants and anyone who aspires to tyranny must die, and because those who kill them cannot be punished. Moreover, Nasica, acting in his capacity as *pontifex maximus*, conferred a particular solemnity on his intervention, casting Gracchus down to the gods of the underworld.[8]

Scaevola speaks without rancor or satisfaction because his speech is what he feels he must say, arising from his profound sense of justice and strict rigor in interpreting and applying the law. Therefore, Scaevola, by criticizing Gracchus, distances himself from the murdered tribune and his friends—if anything, he was so close to them as to be able to call himself one of them—and aligns himself with the majority of the Senate, led, on this occasion, by Nasica. His opinion is taken as gospel by most senators, who recognize it and use it as their own, thus putting an end to the debate.

However, Scaevola's analytical judgment is based on a premise devoid of any connection with reality—an imaginary, false, or, at best, erroneous assessment of a situation that doesn't exist and which, consequently, doesn't allow the *lex Valeria* to be applied. On this basis, a convenient reconstruction of the sequence

---

6   Plut. *Publ.* XII.1.

7   Cic. *Dom.* 34, 91*; Cic. *Planc.* 36, 88*.

8   The hypothesis according to which Nasica coated his actions against Gracchus with sacrality, giving it the merit and meaning of an act of *consecratio*, comes from D. C. Earl, *Tiberius Gracchus: A Study in Politics* (Brussels, 1963), 118–119. It was then taken up by W. Nippel, *Aufruhr und 'Polizei' in Der romischer Republik* (Stuttgart, 1988), 73, and echoed in J. Linderski, "The pontiff and the tribune: the death of Tiberius Gracchus," *Athenaeum* 90 (2002): 339–366. For a similar conclusion, see E. Badian, "The pig and the priest," in *Ad fontes! Festschrift für Gerhard Dobesch zum fünfundsechzigsten Geburtstag am 15. September 2004*, ed. H. Heftner (Vienna: De Gruyter, 2004), 263–272. In effect, "The location of the riot, the moves and gestures of Nasica, and even his decision to wear a toga praetexta and to veil his head all point in this direction." F. Santangelo, "A survey of recent scholarship on the age of the Gracchi (1985–2005)," *Topoi* 15, no. 2 (2007): 465–510, esp. 485. See also F. Pina Polo, *The tyranny of the* Gracchi *and the concordia of the* Optimates: *an ideological construct* (Roma: L'Erma di Bretschneider, 2017), 9.

of events has been corroborated, intentionally exaggerating the importance, scale, and possible effects of the actions attributed to Gracchus, completed by a sprinkling of invented elements. The truth is that Gracchus didn't aspire to tyranny. If he had been elected, it would have been legal and in accordance with the will of the people gathered in assembly. Those who accused Gracchus of illicit conduct were the same ones who impeded a vote on the plebiscite that would have sanctioned his re-election. None of the things Gracchus did during his tribuneship were against the law. The agrarian reforms were approved by the people, not enforced unilaterally. Gracchus called for the observance of a law that had become disregarded, thereby restoring its legality.

Octavius's dismissal, the identification of the people as the correct executors of the legacy of King Attalus III (r. 138–133), Gracchus's renomination to the tribuneship—none of these actions were illegal (at least, not incontrovertibly so). Rather, they were political maneuvers, supported by reasonable arguments and carried out with transparency and in accordance with the law. Before putting Octavius's dismissal to a vote, Gracchus tried several times to convince his colleague to back down from his position, which in no way protected the interests of the lower-class plebeians but instead harmed them. Arguing that the competent constitutional body for deciding what to do with the legacy of Attalus was the people gathered in assembly wasn't a revolutionary act because Rome has no constitution by which to distribute power among the organs of the state. The proposal that the legacy of Attalus be sold and the proceeds be spent on implementing the land reforms favored the plebeians, and its proponent was the man who promoted their interests in the political arena; it was a legitimate initiative that fell within Gracchus's purview because it was consistent with the scope of the tribune of the plebs. Standing for the tribuneship for a second time cannot be considered a revolutionary action either; there were precedents, and no one had been sacrificed for attempting to do so before Gracchus. The suggestion that Gracchus held a meeting the night before to organize the violence is false. It was circulated by a hostile source to charge the tribune with premeditation. There was no meeting, cooperation, or premeditation.

If Gracchus and his friends had planned a violent action, they would have gone to the meeting armed. Instead, when they were attacked, Gracchus wasn't armed. Nor were his friends. All the sources agree that the Gracchans equipped themselves with improvised weapons, found on the spot, when Nasica arrived with his companions, who were armed with clubs.[9] They utilized whatever

---

9   "Tiberius's error, if we may call it that, was in failing to organize a force capable of confronting the violence of the aristocrats with violence […]. Moreover, Tiberius did not have revolutionary

they found not to attack but to defend themselves. It wasn't Gracchus and the Gracchans who sparked the clash on the day of the plebiscite on the agrarian land reforms. The uproar began as soon as Nasica and his followers arrived on the scene, when they started to press en masse on the crowd and kill anyone who shielded Gracchus. Under attack, the tribune didn't defend himself but fled; in doing so, he sought to be seen "to be more intent upon not doing any harm to others than upon not suffering harm himself."[10] Further proof that the Gracchans weren't the attackers but the attacked is that they didn't kill anyone. The only people who lost their lives or were injured in the clashes were Gracchans.

In August 133, Gracchus's politics falls into oblivion. The tribunes of plebs refuse to take up their deceased colleague's political legacy and carry forward his final legislative projects. Plebiscites seeking to obtain a reduction in the length of military service, to increase the number of *equites* to match the number of senators who make up the jury of the magistrates' court,[11] and to extend the right of appeal to persons convicted of political crimes are set aside.

That same month, the Senate carries out another significant political act. As many feared and as many others hoped it would, it accepted the legacy of Attalus. In doing so, it defines the modalities of running the inherited territories—that is, it decides to make a new province out of them, which will be called Asia—and prepares everything necessary to take possession of this inheritance.

A further step down the road toward Gracchus's *damnatio memoriae* consists of reviving the *pax deorum* "broken by Gracchus in his abuse of his functions" and masking the collective crime instigated by Nasica with a semblance of legality. The divinity insulted in this case is identified as Ceres, patroness of the plebeians and often associated with tribunician sacrosanctity. The cult's center is the sanctuary at *Henna* (Enna, Sicily), so the Senate dispatches a delegation to beg the goddess' forgiveness.[12]

The Senate then decrees that those who backed Gracchus in his attempt at a violent overthrow of the *res publica* committed high treason for the purpose of political subversion and, if found guilty, will be punished by death. To this end, a real court of justice will be set up rather than a commission of inquiry.

---

intentions but limited himself to proposing democratic reforms, and the idea of taking recourse to violence was foreign to his political ideals." Perelli, *I Gracchi*, 142.

10   For further similar observations, see Plut. *Comp. Ag. Gracch.* 4–5.

11   Or to transfer control of the jury from the Senate to the group of *equites*. The issue is contentious.

12   Cic. *Verr.* 2.4.108*.

This new *quaestio* will comprise the two consuls in office and an advisor. The consuls will conduct investigations to gather sufficient evidence to support the accusations and will judge the defendants, though they will be able to delegate their duties to other trusted persons (since it is expected that many cases will be brought to trial). The advisor will assist the consuls in issuing the verdict and pronouncing the sentence.

The primary purpose of this process isn't to enact justice by prosecuting, judging, and punishing the enemies of the state (people who acted openly and, therefore, are easily recognizable) but to delegitimize Gracchus's political actions. Had Scaevola still been consul, he wouldn't have agreed to it. Accordingly, the Senate waited for him to leave office before acting. Furthermore, the procedure is conceived in such a way as to avoid conflicting with the judicial necessity of not executing those sentenced to death without them having been judged by the people gathered in assembly. In fact, the death sentence for high treason cannot be challenged by appeal. It goes without saying that the type of crime the "tribunal of the Gracchans" is preparing to prosecute is falsified because the facts show that Gracchus never wanted to make himself king through a *coup d'état*. If anything, Gracchus, in promoting the interests of the common people, set himself against the senatorial oligarchy, which, to defend their own interests, now tries to make him appear as a dangerous subversive. But it is pointless to speak of the law with those who have decided to establish themselves using force.

The "tribunal of the Gracchans" begins its work in October 132 after the elections for the next year's consuls. The new consuls are Publius Rupilius and Marcus Popillius Laenas. They will be advised by Caius Laelius Sapiens. Although Laelius will oversee the Gracchans's suppression, he is Scipio Aemilianus's right-hand man. Thus, the person who will really direct the process is Scipio.

Publius Rupilius comes from a family of enriched plebeians, who became nobles by virtue of his entry into the Senate. Rupilius is, therefore, what the patricians call a "*homo novus*," a term that implicitly carries a moral judgment. Conversely, Laenas is part of an aristocratic, consular family and is a staunch anti-Gracchan. He and the Scipiones may have been behind Octavius's initiative to veto Gracchus's land reform bill.[13] He has taken part in various diplomatic missions. As governor of *Hispania Citerior*, he resumed the siege of *Numantia* but failed to capture the city.

---

13 Earl, "M. Octavius, trib. pleb. 133 B.C.," 657–669. See also Astin, *Scipio Aemilianus,* 346.

The persecution of the Gracchans marks the start of a new chapter in the civic history of Rome dedicated to the political weaponization of justice. Every alleyway in the city is full of people chasing other men. Not even temples are a safe haven. Many wanted people become targets by being falsely denounced, whether out of envy, revenge, or innumerable other reasons. Family members, relatives, and servants are frequently arrested. All those captured are thrown into the *carcer*, Rome's infamous prison, dug into the rock of the Capitoline and accessed from the slope that leads from the two summits of this hill to the Forum.

One of those arrested is the grammarian and Stoic philosopher Blossius of *Cumae*, the former tutor and close friend of Tiberius Sempronius Gracchus. Laelius interrogates him in the presence of the *pontifex maximus* Nasica, seeking to highlight the part he played. The philosopher assures them that he held Gracchus in such high esteem that he would have done anything ordered of him. Laelius considers that, for the sake of convenience and to avoid putting himself in danger, Blossius could have said otherwise, but he wanted to remain faithful to his friend. As such, he pays tribute to him, recommending his acquittal in the preliminary investigation.

In total, a couple of hundred are indicted. The luckiest are sentenced to exile and accessory penalties, such as being deprived of Roman citizenship, dismissed from public office (if they hold one), struck off from the Senate (if they are members), and divested of their family property. Everyone else is put to death. However, as often happens during state purges, it is only the expendable who suffer; the weakest and most defenseless pay the price for the rest. Indeed, not all the Gracchans are prosecuted. Not a finger is lifted against Scaevola, Flaccus, or Carbo, nor against the land reform commissioners, Appius Claudius Pulcher and Caius Sempronius Gracchus.

Nevertheless, the reprisals only cease when the Gracchans have been decimated and the senatorial oligarchy believes they no longer represent a danger, if they ever did. However, after Gracchus's final bills have been shelved and his proposal regarding the use of Attalus's legacy has been rejected, as well as the decimation of the Gracchan movement, anyone who has placed their hope of redemption from a life of misery and exploitation in the agrarian reform of 133 now fears that the Senate will remove this item from the agenda, feeling not so much distressed about it as angry. The political situation is thus very delicate, and the tension is palpable. As the urban plebs mourn Gracchus's death, they maintain that the tribune performed his functions not only out of official duty but also out of a sense of moral responsibility, his sole purpose being to maintain solidarity.[14]

---

14   Plut. *T. Grac.* 9.4.

The Senate and the consuls are aware of the extreme complexity of the moment and know they cannot make a mistake. They agree that the public order situation contains so many unfamiliar aspects that it cannot be managed in the usual way. The possibility of it getting out of control is both certain and significant, so much so that it is no longer considered a risk but a danger. As a result, they decide to make a statement for the lower-class plebeians to reassure them that no backward steps will be taken regarding the land reforms.

This signal consists of appointing Publius Licinius Crassus Dives Mucianus as commissioner of the land reforms to fill the position that became vacant due to the death of Gracchus. Previously, Mucianus was one of those who worked to prepare the reform. Therefore, in 132–131, the land reform commissioners will be Appius Claudius Pulcher, Publius Licinius Crassus Dives Mucianus, and Caius Sempronius Gracchus.

Politics is often referred to as a cattle market in the sense that everything has its price. This maxim also applies in the case of Mucianus's appointment as commissioner. The Senate successfully requests that, from now on, land assignations aren't made in the environs of Rome so as not to interfere with the interests of the senatorial families and the Latin statesmen but in *Picenum* and southern Italy.[15]

Given these premises, the commission's activities to implement the agrarian reforms will only worsen the relations between Rome and its allies in Italy from now on. This issue will become central to the political debate, so it's to this that we must now turn our attention.

---

15 Balbo, *Riformare la res publica*, 94–95.

CHAPTER III

The Italic Question

The Roman conquest is a harbinger not only of massacres and plundering but also of civilization and economic, cultural, technical, and scientific progress. Wherever a state of barbarism exists, it brings cities, written laws, political stability, roads, aqueducts, baths, theaters, etc. Furthermore, it implies the transformation of the vanquished into friends and allies and, later, into Roman citizens, together with all this entails in terms of social integration.

It's worth emphasizing this point. The Roman state typically associates itself with the city-states, tribes, and tribal federations with which it entered into relations, not only those that submitted spontaneously out of a desire for self-preservation but also those that were forcefully subjugated following a war, thus transforming a defeated enemy into a friend and ally. This association takes place through the drafting of bilateral agreements called *foedera* (sing. *foedus*). Every *foedus* is a source of rights and obligations for both parties and integrates the associate (*socius*, pl. *socii*) into a partnership with Rome, although this isn't a political organization like a federation or confederation, but a political and military concept known as *imperium*.

In the second half of the II century, numerous *socii* form part of Rome's *imperium*. In the Italian Peninsula, the northern areas include the Gauls and Veneti, the central areas include the Picentes, Marsi, Peligni, Vestini, and Marrucini, and the southern part includes the Frentani, Samnites, Apulians, Lucanians, and Bruttians.

One of the rights that arise from the *foedus* is mutual defense: if one party suffers from armed aggression in its own territory, all the other *socii* will offer help and assistance through all the means at their disposal. In exchange, the *socius* must support Rome's war effort, paying it the *tributum* and, in times of war, upon request, making available a contingent of soldiers (*auxilia*) and/or other forms of aid, such as shipments of grain. The *tributum* is a type of contribution to the costs of maintaining and equipping the army; it is paid to the treasury quaestors and appropriated by the public treasury. If Rome wins the war, some of the military expenses may be repaid in exceptional circumstances. The contingents of *auxilia* are aggregated to the Roman legions to strengthen them and placed under the command of a Roman officer, normally a prefect.

Being part of Rome's *imperium* is a state that offers many advantages. One is the benefit deriving from an extra-urban road crossing the territory. These are the long-distance roads built on the initiative of the consuls and censors. They serve to facilitate the movement of legions but can also be used by merchants and travelers. Among its other advantages, a *socius* can participate in the economic exploitation of the *ager publicus populi Romanorum*; form part of Latin colonies and, in certain cases, Roman colonies; participate in the division of spoils of war (money is divided up when the victorious commander celebrates his triumph; land is divided up later); come into contact with the Roman state, the patron of which the individual *socius* is a client; and in the event of a dispute with another *socius*, use Rome as an arbitrator—in such cases, Rome will settle the matter by applying the *ius civile*, i.e., the law that applies to Roman citizens, which derives from the *mos maiorum*, the Twelve Tables, the *interpretatio* of the *mos maiorum*, statutory laws, consular edicts, and *senatus consulta*.

Citizens of the member-states of Rome's *imperium* can, individually, become Roman citizens by renouncing their own citizenship. In such cases, they can do everything Roman citizens are allowed to do and enjoy all the legal protections from which Roman citizens benefit. According to Roman law, Roman citizenship can be obtained by birthright, if the individual was born from a legitimate marriage involving a Roman citizen; through *emancipatio*, if this simultaneously involved their enrolment into the register of a *tribus* (a voting unit of the Roman state); from participating in the foundation of a Roman colony; by law; or by naturalization.

Rome's way of dealing with peoples associated with it has always involved establishing preferential relationships, often personal, with the dominant élites because, by doing so, it ensures control over local communities and the straightforward payment of the *tributum*. This guarantees that, in the territory of any *socius*, there may be people who are locally born and speak the local dialect but who are, to all intents and purposes, Roman citizens. Usually, these are eminent individuals due to their social prestige, public role, or economic status.

The possession of *civitas* is proven by the registration of the individual in question and his family members in the census rolls and on the list of any of the 35 territorial tribes. Registration takes place at the request of the person involved, their parent, or ex-owner (and now patron), is performed before a censor, and serves to censor Roman citizens, principally for the purpose of knowing how many young people are theoretically available for compulsory military service—and who those individuals are—and who is legally eligible to be elected to a magistracy. This is followed by their enrolment in the records of a tribe. This attests and certifies that the individual has the right to vote actively and passively and can therefore take an active part in popular assembly meetings and present themselves as a candidate for elections to the magistracies.

Unless it is revoked due to unworthiness in the event of a death sentence or exile, *civitas* is a right that can be inherited by one's heirs. The result is a series of active and passive legal positions: active positions are rights (everything that can be claimed) and freedoms (everything that can be done without constraint, i.e., without going against the law), and passive ones are obligations. Among the rights and freedoms deriving from the possession of *civitas*, the following are worth noting:

- participate in public assembly meetings, including the right to vote in elections for the renewal of magistracies, to approve or reject bills, to declare war, to ratify a peace agreement, to confer military command (*imperium*), and to confirm or reverse a conviction in the first degree;
- run for public office;
- enter a marriage that is entirely valid in the eyes of the law;
- operate freely in the business world (commerce, crafts, industry, currency exchange, contract management, etc.) and, more generally, establish legal relationships involving patrimonial content with other Roman citizens and foreigners;
- make a will, receive an inheritance, and be appointed a guardian in a will, all according to Roman law;
- use the *mancipatio*;
- seek justice according to the norms of Roman civil law or be judged by a Roman court according to Roman law;
- not be subjected to corporal punishment in the event of arrest;
- appeal to the people gathered in assembly in the event of a death sentence or a fine requiring payment exceeding a certain amount;
- apply for enlistment in the army as a fixed period of service; and
- emigrate from the territory of one rural tribe to another, or from a rural tribe to an urban tribe.

However, not all those with *civitas* have the same rights and freedoms. Some are Roman citizens but cannot stand as candidates in the elections for the magistracies, nor are they entitled to vote on any matter of public importance. Female Roman citizens and anyone else born as a free citizen who has been legitimately deprived of their liberty do not have the right to vote. A distinction can thus be made between *civitas cum suffragio* and *civitas sine suffragio* (respectively, Roman citizenship with and without voting rights). Furthermore, women cannot enter into legal relations involving patrimony, make a will, or receive an inheritance, let alone be named as a guardian in a will, without a male guardian's intervention.

The obligations arising from being a Roman citizen consist of compulsory military service, which is required of all males aged 17 and older, and the payment of taxes, according to the provisions of Roman law.

The possession of *civitas* confers a privileged, much-coveted status on the bearer because it justifies a Roman citizen doing what isn't allowed to those who aren't Roman citizens and who, from the Roman perspective, are foreigners, even if they are friends and allies. Additionally, Roman citizens who find themselves in a foreign state that has good relations with Rome enjoy a form of respect. This means that Roman citizens are proud of their legal status and are envied by many foreigners when they say, "*ego civis romanus sum*" ("I am a Roman citizen") while wearing the *toga*, the symbol by which the Roman citizen is defined and distinguished (slaves and foreigners are forbidden to wear it).

Ultimately, possessing *civitas* marks a fundamental difference between Roman citizens and foreigners. However, the Roman system provides for another type of citizenship, so-called *latinitas* ("Latin citizenship"), which is also a source of rights and freedoms. Possession of *latinitas* facilitates relations with Roman citizens. Those with *latinitas* can:

- enter into a marriage and inherit according to Roman law;
- trade with Roman citizens, with the stipulation of sales agreements regulated by Roman law and the use of the *mancipatio*;
- emigrate to Rome or a Roman colony, be registered in the census, and request enrolment in an urban tribe (because this enrolment entails the attribution of *civitas*);
- vote in the elections for the Roman magistracies (in a tribe drawn by lot) if they happen to be in Rome on election day;
- stand as a candidate in the elections for the Roman magistracies (their election will entail the automatic acquisition of *civitas*); and
- under certain conditions, to appeal first-degree criminal sentences involving them.

Latinitas is an inferior class of citizenship compared to *civitas* but still a privileged status compared to foreigners, non-citizen freedmen, and slaves. The communities of Latins, Italics, and Italiotes who do not possess either *civitas* or *latinitas* are governed by their own regulations, which are also valid for all that is not foreseen by *latinitas*. They are required to observe Roman private law only if, and to the extent that, they have formally incorporated it into their own legal system.

The legal relationship that arises from any *foedus* is different from the contractual one, in which the parties are on the same level (a contract is an agreement between two or more parties to create, regulate, or terminate a legal patrimonial relationship between them). Here, the relationship is biased in Rome's favor. This has important implications, as the *socius*'s subordination can be a cause of discrimination and exploitation.

Indeed, Rome constantly profits from its position of strength to secure greater advantages over the *socii*. It makes decisions—by law or by issuing consular edicts, based on the concurring opinion of the Senate (*senatus consultum*)—on anything concerning itself, *imperium*, war, victory, and security before imposing them on the *socii* without having consulted them previously or even asking them to consider the measures adopted. Only occasionally does Rome ask its *socii* to suggest their own proposals.[1] Moreover, Rome demands the *socii* support its war effort to the extent that it has determined unilaterally.

Each year, at the consuls' request, the Senate establishes how many men the army should consist of in the event of war, distinguishing the Romans' share from the number that must be ensured by the *socii*, which oscillates between 55% and 59%. In absolute terms, the *socii* must be ready to supply around 89,000 men every year, whom Rome will use as it sees fit.[2] In 225, faced with the Gallic threat, Rome asked its allies to provide it with all the *auxilia* possible. The Latins provided around 100,000 men, roughly 20% of those made available by Rome's Italic allies and just under 25% of the army formed through the conscription of Romans.

Furthermore, the *socii* must continue to pay the *tributum*, unlike Roman citizens, who were exempted from paying it in 167 following the conquest of the eastern provinces, which led to a considerable influx of money into the treasury's coffers.

The Romans also apply less favorable legal, economic, and disciplinary treatment to the *auxilia* compared to the legionaries. The *auxilia* are kept

---

1   Cic., *Balb.*, 8.20.

2   See C. Nicolet, *Rome et la conquete du monde mediterranèen*, vol. 1: *Le structures de l'Italie romaine* (Paris, 1993), 214.

in service for longer, they receive less money, they are given a lower share in the division of the spoils of war than the legionaries, and the disciplinary sanctions imposed on them are harsher. On the other hand, some *auxilia* may be rewarded with naturalization for particularly outstanding actions.

Some Roman magistrates behave in their allies' territory as if they were at home, even lording it over the territory: they commit sacrilegious thefts, demand services without offering payment, and mistreat and humiliate magistrates and ordinary citizens. Abuses of this kind are quite common, but the Senate ignores them, neither endorsing nor punishing them. In some cases, it encourages them, acknowledging its most illustrious members' privilege when traveling abroad to enjoy ambassadors' rights (*libera legatio*) when they have no such status. This implies that when a Roman magistrate or private citizen who enjoys *libera legatio* is traveling in the territory of a *foederatus*, he can expect it to supply him with everything he needs, potentially leading to awkward situations.

Rome has interfered in the internal affairs of particular *socii* on numerous occasions, whether directly or through local authorities, to quash crimes that threatened public safety and offended the authority of the Roman state. In other words, it has behaved like a law enforcement authority in a territory that was not its own.[3]

This was exemplified in its repression of the orgiastic rites in honor of Dionysus (Bacchanalia).[4] Dionysus is the Greek god of wine, ecstasy, and wild abandon and was assimilated into the Roman pantheon as Bacchus. He represents man's natural state, his primordial, animal, wild, spontaneous side, which remains present even in the most civilized man as an irrepressible kernel of his origins. The cult of this divinity, once widespread throughout Greece but especially in Boeotia and Attica, was introduced to Italy by Greek colonists and reached Rome via *Magna Graecia*. At first, the Senate restricted it to women, foreigners, and slaves, before losing interest in it for a long time. Then, in 186, news reached the ears of the Senate and the Roman consuls that the devotees of Dionysus gathered at night and drank themselves into a stupor, dancing, singing, loudly invoking promises of liberation, rebirth, and immortality, handling snakes, and on such occasions, crimes were

---

3 Polyb. 6.13.4.

4 This episode is reported in considerable detail in Liv. 39.8–19 and an epigraphic text from the *ager Teuranus*, known as the *senatus consultum de Bacchanalibus* (CIL, I(2), 581=IL, 18=ILLRP, 511). J.-M. Pailler, *Bacchanalia: la répression de 186 av. J.-C. à Rome et en Italie. Vestiges, images, tradition* (Rome: École française de Rome, 1988); P. V. Cova, "Livio e la repressione dei Baccanali," *Athenaeum* 52 (1974): 82–109.

committed, and conspiracies were formed against the established order. The Senate launched an investigation and discovered that Dionysus was a very popular deity among rebels and conspirators, who saw him as a symbol of hope in a better, otherworldly world. It ruled that the cult of Dionysus had the potential to destabilize the Roman state and took drastic measures to ensure its security. During the crackdown, numerous people were sentenced to death and executed, and many others were imprisoned.[5]

It is important to note that the repression of the Bacchanalia didn't just apply to Rome but to all of Italy, including the lands of its *socii*, and it involved the local authorities not only for the purpose of publishing the deliberations of the Senate but also carrying them out, including sentencing offenders. These interventions seriously compromised the internal sovereignty of the *socii*, albeit with the mediation of local authorities.

This wasn't the first time the Roman government forcefully intervened in allied territories, and it certainly wouldn't be the last. Other occasions on which it occurred include the repression of a slave insurrection connected to the cult of Dionysus in *Apulia* (Puglia) in 185–184,[6] quelling bread riots in *Apulia* in 172 (a plague of locusts had caused a famine),[7] and a series of murders committed in the Silan Forest in *Brutium* (Calabria) in 138.[8]

Rome's tendency to steamroller the *socii* goes beyond the contractual clauses that regulate their relations and this causes recriminations, resentment, and poisonous gossip, undermining the foundations of the relationship of mutual trust that represents the glue of the *imperium* and guarantees its stability. Over time, relations between the *res publica* and the Italic *socii* have become increasingly tense, leading to outbreaks of rebellion. The *socii* reproach Rome for constantly taking advantage of its position of strength to ensure the greatest advantages for itself. The *socii* feel a sense of political exclusion and inferiority. They make overtures to leave their position of marginalization and exploitation to be able to fully enjoy the benefits deriving from their association with the *imperium* in terms of legal protection, economic opportunities, and political participation.

The Etruscans, Gauls, Italics, and *Italiotes* make increasingly loud requests that the balance of relations between Roma and its friends and allies must

---

5   P. A. Fernandez Vega, *Bacanales: el mito, el sexo, y la casa de brujas,* (Madrid: Siglo XXI, 2018).

6   Liv. 39.29.8–10 41.6–7; M. Capozza, *Movimenti servili nel mondo romano in età repubblicana,* vol. 1: *Dal 509 al 184 a.C.,* (Rome, 1966), 143–159.

7   Liv. 42.10.6–8.

8   Cic. *Brut.* 22.85.

change. The petition they address to Rome aims at their complete integration into the Roman system through the adoption of a mass naturalization measure. All *socii* must become fully-fledged Roman citizens to enjoy the related rights and freedoms. The petition is backed particularly by the Italic and Italiote *socii*, that is, the peoples of *Latium* (Lazio), Umbria, *Picenum* (the Marche), *Samnium*, *Apulia*, *Lucania* (Basilicata), and Brutium (therefore, by the Marsi, Peligni, Vestini, Piceni, Samnites, Lucani, Apulians, and Brutians), as well as the inhabitants of the cities of *Magna Graecia*.

Of the *socii* who are most tireless in asking for mass naturalization are the swathes of merchants and businessmen who have recently enriched themselves thanks to their ability to fill the increasingly numerous opportunities that have opened since the enormous increase of money in circulation.

But the Senate, the consuls, and large sections of Roman society are against making concessions to foreigners in matters of citizenship. They are against the mass naturalization of *socii* principally because:

- there would be many more new citizens than old ones, and they would obtain majorities in the Senate and the popular assemblies, thus depriving the old citizens of control of public affairs concerning them, preventing them from legislating as they see fit, and causing severe problems for the management of the state—with unpredictable consequences;
- they don't want a large-scale and indiscriminate attribution of rights to jeopardize their own privileged position, which they tend to bolster by only conferring fully-fledged Roman citizenship on prominent figures from Latin and Italic society, allowing them to enter the client-patron system of the great Roman families; and
- they believe that many new voters, which would be difficult to reconcile with the urban citizenry, would create inconveniences and imbalances, especially in weakening the personal power of influential local figures.

The request of the *socii* for legal equality and most of the Romans' opposition to this is a political affair that will go down in history as the Italic Question. In 187 and 177, we recall, it was fed by the mass expulsion of immigrants from Rome who had fraudulently obtained membership of an urban tribe.[9]

---

9   On the mass expulsion of Italic immigrants from Rome in 177: Liv. 42.10.6–8.

CHAPTER IV

A Mysterious Death

Early in the morning

After the Capitol massacre, the Senate's attempt to demonstrate the unprovable (that is, that Gracchus, in order to make himself king, conspired against the State and instigated his supporters to violently overthrow the *res publica*) has the effect of deepening the abyss that has long divided Roman society into two parts. On the one side are the *populares*, i.e., those who constitute the basis of the authority of the plebeian tribunes, who support the interests of the common people. On the other side are the so-called *boni*, or *optimates*, i.e., those who have appointed themselves defenders of the *mos maiorum* and the values of *romanitas*, who consider the *populares* as demagogues and populists who are endangering the community of citizens.[1]

Following the massacre, the *optimas* Publius Cornelius Scipio Aemilianus made a statement that amounted to pouring fuel on the fire. Asked to comment on the news of the killing of Gracchus, his cousin, he responded by citing a Homeric verse: "So, too, may any other also be destroyed who does such deeds!"[2] In other words, "If Gracchus intended to take over the state, he had to be stopped."[3]

The meaning of Scipio Aemilianus's declaration that it was legal to kill Gracchus if he had attempted to overthrow the *res publica* to make himself king was not clear-cut. However, it was sufficient to throw things into disarray. After the lower-class plebeians closed ranks to protest against Scipio

---

1   Cic. *Rep.* I.31*. App. *B. Civ.* I.2.17*.

2   Plut. *T. Grac.* 21.5. The verse originates from *Od.* I.47. Scipio Aemilianus had perhaps been induced to think in this way because, at the time, he was far from Rome and the only news that reached him about Gracchus dragged the slain tribune's reputation through the mud. Later, however, he would add that he had never liked Gracchus's politics.

3   Vell. Pat. II.4.4.

Aemilianus,[4] Caius Laelius Sapiens came to Scipio's aid, urging his fellow citizens to forget about Gracchus's land reform policy so as not to worsen the dissent it had provoked.[5] The incident, however, left a mark.

In 129, Scipio Aemilianus is 56 years old. His popularity with the urban plebs has declined due to him justifying the killing of Gracchus as well as supporting a bill that sought to deprive the land reform commissioners of their control over its implementation. Most recently, the political majority in the Senate, dominated by the ultra-conservative *optimates*, has seen in him the man most capable of effectively protecting the land-related interests of the senatorial families, under threat from this law, and it has nominated him for the dictatorship.

Scipio Aemilianus has called a *contio* to declare publicly he was inclined to accept and justify why, in his opinion, it was necessary to transfer the competencies of the land reform commissioners to the consuls. He prepared a speech, which he worked on for many hours in his house that evening before going to sleep.

Scipio's house is in the exclusive district of the *Palatium*. It has a regular layout: in the center of the atrium is the marble impluvium, on the edge of which is an elegant table with feline feet. At the back is a peristyle with Doric columns. There is also a marble portrait bust of the owner in the atrium. It is assumed that something happened in that house after Scipio retreated into his bedroom. We don't know what exactly, much less whether there was any involvement of outsiders, but something must have happened during the night as, a few hours later, Scipio is dead.

Early in the morning, a *valet de chambre*, who had entered the room at dawn to wake his master and say good morning, found Scipio's body devoid of signs of life and with the extreme pallor of the deceased. When he realized what had happened, he stopped in his tracks before raising the alarm. The family physician was sent for but was unable to do anything except certify the death.

The cause of death

The news of Scipio Aemilianus's passing spreads quickly through the city, sparking disconsolation in relatives, friends, and allies. His political opponents, especially his personal enemies, are unfazed.

---

4   Vell. Pat. II.2.4*.

5   The 59-year-old Sapiens is a childhood friend of Scipio Aemilianus and the son of Caius Laelius, a man of great culture and eloquence and consul for 190. Laelius was one of Scipio Africanus's closest friends and a general in his army.

The news that it wasn't his wife who found her husband's body in the unmade bed but a manservant doesn't surprise anyone. It was common knowledge the couple didn't sleep in the same bed. It is said they lived apart at home, maintaining a certain level of detachment and a respectful, non-confrontational relationship. The 41-year-old Sempronia, the sister of the Gracchi, was unhappy. Scipio Aemilianus disdained her, saying she was ugly and barren. All the conditions for divorce were there, including a lack of children and the husband's frequent absences, often for long periods, due to war or diplomacy. But neither spouse had considered taking the step.

The great mass of citizens wonder what Scipio Aemilianus died from. Speculation increases when some slaves from the dead man's house reveal that, in the dead of night, someone let some strangers in through the back door.[6] Another detail attracts attention: when the deceased was found, his eyes were open. Sempronia later closed his eyes. This is an oddity since anyone who dies in their sleep does so with their eyes closed. There is also an unverified rumor that suggests the corpse had bruising on its neck, as if strong pressure had been exerted on it. Commentators deduce that Aemilianus was asleep, awoke, or was woken, then died.

At first, the most fervently circulating hypothesis suggests Scipio was strangled.[7] This suggests it was a political murder, or, more accurately, the response of the *populares* to the assassination of Gracchus. This is supported by the fact that the victim was widely known not to be on Gracchus's side, going so far as to justify his killing, even though he was his cousin and a fellow aristocrat. Moreover, Scipio had sided in favor of the proposal to transfer the competencies of the land reform commissioners to the consuls. Further indirect proof comes from the fact that the commissioners—Caius Sempronius Gracchus, Marcus Fulvius Flaccus, and Caius Papirius Carbo—were unmoved by the news of his death.

Given this, it's reasonable to assume that the ones behind the deed, who gave orders to the killers (the people let in at night through the back door?), are among the victim's closest acquaintances. One theory suggests Cornelia, the mother of the Gracchi, instigated the conspiracy to have her son-in-law (who was also her adopted nephew) killed to save her son Tiberius's land reforms. Sempronia may have taken part in the crime for another reason: to take revenge on her neglectful husband. The land reform commissioners apparently complied with Cornelia's and Sempronia's wishes by hiring unnamed

---

6   App. *B. Civ.* I.20.

7   Vell. Pat. II.4. Plut. *G. Grac.,* 10.

killers. The involvement of the two women is likely, the rumor goes, because in 132, Flaccus and Gracchus litigated against Tiberius's assassins.

This insouciant reconstruction is based on a non-existent assumption: the suggestion that the body showed signs of violence at the time of its discovery has, in fact, not been confirmed. Therefore, no one can know for sure if the report of bruising on the neck is false. In all likelihood, it was circulated by an anonymous source to give credence to an otherwise untenable hypothesis, that of political murder, to instrumentalize the tragic event for political purposes (there were cries of political murder so as to be able to place the blame for the death on the Gracchans).

Laelius Sapiens reconstructs the sequence of events entirely differently. In his opinion, Scipio Aemilianus committed suicide because he had been worn out by the effort to reconcile the competing collective interests and was tormented by having been hit by an avalanche of malicious criticism, which had caused him to lose much support. But this explanation is even less convincing than the first. Scipio was a man of supreme temperament and experience. He was certainly not the type to become disheartened in the face of adversity.

There remains only one plausible explanation: a natural death. Scipio Aemilianus likely passed away from a sudden illness, perhaps a heart attack or a stroke.[8] Consequently, the diagnosis is this: the most powerful man in Rome lost his life to a fulminant disease. There is no mystery, only a natural death.

The funeral

The funeral is impressive. The body, placed feet first on a catafalque, is carried on a black hearse to which three pairs of black horses are yoked. A coin has been placed in his mouth as an offering for Charon, who carries the shades of the deceased from one bank of the river separating the world of the living from the Underworld to the other.

The funeral procession leaves the house of the deceased and passes through the city streets. All Rome takes part in the funerals of illustrious citizens. In addition to his family, relatives, and friends, political adversaries are also in attendance; despite opposing Scipio Aemilianus, they still respected him. Finally, the procession reaches the Forum and stops at the foot of the Orators' Tribune, from which official commemorative orations are delivered.

---

8   A. Everitt, *Roma. Nascita di una grande potenza* (Milan: Hoepli, 2013), 388.

The content is delivered by the nephew of the deceased—Quintus Fabius Maximus—based on a text by Laelius Sapiens, written in a convoluted form.[9]

Amid the crowd that fills the Forum are Quintus Caecilius Metellus Macedonicus and his four sons: Caius (later known as Caprarius), Lucius (later known as Diadematus), Marcus, and Quintus (later known as Balearicus). Not long ago, Metellus Macedonicus criticized Scipio Aemilianus for his tardiness in standing against Gracchus's agrarian reform, but neither before nor after this incident did he ever deny his outstanding achievements in service to the state. As he pays his last respects to the deceased, his attitude is marked by *pietas* (to be understood in this instance as a feeling of respect for the deceased, who, in turn, was respectful of his family, homeland, and religion). When the procession sets off again to go back through the city streets, through the *Porta Capena* and start down the Appian Way for the cremation, he orders his sons to lift the body from the catafalque and carry it on their shoulders.

During the Republican Period, the Romans' funerary practice is cremation. Only babies whose baby teeth have not yet come it are not cremated and there is only one exception to this rule: the *Cornelii* bury their dead. The body of Scipio Aemilianus is placed on the pyre with his eyes open to commune with the heavens, a coin in his mouth, and his most precious equipment (clothes, objects, and armaments) beside him. Not even now is his body deprived of the foulard covering his neck, which, according to some diehard adherents of the murder thesis, hides the signs of strangulation.[10]

The pyre is a heap of wood soaked in pitch and stacked very high, reflecting the elevated social status of the deceased. After shouting her husband's name several times, Sempronia lights the pyre, then looks away. The flames catch almost immediately, helped by the breeze and the dry and seasoned wood. Before long, the pyre is engulfed in flames and smoke, and the sweetish smell of burned meat spreads through the air. While the pyre burns, ointments, flowers, and cypress branches are thrown onto it.

Much later, when the last flames are extinguished with water and wine, the half-burned bones are cleaned of ash by washing them in milk and wine and sealed in an urn together with the ashes, carefully removed from the pyre. Usually, the urn is placed in a niche in a collective tomb called a *columbarium*. However, this rule doesn't apply to nobles, whose ashes are placed in a monolithic tufa sarcophagus in the family tomb, usually monumental. The

---

9   A fragment of this oration is preserved in ORF 4.22. On the convoluted tone and related hypothesis: App. *B. Civ.* I.83–85.

10   T. Mommsen, *Storia di Roma* (Firenze: Sansoni, 1960), 123.

urn containing Scipio Aemilianus's ashes is thus carried into the Tomb of the Scipios and placed inside a limestone repository.

The Tomb of the Scipios is a hypogeum dug into the tufaceous rock with a monumental façade that documents the Scipio family's early openness to Hellenism. It is located on the Appian Way, just beyond the *Porta Capena*. Both the external and internal parts of the tomb have changed over time. The oldest element of the external part is the lower part of the façade, which contains the entrance to the hypogeum and two windows that flank the entrance. Then, in around 150, Scipio Aemilianus raised the façade. Originally, the entrance led to a single room with a rectangular plan. When the façade was raised, a second rectangular room was dug adjacent to the first. As time passed, both rooms were filled with sarcophagi, some bearing inscriptions. The tomb of Lucius Cornelius Scipio Barbatus, who built the tomb, occupies the place of honor in the center of the original room.[11]

---

11 There were once about 30 sarcophagi in the Tomb of the Scipios, all dating back to the late III and early II centuries. The sarcophagus of Scipio Aemilianus has not been found. On the Tomb of the Scipios: F. Coarelli, *Revixit Ars. Arte e ideologia a Roma* (Roma: Qasar, 1997). See also H. I. Flower, *The Art of Forgetting: Disgrace and Oblivion in Roman Political Culture* (Chapel Hill, NC: University of North Carolina Press, 2006).

CHAPTER V

The Massacre on the Aventine

Marcus Fulvius Flaccus is 46 years old. We know him. He descends from a senatorial and consular family that was particularly prominent in the early II century. He is a judicial orator of no ordinary ability with a powerful, energetic personality and a substantial following.[1] A close friend of Tiberius Sempronius Gracchus, he became an agrarian reform commissioner in 130, replacing Publius Licinius Crassus Dives Mucianus. For the most part, the attitude of his senatorial colleagues toward him is characterized by hatred and suspicion. They accuse him of sowing discord between Rome and its Italian friends and allies and secretly instigating the *socii* to revolt.

When Flaccus was consul in 125, he presented a bill that aimed to introduce changes to the agrarian law of 133 to defuse the tension between Rome and some of its friends and allies, which was fueled by the Italic question and put the *imperium* at risk. Specifically, this initiative sought to ensure that anyone in the *municipia* and federated cities in Italy who had to renounce part of the land they owned to comply with the agrarian reforms would be compensated for the losses suffered with a choice between naturalization or a recognition of their right to appeal to tribunes of the plebs against the abuses of Roman magistrates. However, Flaccus was forced to abandon the project due to the robust opposition of the Senate, the consul Marcus Plautius Hypsaeus, and large swaths of Roman society.

Later, Flaccus was active in *Gallia Cisalpina*, founding colonies, distributing land (outside the allocations envisaged by the agrarian law of 133), and developing extra-urban roads. At the same time, he defeated the Salluvii, a Ligurian tribe, and the Vocontii, a Celtic or Celtic-Ligurian people, who had attacked the federated city of *Massilia* (Marseille) and its eastern colonies.

---

1   F. Santangelo, *Roma repubblicana. Una storia in quaranta vite* (Rome: Carocci, 2019), 173–180.

Although Flaccus is 14 years older than Tiberius's brother, Caius Sempronius Gracchus, brother of Tiberius, the tribune of the plebs murdered in 133, he treats him as an equal. Politically, he supports him unreservedly, passionately, and openly, but also impulsively and, at times, intemperately, as is his wont.[2] Caius Gracchus leans more toward the plebs than the nobility to which he belongs. He was elected as tribune of the plebs in 124 for 123 and was re-elected in 123 for 122. He was the first beneficiary of a law allowing a tribune to serve consecutive terms, which he himself proposed and obtained approval for.

Another close friend of both the late Tiberius and of Caius Gracchus is Caius Papirius Carbo. He was tribune in 131 and therefore must have been born around 160. So in 123, he is about 37 years old. He joined the triumviral commission established in 130 to oversee the implementation of the agrarian reform law of 133, filling the post made vacant by the death of Appius Claudius Pulcher.

One of Gracchus's colleagues in the tribuneship of the plebs is Marcus Livius Drusus. He has a strong character and is a very eloquent judicial orator. He lives in a *domus* that occupies a lot in the northwest corner of the *pomerium* of *Roma Quadrata*, outlined by Romulus himself.[3]

The *Livii* are a family clan who arrived in Rome from lower *Latium*, seemingly from near *Praeneste*, whence the *Caecilii Metelli* also originated. This *gens* brings together five plebeian families: *Denter, Drusus, Libo, Macatus,* and *Salinator*. The most prominent family in the *Livii* clan are the *Drusii*. Their name originates from the fact that one family member killed a Gallic chieftain called Drausus in battle (over time, the surname Drausus became Drusus). This Drusus is also said to have recovered the ransom gold paid by the Romans to the Senones and kept in *Pisaurum* (Pesaro), a city overlooking the Adriatic Sea between two coastal hills, rising near a long, sandy beach at the mouth of a river. Pisaurum, previously a Gallic settlement and an important village of the Piceni, was refounded as a Roman colony in 184 to control—together with the other Roman colonies of *Ariminum* (Rimini), *Fanum Fortunae* (Fano), and *Aesis* (Jesi)—the nearby *ager Gallicus*, an area of *Picenum* (the Marche) peopled by Piceni and Gauls, non-Roman populations, subjugated by the Romans after their victory at the Battle of *Sentinum* in 295.[4]

---

2   Plut. *C. Grac.* 10.2.

3   A. Carandini, *Angoli di Roma. Guida inconsueta alla città antica* (Rome: Laterza, 2016), 61.

4   An annalistic tradition, preserved in Serv. 6.825*, suggests the Gauls kept the gold plundered during Brennus's sack of Rome in *Pisaurum*.

One of the family's most famous members is the jurist and legal expert Caius Livius Drusus.[5] In 147, he became consul with his first cousin, Scipio Aemilianus. Generations of legal students studied Drusus's works, and his judgments were taught and cited by other masters of law. In later life, he lost his sight, but crowds of people continued to seek him out at his home to ask him for advice.

In 122, Marcus Livius Drusus is a tribune "loyal to the Senate,"[6] which charged him to rival Caius Gracchus for the favor of the common people in order to neutralize his influence and deprive him of his considerable support. For brevity, we will refer to him simply as Drusus. Drusus was not to use violence, nor offend the masses, but to please them and dispense favors by promoting demagogic and populist legislative proposals.

He plays his part with aplomb. He claims to be a friend of Gracchus and support his policy of reforms, especially regarding the founding of new colonies, the involvement of the less well-off in the economic exploitation of the *ager publicus* and enfranchising the colonies of Latin law. He promotes a series of plebiscites similar to Gracchus's own legislative initiatives but more daring. Unlike Gracchus, who has reserved the management of colonial enterprises for himself and his friends and assigned the expenditure of moneys to himself, Drusus proposes nothing that could be to his own advantage or tied explicitly to him.[7] This speaks favorably of him, and people are persuaded that Drusus is honest and trustworthy. The Senate, meanwhile, opposes Gracchus, saying he is humiliating the people and dealing in base demagoguery while it shares and adopts Drusus's proposals. It exalts Drusus to discourage and demean Gracchus.

One of the interventions proposed by Gracchus concerns the foundation of *Colonia Junonia*; in practice, the refoundation of *Carthago*. This was regulated in detail by the *lex Rubria de colonia Carthaginem deducenda*. Gracchus had this bill promoted and brought to approval by another tribune named Rubrius.[8] Once again, he assigned the role of the colony's administrator to himself, uniting distinct things that ought to have remained separate. The other two *triumviri coloniae deducendae* (the leaders responsible for founding the colony and making its laws) are Carbo and Flaccus.

---

5   Drusus has been identified as the jurist mentioned by Cicero in his *Tusculanae Disputationes*.

6   Plut. *C. Grac.* 8.

7   Plut. *C. Grac.* 10.

8   Neither the *praenomen* nor the cognomen of this individual is known.

In 122, Gracchus, Carbo, and Flaccus lead the enterprise that will lead to the foundation of *Colonia Junonia*, settling numerous colonists on the eastern shore of Lake Tunis, just beyond the "accursed soil" of *Carthago*. Shortly afterward, they learn that Drusus, speaking in the Senate, has exaggerated the importance of some episodes that occurred on the site of the nascent colony: a gust of wind caught the colony's standard and tore it, broke the pole that supported it; swept ritual offerings from an altar; burst open the flaps of tents and whistled so loudly that people struggled to sleep. Furthermore, the boundary marks themselves were set upon by wolves and scattered.[9]

In addition, Drusus has fanned the flames of suspicion that Flaccus was involved in Scipio Aemilianus's death, emphasizing the fact that Flaccus had publicly argued with Scipio shortly before the latter was found dead. The Senate acted as a sounding board for Drusus's words, revitalizing the idea that Scipio had been killed for political reasons, even though his death had been judged to be the result of natural causes.

Gracchus understands that the occurrences while setting up the colony, if read through the lens of ignorance and superstition, may be interpreted as unfavorable omens and suggest the gods are angry with the Romans' foundation of *Colonia Junonia*. He also understands that Drusus is seeking to ensure that the accusation brought against Flaccus reflects poorly on him because it was he who advocated Flaccus's appointment as a *triumvir coloniae deducendae*. He infers that the political situation has worsened, that Drusus's muckraking against Flaccus has reached him too, and that it is therefore time to return home.[10]

Shortly after returning to Rome, Gracchus is approached by some individuals with considerable political weight—Italics who live in the city or are passing through—who let him know that Drusus's recent attack on Flaccus has strengthened the already strong resentment of the Italic *socii* against Rome, exacerbated most recently by the ditching of Flaccus's legislative initiative on citizenship, which had initially aroused great enthusiasm and collected widespread acclaim in the Italic territories. Now that it has been dropped, the increasing tension has reached dangerous levels; there are fears of large-scale demonstrations of dissent with unpredictable outcomes.

Gracchus decides to tackle the issue head on and presents a plebiscite that, in terms of content, motivation, and purpose, imitates that of Flaccus, despite knowing that the Senate, the consuls Cnaeus Domitius Ahenobarbus and Caius

---

9   For these rumors: App. *B. Civ.* I.3.24. Plut. *C. Grac.* 11. Oros. V.12. Liv. LX.

10   Plut. *C. Grac.* 13.

Fannius, and large swathes of Roman society are *a priori* opposed to making concessions to Italics in matters of citizenship, if what is being discussed is mass naturalization. He doesn't realize that in doing so he is committing a severe political error, which will soon have consequences. Indeed, shortly thereafter, many people who had previously supported him turn away from him, including Fannius and Papirius Carbo.

Fannius is a mediocre orator, yet he delivers a speech—perhaps not his own—that will go down in history as a rhetorical masterpiece. Forgetting that he obtained the consulship thanks to Gracchus, he openly criticizes the action of his benefactor. At the Senate's request, he also expels all foreigners who had arrived in the city to support Gracchus's plebiscite. The act isn't without precedent—we have repeatedly mentioned that two mass expulsions have already taken place in 187 and 177—but it's the first of its kind that isn't aimed at sanctioning illicit behavior.

Gracchus protests at Fannius's interference (but doesn't use his veto) and defiantly promises to help the foreigners who have remained in Rome. But he doesn't keep his commitment. To justify himself, he claims that he didn't want to give his political opponents the pretext to attack him. He probably fears that, by engaging in a fight, he may not appear to be as strong as he claimed. In effect, Gracchus's electorate—constituted primarily of the *equites* and lower-class plebeians, and which has hitherto been a solid bloc—is starting to fall apart.

As the end of his electoral mandate approaches, Gracchus puts himself forward as a candidate for the tribuneship for 121. To boost his support, as evidence of his willingness to distance himself from the rich and powerful and become physically closer to ordinary people, he moves out of his house on the slopes of the Palatine, near Flaccus's own home, and rents another near the Forum.[11] This is clearly a piece of propaganda. But his demagogy leads him to make another political error when he sparks the ire of several magistrates, who respond vengefully by henceforth describing him as a bad man.

When, in October 122, the people gather in assembly vote for the tribunes of the plebs for 121, Gracchus isn't elected. This failure is a severe blow; Gracchus is now on the ropes—especially since, in the same round of elections, Lucius Opimius, one of his main political opponents, is elected to the consulship, together with Quintus Fabius Maximus Allobrogicus.

As time goes on, the political climate heats up. The tribune of the plebs Marcus Minucius Rufus, probably in agreement with the Senate and Opimius,

---

11   On Gracchus's house on the Palatine: Plut. *C. Grac.* 12.1. On Flaccus's house: Cic. *Dom.* 38.

puts forward a plebiscite that seeks to abrogate the *lex Rubria de colonia Carthaginem deducenda*, primarily for the purpose of provoking Gracchus to anger and losing control.[12]

Rufus is known among his fellow citizens for having had a column surmounted by a statue erected in front of the *Porta Trigemina* to commemorate his ancestor Marcus Minucius Rufus. The Minucius Rufus family are wholesalers of grain, which it imports from North Africa, and thus play an active role in Rome's food supply. Before the *lex Sempronia frumentaria* was introduced, his family could speculate on prices and increase their wealth. Afterwards, they were no longer able to do so.

The *lex Sempronia frumentaria* was issued in 123 on the proposal of Caius Gracchus. According to this law, the public treasury purchases grain in Sicily and takes care of its transport to Rome by sea, via the port of Ostia. It is then distributed to Roman citizens in the Porticus Minucia, where it is sold in strict quantity limits (5 *modii*?) at the controlled price of 6⅓ asses per *modius* (the *modius* is a Roman unity of measure, equivalent to about 8¾ liters).

Rufus argues that this law has harmed him and his family. Therefore, the attack that he launches on Gracchus to have the laws repealed is motivated by his own material interests and his desire to take revenge for the losses suffered.

Gracchus sees his approval visibly diminishing and becomes increasingly nervous and less lucid. He begins to suffer from the same psychosis that his brother Tiberius did in the last days of his life. Caius fears he will be killed on the orders of his political opponents when his mandate expires, and he no longer enjoys the legal protection afforded to magistrates. In a situation of great tension, he makes a third political blunder by publicly addressing his opponents with an obscure threat, as if referring to a secret plot.[13]

Gracchus looks at the calendar with growing concern, given that 9 October 122, the final day of his second electoral mandate, is inexorably approaching. He is increasingly tormented by the thought of his life being in danger. The suspicion that Opimius is plotting against him deeply distresses him. When he thinks about it, he swallows hard and gets dizzy. It seems to him as if he's sliding inexorably into a downward spiral.

At the instigation of his friends, mainly Flaccus, he surrounds himself with bodyguards. The move is used as a pretext to launch another attack against him as his political opponents accuse him of building up another faction to oppose Opimius. Some bring Cornelia Africana, the Gracchi's mother, into

---

12 Plut. *C. Grac.* 13*.

13 Plut. *C. Grac.* 12.5.

play, saying that she is "secretly hiring from foreign parts and sending to Rome men who were ostensibly reapers" and that "obscure allusions in her letters to her son" are proof of this.[14] Others, however, dismiss Cornelia's involvement because she doesn't endorse her son's conduct and, indeed, looks upon it with displeasure.[15]

Rufus convenes the *comitia tributa* and puts the vote on his bill on the meeting's agenda. As dawn breaks, a large crowd swarms into the *Area Capitolina*, cramming into the open area in front of the Temple of Jupiter Optimus Maximus, up to the foot of the stairway leading up to it. In the thick of it are both supporters and political opponents of Gracchus, each with a retinue of friends, clients, and slaves. Crowded on the platform, between the columns of the temple façade, are Gracchus, his bodyguards, the tribune's various assistants, a crowd of his friends and sympathizers, Opimius, his lictors, and other senators and magistrates. Other men from the tribune's personal guard protect the outer perimeter of the *Area Capitolina*, within which the crowd's excitement is growing into a loud, confused clamor.

Since the auspices aren't unfavorable, the meeting can begin. But a strange thing happens. One of the consul's servants, Quintus Antyllius, is going back and forth through the crowd, carrying a tray with the entrails of the sacrificial animal in his hand, shouting, "Make way for honest citizens, ye rascals!" The Gracchans shout in defiance and protest loudly. Antyllius places the tray on the ground and makes a rude gesture at Flaccus and those around him. They react instinctively, without thinking about the consequences, leaping on Antyllius and fatally wounding him.[16]

Enraged, Gracchus's political opponents hurl themselves onto the killers, followed by their friends, clients, and slaves. Gracchus watches the scene,

---

14 Plut. *C. Grac.* 13.2. There are some fragmentary references in the correspondence between Cornelia and her son, but their authenticity is contentious. On this, see: J. P. Hallett, "Matriot Games? Cornelia, Mother of the Gracchi, and the Forging of Family-Oriented Political Values," in *Women's Influence on Classical Civilization*, eds. F. M. Chardy & E. Marshall (London & New York, 2004), 26–39; J. P. Hallett, "Women Writing in Rome and Cornelia, Mother of the Gracchi," in *Women Writing Latin from Roman Antiquity to Early Modern Europe*, eds. L. J. Churchill, P. R. Brown & J. E. Jeffrey (New York & London, 2002), 13–24. E. A. Hemelrijk, *Matrona docta: Educated women in the Roman élite from Cornelia to Julia Domna* (London-New York, 1999), 193–197.

15 Plut. *C. Grac.* 13.2: "Others, however, say that Cornelia was very much displeased with these activities of her son."

16 On the attack on the consul's assistant: Plut. *C. Grac.* 13. At this point, the sequence of events becomes unclear. An entirely different narrative, hostile to Gracchus and hardly credible, is offered by Diod. Sic. XXXIV.28a.

alarmed. Then, more loudly, he strenuously condemns the murder of Antyllius and reproaches his supporters for giving his opponents a pretext to attack him. Frantically, he tries to restore calm from his position at the top of the temple steps, at the foot of which the brawl continues. But his efforts are in vain. Opimius suspends the meeting and adjourns it until the following morning. Antyllius's body remains on the ground, with the tray and sacrificial entrails scattered around him.

Gracchus heads for the Forum, taking the *clivus Capitolinus* down the hill. As he arrives at the foot of the slope, he stops in front of the statue of his father, placed at the corner of the *Basilica Sempronia*. He stays there for a long time, looking at it silently. Then he continues, forlorn and tearful.[17]

Opimius rejoices: he has the opportunity to exploit all the miserable potential of Antyllius's death for political ends and incite the people to revenge against Gracchus and the Gracchans. It is in this context that we must view what happens next.

At dawn the following day, some people place Antyllius's body at the foot of the stairway leading to the *Curia Hostilia*.[18] As the sun slowly rises above the horizon, a crowd gathers around the catafalque, gradually swelling. The Senate meets in the *Curia*. By mid-morning, the square is teeming with people, at which point Opimius suspends proceedings, leaves the building, stands beside the bier, and whips up the crowd to take revenge against the servant's murderers. Then he returns to the *Curia* and attempts to convince the senators of Flaccus's guilt with a speech of great oratorical fervor. He accuses Gracchus of having carried out violent acts that sought to undermine the stability of the *res publica* and denounces his work, worsened, he says, by his violation of a civil magistrate's duties. The senators leave the building en masse, though they remain at the top of the wide staircase outside under the portico that keeps the façade in the shade.

In the meantime, the crowd around the bier has grown denser. The whole Forum is chockfull. The crowd fidgets menacingly and seems to be rising and falling. Senators speak one after another, addressing the crowd. They describe the crime committed against poor Antyllius as monstrous, atrocious, of unspeakable gravity. Then they gather around the bier, intone a funeral dirge, and offer to carry it on their shoulders. Thus, Antyllius, a simple servant, receives honors usually reserved for those who can boast of providing considerable benefits to the citizenry, such as having done good

---

17 Plut. *C. Grac.* 14.4.

18 Plut. *C. Grac.* 14.2–3.

works in public service, increasing the territory of the state through great military conquests, or rendering other services in the political, economic, administrative, or diplomatic areas.

The contrast between what is happening now and what happened on the day of Tiberius Sempronius Gracchus's death is stark. This observation agitates the Gracchans in the Forum and rekindles their hatred for most of the Senate. Suddenly, a great clamor arises from the square, which at first is a lot of confused shouting before growing in tone and becoming a roar. The senators, suddenly frightened, return to the *Curia*.

After a short discussion, at Opimius's suggestion, they resolve to declare a state of national emergency,[19] arguing that they must deal with a tragic event that has a human cause and which, due to its intensity, requires the exercise of exceptional powers in derogation from standard regulations. To this end, they instruct Opimius to act to prevent the *res publica* from harm, authorizing him to do whatever he deems necessary, useful, or opportune, and grants him, for this purpose, full powers, relieving him of all responsibility inherent and consequent to their exercise.

Opimius immediately gets to work. First, it is necessary to form a militia. Therefore, Opimius urges the senators to arm themselves and summons the *equites* for the following day; at first light, each of them must bring along two well-armed servants.[20] Opimius then appoints Decimus Junius Brutus Callaicus as the commander of this militia. (Brutus had been consul in 138 and later "pacified" *Lusitania*, extending Rome's sovereignty to southern *Gallaecia*.) Opimius also arranges for a contingent of Cretan mercenary archers to be ready for action.[21]

We can get an idea of how many armed men respond to Opimius's call if we consider that there are no more than 300 senators, mostly elderly; there are no more than 2,500 *equites*, though many of them may not be in Rome at this moment;[22] and the *equites*'s servants number no more than 5,000. In any event, they are two or three times more numerous than the Gracchans.[23]

---

19 G. K. Golden, *Crisis Management during the Roman Republic: The Role of Political Institutions in Emergencies* (Cambridge: Cambridge University Press, 2013); W. Nippel, "Emergency Powers in the Roman Republic," in *La théorie politico-constitutionelle du gouvernement d'exception*, ed. P. Pasquino (Paris, 2000), 5–23.

20 Plut. *C. Grac.* 14.4.

21 Plut. *C. Grac.* 16.3–4.

22 C. Nicolet, *Rome et la conquete du monde mediterrànèen*, Presses Universitaires de France, Paris, 2001, 197–198.

23 Plut. *C. Grac.* 35.4.

Furthermore, these are men to whom weapons of war and military equipment, taken from the public armories, have been distributed.[24] As for the Cretan archers, they are armed and equipped as befits military professionals.

The Gracchans, in contrast, aren't armed or equipped for combat, except for a few, who are only outfitted to attack with edged, blunt, or slashing weapons and protect themselves with helmets, shields, and chain mail, at most loricated armor. The Gracchans thus face the dual disadvantages of inferior weaponry and numerical inferiority.

The Senate summons Gracchus and Flaccus to explain what happened, but neither appears.[25] Instead, they call on the Gracchans to rally and instigate a public demonstration on the Aventine,[26] the lowest and most impenetrable hill in the urban area of Rome. The Aventine has been a district inhabited by families of modest living standards. It is now a working-class and mercantile neighborhood, partly because it is close to the *Forum Boarium* and the *Emporium* fluvial port and is thus the antipode of the *Palatium*.

Gracchus and Flaccus have called their supporters together on the Aventine for two reasons. Firstly, the Temple of Ceres, Liber, and Libera, located there, is the heart of the political and economic organization of the plebs, whose historical stronghold is on the Aventine. In this regard, the Aventine is opposite the *Area Capitolina*, one of the two summits of the Capitoline, which is traditionally identified with the patriciate. Secondly, the Aventine is an extra-urban space for arbitration. In 494, Agrippa Menenius Lanatus, who was consul in 503, mediated between the patricians and plebeians to re-establish concord between the classes. He managed to channel the complaints to a happy and peaceful resolution, telling the plebeians the fable of the stomach and the limbs, which later became very well known. Subsequently, it was common for the organizers of plebeians' public demonstrations to strike a deal with the Senate and the consuls on the Aventine.

Therefore, Gracchus and Flaccus convened a demonstration not as an incitement to revolution but to evoke the era of plebeian secession and reach a compromise agreement with the Senate. They hope the Senate will dispatch a conciliator—a man of moderate ideas, universally esteemed and liked by both parties—to conduct negotiations.

---

24   See N. Barrandon, *Les massacres de la République romaine*, Fayard, Paris, 2018, 162, n. 166. This theory is based on the military provisions laid out for the fulfillment of the *senatus consultus ultimum* of 100. See Cic. *Rab. Perd.* 7.20.

25   App. *B. Civ.* I.26.

26   App. *B. Civ.* I.25; Plut. *C. Gracc.* 15; Flor. II.3; Oros. V.12.6.

The night passes peacefully, like the calm before the storm. Some supporters spend it at Gracchus's house.[27] Others stay with Flaccus at his house on the Palatine.[28] As day breaks, Gracchus is in a hurry to meet his fate. His wife Licinia tries to dissuade him from going to the demonstration. Gracchus doesn't listen to her and leaves. In the company of Flaccus and other friends, he sets off on foot toward the Aventine with Flaccus's two sons. All the Flacci have hidden the weapons Flaccus kept at home under their clothes. Gracchus, on the other hand, has only a writing stylus in his pocket. By the time the group reaches the top of the Aventine, a multitude of people have already gathered there to show their support for Gracchus. Mingling among the crowd are "the boldest of the plebeians,"[29] armed with daggers and ready for anything.

Flaccus sends his youngest son to Opimius, who is in the Temple of Castor and Pollux,[30] to urge him to avoid bloodshed. Flaccus's son is little more than a boy.[31] After receiving him, Opimius sends him back, telling him to return with his father or not at all. Gracchus offers to go to Opimius to persuade him of his innocence and his good intentions, but Flaccus detains him and sends his young son back to Opimius, together with an escort. The move is miscalculated and will have grave consequences.

Opimius orders his lictors to seize the young man, intending to use him as leverage against his father. They are about to lay their hands on Flaccus's son when his companion tries to stop the kidnapping, pulling a weapon from under his tunic, hurling himself against a *lictor* and mortally wounding him. The attack lights the fuse that will set off the bomb.

Enraged, Opimius orders Brutus and the Cretan archers in the *Forum Boarium* to bring him the heads of Gracchus and Flaccus, promising to pay them their weight in gold.[32] A mass of armed men surrounds the crowd gathered before the temple of Ceres's steps and orders them to disperse. Then something unexpected happens. A chorus of menacing shouts rises from the crowd, directed at Gracchus and blaming him for the situation that has arisen, which is one he certainly didn't want. This marks a turning point. Having supported and praised Gracchus, the urban plebs are now openly critical of him.

---

27   Plut. *C. Grac.* 14.6.

28   Plut. *C. Grac.* 14.5.

29   App. *B. Civ.* I.24.

30   App. *B. Civ.* I.25.

31   Vell. Pat. II.7.2; Plut. *C. Grac.* 16.1.

32   Plut. *C. Grac.* 17.3–4.

Many of those present move away in dribs and drabs. Around 250 people remain, among whom are Gracchus, his bodyguards, and Flaccus. Once the ultimatum expires, the archers loose their arrows at the Gracchans, striking them with precision.[33] Then the militia launches its attack. Many Gracchans die, others flee or surrender and are arrested or executed on the spot.

One group of fugitives, running at breakneck speed and fearing for their lives, are followed by elements of the militia. The group comprises Gracchus, a trusted servant named Philocrates, two of his most loyal companions named Pomponius and Licinius, and Flaccus and his eldest son. The pursuers track down Flaccus and his son, who, helpless and at the militia's mercy, are killed and beheaded.

In the meantime, Gracchus, Philocrates, Pomponius, and Licinius have taken refuge in the Temple of Diana. The pursuers don't hesitate to violate the temple's sacrality but come away empty-handed—the four have resumed their flight. They enter the Temple of Luna, close to the Temple of Diana, where they pause. Gracchus is shocked and cannot resign himself to the thought that the plebs have turned their backs on him. He is deeply distressed, even desperate. He would prefer to commit suicide, but Pomponius and Licinius rush at him, console their friend, and manage to convince him to resume his escape.

Jumping down from a platform, Gracchus sprains his ankle. He feels a sharp pain in his foot, which is shortly followed by swelling. Despite that, he continues his escape. The fugitives take the *clivus Publicius* downhill, reach the foot of the Aventine, and pass through the *Porta Trigemina* at a sprint. Their target is the Janiculum, the highest hill in Rome, located on the Tiber's west bank and therefore outside the Servian Walls.

Still running to escape their pursuers, Gracchus, Philocrates, Licinius, and Pomponius cross the *Pons Sublicius*. Gracchus is noticeably limping. Philocrates puts an arm around his waist to support him. When they reach the middle of the bridge, Pomponius and Licinius suddenly stop, turn around, and face their pursuers to give Gracchus time to gain an advantage. Both sacrifice themselves on the altar of friendship.

Gracchus and Philocrates climb up the lower slopes of the Janiculum, where there is a grove with a spring and a sacellum. Exhausted, they stop at the spring to catch their breath, and Gracchus falls into despair again. This time, though, his story is at its end. It ends tragically shortly after. Everything happens within a few moments. When the pursuers arrive at a run, Gracchus

---

33 Plut. *C. Grac.* 16.4.

realizes all is lost and orders Philocrates to kill him. The obedient slave mortally wounds the tribune, then he turns the weapon on himself and falls onto his master's body.[34]

One of the attackers, Lucius Septimuleius, sticks Gracchus's head on a pike and walks away. Before delivering the macabre trophy to Opimius, he empties the skull of its brains and fills it with lead. His swindle will benefit him. Opimius pays its weight in gold as promised.[35] Cornelia, the mother of the Gracchi, will receive her son's headless body after it has been dragged through the streets and thrown into the Tiber. The vilification of the victims of the massacre on the Capitoline in 133 is thus repeated.[36]

But it isn't over. The Gracchans are accused by Opimius of complicity in an attempted *coup d'état*, thrown into prison, and strangled, except for Flaccus's younger son, the herald whose attempted kidnapping sparked the massacre on the Aventine,[37] who dashes his brains out against the wall.[38] Moreover, Flaccus's home is ransacked and razed to the ground, and it is forbidden to build on the site ever again.[39] The house that Gracchus rented and where he lived out his final days with his wife and young son is looted and devastated but left standing.[40]

This extreme and ruthless repression ceases only when Opimius is convinced that he has successfully completed the mandate he received from the Senate. The list of casualties is terrifying: 3,000 people are missing, including those who were killed in the Aventine massacre and those who were executed later. The victims' families are subjected to sanctions to discourage any further attempt at political subversion. They will not be able to organize ostentatious funerals, widows will not be able to mourn, and family estates will not be

---

34 The circumstances and way in which Gracchus lost his life are described in Oros. V.12*.

35 On the death of Gracchus and the payment of his head's weight in gold: Plut. *C. Grac.* 17*. See also Aur. Vict. 65.1.6*. Flor. 2.3* highlights the affront to the victims' bodies. On this point: W. V. Harris, "A Revisionist View of Roman Money," *JRS* 96 (2006): 3–4 and n. 21.

36 Some authors say that the bodies of Gracchus, Flaccus, and everyone else (in all, 3,000 men) were thrown into the Tiber: Plut. *C. Grac.* 17*; App. *B. Civ.* 1.16. Vell. Pat. 2.6.7* only mentions Gracchus's body. Oros. 5.12.9* is the only source that reports that Gracchus's body was brought to his mother in her villa in Cape Miseno. On the bodies left unburied: Val. Max. 1.4.2, 6.3; Sen. *Min.* 16.3*.

37 Plut. *C. Grac.* 17.5.

38 Vell. Pat. II.7.2.

39 On the house's demolition: Cic. *Dom.* 102*; Val. Max. 6.3.1*. M. B. Roller, "Demolished Houses, Monumentality and Memory in Roman Culture," *CA* 29 (2010): 117–180.

40 See Flower, *The Art of Forgetting*, 77. See also Roller, "Demolished Houses," 132–133.

inherited by the eldest son but confiscated and auctioned off for the public treasury.[41] Marital dowries will also be confiscated, thus preventing widows from remarrying.[42]

The slaughter on the Aventine marks the collapse of the Claudii–Fulvii Flacci axis that played such an influential role in Rome's history. As for the ambitious Claudii, they will re-emerge from anonymity only as followers of a more powerful political group.[43] The Gracchi disappear from the public scene and will die out soon after.

At present, this family survives through Cornelia Africana, Sempronia, the eldest son of Tiberius (of the latter's three sons, the youngest disappeared in Rome shortly after his father's death, while his second son died at an early age in *Praeneste*), and Caius's young boy. Tiberius's eldest son dies in Sardinia while serving as a military tribune, while all traces of Caius's boy are lost soon after his father's death.

Cornelia receives the tragic news of her son's violent death in her villa at *Misenum* (Capo Miseno, Campania). *Misenum* is a maritime promontory near *Baiae*—a holiday resort for wealthy Romans where people go to undergo spa treatments, take sea baths, meet other people, try to get noticed, and indulge in vices—but distinct from it, a place where nature still reigns supreme. Villas of high-ranking families, half-hidden among the vegetation, peek out among the greenery. It faces the Gulf of Naples and the islands of Ischia and Procida and, much farther away, Capri. Cornelia owns one of the villas in the area, which, owing to her control of her patrimony, remained her property even after the Gracchi family assets were confiscated. At first, Cornelia loved to spend holidays there with her husband and their children. After Tiberius's death, she chose to live there permanently. After the death of her husband in 129, Sempronia joins her mother.

Cornelia lives in seclusion but not in isolation. She keeps a good table to honor her guests, and her living room continues to be frequented by famous individuals and a cosmopolitan entourage of friends and intellectuals, especially literary men, most of whom are Greek. Cornelia is full of charm when her visitors discuss her father's life and customs with her, and she speaks admirably

---

41 Plut. *C. Grac.* 17.5; Oros. 5.12.9. See also Dig. 24.3.66.

42 Plut. *C. Grac.* 17.5.

43 E. S. Gruen, *Roman Politics and the Criminal Courts, 149–78 B.C.* (Cambridge, MA: Harvard University Press, 1968), 98.

when she remembers her sons, so much so that some believe that she has lost her senses and no longer realizes her misfortune.[44]

Sempronia will reappear in Rome in 101 to testify in a trial (we will examine this issue later), while Cornelia will die in approximately 110. A few years later, the Gracchans dedicate a bronze statue to her to honor her virtues. This is an unprecedented and unparalleled gesture: no statue in Rome had ever previously been dedicated to a woman. The monument will be placed in the *Porticus Metelli* and will bear a simple inscription on its base: *Cornelia Africani F(ilia) (Mater) Gracchorum*, "To Cornelia, mother of the Gracchi."[45]

When the Romans speak of *concordia*, they may mean one of two things: civil coexistence, or the goddess responsible for it. The goddess Concordia is the result of traditional Roman religion's assimilation of the Greek goddess Homonoia (the correspondence between Homonoia and Concordia can be seen in the way the two divinities are depicted). Several places of worship are named after Concordia in Rome. One is the temple that overlooks the *Scalae Gemoniae* (Gemonian Stairs), opposite the *carcer*. Another was erected in the *Area Volcani* in memory of Cnaeus Flavius, a jurist, son of a freedman and scribe of the famous Appius Claudius Caecus,[46] who had disseminated the text of the procedural formulas and the calendar of the *fasti*. In 216, an altar dedicated to Concord was placed on the *Arx*, one of the two peaks of the Capitoline.

The Temple of Concord by the *Scalae Gemoniae* was seriously damaged by the fire that destroyed two sides of the Forum in 210. After putting an end to his persecution of the Gracchans, Opimius had works carried out on it and, on 22 July 121, the day of the celebration of his triumph, returned the rejuvenated temple, the result of the radical and comprehensive transformation of the pre-existing components, to the city. The restored temple consists of a cella surrounded by columns on three sides, with eight columns on one of

---

44 Plut. *T. Grac.* 19.1–3.

45 This is suggested by the discovery of a statue base with an inscription in the *Porticus Octaviae*. The attribution of the monument to Cornelia as the person to whom it was dedicated, the admirers of the Gracchi as the dedicants, and the dating (end of the II century) are by F. Coarelli, "La statue de Cornélie, mère des Gracques et la crise politique à Rome au temps de Saturninus," in *"Revixit ars". Arte e ideologia a Roma. Dai modelli ellenistici alla tradizione repubblicana* (Rome: Quasar, 1996), 280–299.

46 Appius Claudius Caecus (350–271) served as military tribune (three times), quaestor (twice), *curule* aedile (twice), consul (twice), dictator, *interrex* (three times), and censor. He was a judicial orator and jurist and encouraged the publication of civil procedure formulas and a calendar that distinguished auspicious days from inauspicious ones. Caecus was the first Latin intellectual and the first Roman philhellene.

the short sides. The columns are in travertine, and the masonry is made of concrete, a mixture of lime, pozzolana, and cement. Given its large size, it will host sessions of the Senate.

Many temples have been built in Rome to celebrate the Romans' military victories over their enemies and record the names of their victorious generals in history, but Opimius's Temple of Concord is the first structure of this type to be erected to commemorate the extermination of internal enemies of the state, i.e., other Romans.

In his inauguration speech, Opimius draws attention to the temple's dedicatory inscription, placed on the architrave resting on the capitals of the main façade's columns, which reads: "An act of concord produces a Temple of Concord." Opimius also explains that the restoration work is in line with the wishes of the Senate and the consuls, who made a solemn appeal to their fellow citizens to put aside all resentment, dissent, rancor, and interests conflicting with the project to re-establish societal peace and national concord. But the plebeians don't allow themselves to be deceived by Opimius's flowery words, intended to celebrate the rediscovery of societal "peace," which they consider merely propaganda. So, one night, someone changes the temple's dedication, substituting *concord* with *discord*, rendering the inscription as follows: "An act of discord produces a Temple of Concord."

Fortune is fickle, especially in environments such as the political world, where changes in fortune are unpredictable but frequent. Proof of this comes in 120, when Opimius is tried on the charge of having violated the *ius provocationis* (the right of Roman citizens to appeal to the people gathered in assembly for their final judgment if sentenced to death or a fine higher than a certain amount). The case is brought against him by the tribune of the plebs Publius Decius, who believes that the *senatus consultum ultimum* of 122 gave plenipotentiary powers to Opimius but didn't suspend the citizens' right to *provocatio ad populum* (Opimius had the Gracchans incarcerated after the massacre on the Aventine executed, violating their right to appeal against their death sentence, which, moreover, was imposed unilaterally and without a trial). However, he is acquitted thanks to the effective petitioning of his defense lawyer, Caius Papirius Carbo,[47] who, during his speech, said

---

47 Since being a partisan of the Gracchi, an agrarian reform commissioner (133 and 123–122), and suspected of involvement in the death of Scipio Aemilianus (129), Carbo has switched sides and joined the *optimates*. The *optimates* welcomed him into their ranks, but they didn't trust him. Proof of this came in 119 when Carbo was tried on similar charges to those brought against Opimius. Carbo committed suicide when he realized he would be found guilty and his "friends" among the *optimates* wouldn't lift a finger to prevent this.

that Gracchus's killing had been just(!). Nevertheless, the issue that fueled the debate will remain on the agenda until the fall of the *res publica*.[48]

While Opimius consecrates his success to Concordia, the populace ordains the Gracchi as martyrs of the plebs.[49] To this end, numerous effigies of the two brothers are made to act as protective totems to be distributed to ordinary people, who place them on private altars,[50] or are publicly displayed at the corners of buildings or on crossroads to be venerated with the *Lares Compitales*.[51] Furthermore, the plebeians declare the places where the Gracchi met their deaths as places of worship. They bring them the first fruits of the season and make sacrifices there as if they were altars dedicated to the gods.[52] This spontaneous hero cult contradicts the negative image of the murdered tribunes applied by their political opponents to make them appear as unworthy elements of the citizenry.[53]

Because the Gracchi are now considered tutelary deities of the lower-class plebeians, the Senate, fearing a strong popular reaction, doesn't dare to repeal the agrarian law of 133 but instead deprives it of meaning. The law will remain, but its purpose, which is to reduce the scale of poverty, revitalize rural smallholdings, and make the army more efficient, will fade away.[54] A tribune of the plebs—evidently "loyal to the Senate"—presents a plebiscite that provides that anyone holding portions of *ager publicus* that exceed the legal limit will no longer be required to return the excess, even if a portion of the *ager publicus* is held illegally. The plebiscite also provides for the suspension of land distributions and that anyone still entitled to land assignations is compensated, using the revenues deriving from the collection of this tax for this purpose. The amount of this duty is reduced (and will later be abolished), and Gracchus's legislative provisions that valorize the group of *equites* aren't touched.

---

48 As for Opimius, he headed a Senate commission in 115 charged with looking into allegations of corruption on the Numidian front but allowed himself to be bribed in turn. His subsequent prosecution was supported by Marcus Licinius Crassus, who demonstrated great honesty, returning various letters—still unopened—to the accused, which he had received from a disloyal slave, and which proved his guilt. Opimius was found guilty and died in exile in *Dyrrachium*.

49 See Pina Polo, *The "Tyranny" of the Gracchi*, 20.

50 See Flower, *The Art of Forgetting*, 79; F. Marco & F. Pina Polo, "Mario Gratidiano, los compita y la religiosidad popular a fines de la Republica," *Klio* 82 (2000): 154–170, esp. 155.

51 See Plut. 18.3; Flower, *The Art of Forgetting*, 79; Pina Polo, *The "Tyranny" of the Gracchi*, 19–20.

52 Plut. *C. Grac.* 18.3.

53 Flower, *The Art of Forgetting*, 80.

54 App. *B. Civ.* 1.27*.

Finally, the constraint of the allocated funds' inalienability is removed. This last provision is the one that sinks the agrarian land reforms for good. In fact, many assignees will see it as an incentive to sell their land and return to live in the city. Who will buy the land for sale? Naturally, the large landowners, in whose hands the lands previously assigned to the poor will once again be concentrated.

CHAPTER VI

Saturninus's Tribuneship

At the end of the II century, Rome's population likely exceeds 200,000, perhaps far more.[1] The difficulty with establishing a firm number arises because the censuses refer only to those registered on the census rolls and therefore omit the *capite censi* (the "have nothings"), slaves, freedmen without citizenship, and foreigners.

Supplying food to such a large community requires the regular and massive import of wheat and related produce since the Romans' diet is largely based on wheaten bread. Cereal arrives in Rome mainly from Sicily, Sardinia, southern Spain, and North Africa, as well as from various parts of Italy, primarily Campania. It is transported by sea on ships designated for the purpose, the largest of which have a load capacity of 450–500t. Depending on the wind's direction and sea conditions, navigation may be slow and indirect or quick and direct. Ideally, it takes place along the coast, but on certain stretches, crossing the high seas cannot be avoided.

The main ports of arrival are Ostia for grain imported from the West, and *Puteolis* (Pozzuoli) for grain from Sicily, unless the latter is exported on the Sardinia route, skirting the island's eastern edge before cutting across toward Italy. Wheat from the rest of Campania and Sicily converge at *Puteolis* before continuing toward Rome via Ostia.

Ostia is located at the mouth of the Tiber, about 30km from Rome. Ships drop anchor off the estuary. Their cargo is moved onto smaller boats, which transport goods over the short distance to the warehouses of Ostia. It will later be transported up the Tiber to Rome aboard large barges, towed from the shore by groups of slaves dressed in rags, who pull on their long ropes

---

1   See A. Giardina ed., *Roma antica* (Rome-Bari: Laterza, 2014), 89–90. In any case, the population of the urban area within the Servian Walls, i.e., excluding *Trans Tiberim*, could not have exceeded 400,000 due to its size (426ha).

with considerable effort. The cargo's destination is one of the river ports of the urban area of Rome, all of which are located downstream of Tiber Island on one bank or the other.

The urban area of Rome has three main river ports: Tiberinus, *Emporium*, and *Vinarius*. The former is the oldest. It is located farthest upstream, near the *Pons Aemilius (Ponte Rotto)*. *Emporium*, the largest and busiest, is the newest. It is on the east bank, near the *Forum Boarium*, between the Aventine and Testaccio, on the edge of a large, open, flat space. It contains a quay that runs along the shore for about 150m, is paved with stone slabs fixed to concrete foundations, and has wooden piers and mooring rings with bronze heads of lions, wolves, and snakes.

There are two large architectural complexes nearby: the *Porticus Aemilia* and the *Horrea Sulpicia*.[2] The former serves as an arsenal, shipbuilding yard, and naval base. Its rectangular plan measures 487m on the long sides and 60m on the short sides. The total area (25,000m^2) is divided into 50 barrel-vaulted naves with 294 pillars arranged in seven rows. The immense building is accessed via stairways and ramps leading to and from the Tiber, about 90m away. The *Horrea Sulpicia*, a complex of warehouses used for storing goods, is arranged around three large rectangular courtyards with arcades, under whose vaults are long rooms.

In summer, the seafaring season, the comings and goings of boats, sailors, slaves, goods, pack animals, and ox-drawn carts are ceaseless. The quays come alive with crowds from the early hours of the morning. Dozens of slave porters carry goods on and off the ships. Before long, the docks and quays are cluttered with merchandise. The grain unloaded at *Emporium* is stored in the *Horrea Sulpicia*, where it is safe from humidity, before being distributed in the city or sent to other destinations.

Based in the ports of *Ostia* and *Puteolis*, two quaestors supervise the shipments and distribution of grain, control the quantity and quality of incoming grain, set the prices, and handle relations with the merchants involved in the trade. The task of supplying Rome is left to private individuals.[3] Some of the imported grain is owned by the wholesalers. Some of it, however, is public grain and represents the payment in kind of the *decima*, the tithe on agricultural production levied in the colonies of Latin law, allied cities, and provinces, or was purchased by the authorities in the places of production with the money obtained from the collection of taxes.

---

2   The complex was initially named the *Horrea Sulpicia* but later renamed the *Horrea Galbae*.

3   See I. Tantillo, "Gli uomini e le risorse," in *Roma Antica*, ed. A. Giardina (Rome: Laterza, 2014), 100.

Some of the public grain is distributed to the army. Some is set aside to prevent market manipulation and price speculation. What remains is sold to the public at a subsidized price. During the tribuneship of Caius Sempronius Gracchus (123–122), a system for the public distribution of grain at a lower price than the market price was introduced by law (*lex Sempronia frumentaria*). One of the buildings used for the sale of subsidized grain is the *Porticus Minucia Vetus*, a *quadriporticus* in the *Campus Martius* that encloses a square with three temples.

Rome's food supply system demands great energy and requires complex organization. If it breaks down, there will be consequences both politically and in terms of public order. The history of Rome is marked by periods of famine and "bread riots," often very violent. There may be food shortages for a variety of reasons: bad weather, an epidemic, war, an economic crisis, the incompetence or corruption of those responsible for the food supply, or speculative maneuvers, including agiotage, that is, speculating on the increase or decrease in the price of certain goods. Agiotage is carried out by exploiting confidential information or divulging false or tendentious news to raise or lower prices and profit from this to the detriment of wholesalers and consumers. It is a crime foreseen and punishable by law.[4]

In 105, a grain crisis occurred in Rome due to a decrease in wheat imports from Sicily, caused by a slave revolt that broke out on the island. The insurrection was so vast and ferocious and lasted for such a long time that it will eventually be considered a war (Second Servile War, 105–100). To explain its origins, we need to take a step back.

Previously, the Senate had decreed the release of all those who had been reduced to slavery after being taken from a people allied to Rome. After having freed many slaves, the governor of Sicily, based in *Syracusae* (Siracusa), refused the release of others entitled to manumission so as not to upset their masters (large landowners). The vast number of enslaved people, mostly Syrians, who had the right to freedom but were not released, rose up, obtained armaments, horses and supplies, formed action squads, and put large swathes of the island to the sword. The rebels proclaimed a Greek (or Italic) named Salvius as king, who assumed the royal name Tryphon, adopted regal *regalia* and *insignia*, surrounded himself with lictors in the Roman style, and, having proclaimed the independence of the territory under his control, intended to liberate the whole of Sicily from Roman rule.

---

4   Ibid., 100.

Over time, many other fugitive slaves and a few large groups of free, low-class proletarians joined the rebels. This uprising inflames Sicily, and the provincial militias are overwhelmed. The Senate reacts by sending reinforcement troops, but this army continues to be a stern test for the legions sent to counter it. As a result of the rebellion, the previously well-cultivated countryside has been transformed into desolate lands where no one sows or harvests, causing severe damage to the island's economy and grain exports.

The amount of wheat available on the Roman market has decreased so much that it's now impossible to produce bread in sufficient quantities to feed the entire population. This leads to a rise in cereal prices, which the massive sales of public grain at subsidized prices are unable to control. This weakens and exasperates consumers, especially the less-well-off, and arouses discontent and anger toward the authorities. The protestors accuse the consul Caius Flavius Fimbria and the urban prefect Caius Memmius of shirking their duties due to negligence or ineptitude as well as tolerating the frequent instances of corruption and price speculation because they are personally involved. There are protest marches, which often degenerate into violence, with collateral damage and injuries, and attacks on bakeries, which are increasingly frequent. Occasionally, in the background, we can glimpse the promises and incentives of individuals who aim to gain the approval of the masses by flattering their aspirations, especially financial ones, with promises that are difficult to achieve.

The authorities targeted by the protests are principally the aediles. During periods of social and political tension, these magistrates should be able to intervene to disperse gatherings, quell riots, repress crimes, identify the guilty parties, and arrest them. However, they cannot because there is no urban police force, save for the *tresviri capitales*, or *tresviri nocturni*. Furthermore, the aediles cannot make use of any legions camped outside the city to restore public order. In fact, it is strictly forbidden for soldiers to cross the *pomerium*. The reason for this is to prevent *coups d'état*.

Inevitably, therefore, the gaze of those attempting to solve Rome's riot problem falls on the removal of the cause of the discontent that caused them. So, what can be done to restore the management of the food supply system to optimal levels? The Senate discusses it and selects its most esteemed member, Marcus Aemilius Scaurus, to make inquiries.

Born in 161, 56-year-old Scaurus is one of the most influential men in the *res publica* in 105. He has been a politician for some time and is a political animal with highly attuned senses, unaccustomed to making rash decisions. Scrupulous, ever vigilant, and well-informed, he tends to act as a driving force and, in the event of a dispute, as a mediator between the parties involved.

Having become *princeps senatus*, succeeding Quintus Cornelius Lentulus, he is required to deal with disputes with foreign states, among other duties. Scaurus loves to read and is the author of a *commentarius*, entitled *De vita sua*.

During his investigation, Scaurus avoids confrontation with Fimbria and Memmius: either he isn't convinced that they are guilty or—as the experienced politician he is—he has other reasons for not doing so. Instead, he identifies the person responsible for the disruption to the city's food supply, leading to the grain crisis, as the quaestor *ostiensis* Lucius Appuleius Saturninus.

Saturninus is a 28-year-old with brown hair, a sharp mind, and deep intelligence.[5] Scaurus declares that Saturninus, due to his position and role, was able to know before and better than anyone else what was transpiring regarding the city's food supply. Due to his negligence, if not his self-interested silence, Scaurus says, the treasury wasn't alerted in time and, consequently, couldn't buy more grain before the prices rose.

But Scaurus was deceived into turning his attention to Saturninus by people who had an interest in misleading his inquiries. Therefore, although Saturninus is innocent, he is declared guilty. In early October 104, the Senate, on Scaurus's proposal, decides by a large majority to establish a commission to deal with the city's grain supply and appoint the *princeps senatus* as its leader. In other words, it effectively ousts Saturninus from office, although there appears to be no proof of his dereliction of duty.[6]

What is said about Saturninus's alleged culpability harms his public image. He is insulted in public, his wife and daughter are forced to shut themselves away in their house out of shame, and his slaves behave toward him as they would toward a person without honor or prestige. The office to which he was appointed has now become an obstacle to his future career. His pride wounded, Saturninus is embittered and dejected. He harbors a dark grudge against the nobility, of which he himself is a part, and ponders his revenge. He decides he will run as tribune of the plebs for 103 to manipulate the people for the purpose of personal revenge and moral restitution.[7] To increase his chances of election, he asks the consul Caius Marius for help and convinces

---

5   Since Saturninus was quaestor in 104, he must have been born in 132 at the latest. Not everyone managed to be elected at 28; consequently, it cannot be excluded that Saturninus was older than 28 in 105.

6   The exact reason why Saturninus is removed from office is unknown. According to Diodorus, it was incompetence.

7   Cicero remarks that the Senate's punishment of Saturninus is unjust and sees it as the cause that prompted Saturninus to side with the *populares* against the *optimates*.

him that he is innocent of the faults attributed to him, so Marius promises him electoral support.

Marius is a self-made man. Without a family or a group of friends to lean on, he rises from the bottom to increasingly high positions. Born in 157 in lower *Latium* into a humble family (his father worked the land and offered himself as a laborer to earn some extra money; before undertaking military service, Marius himself worked as a blacksmith). He served in the Numantine War, the Jugurthine War, and the Social War, was consul in 107, celebrated a triumph for having successfully ended the Jugurthine War, and is currently consul (104). He is now one of the Senate's most renowned and prestigious members, acclaimed and revered, but while he is a former magistrate and a magistrate in office, and thus a politician, he feels that he is also, and above all, a soldier. He can be described as a dog-faced soldier in that his way of thinking and behaving is closer to that of enlisted men than senior officers. His support comes from the people he belongs to and among whom he grew up. They admire both his qualities and the luck that has constantly followed him. The time and place in which Marius is perfectly at ease, like an animal in its natural environment, is the battlefield amidst the orgy of violence and bloodshed.

Marius is a poorly educated man with two sides to his character. As a soldier, he is a protagonist on the battlefield: he faces danger head-on, often pushing himself to the front line to instill courage and determination in his men. As a politician, Marius keeps a low profile. He prefers to stay behind the scenes and is very good at plotting and manipulating men and situations while remaining in the shadows. This, however, does not limit his sphere of influence; if anything, it improves it. Indeed, this is precisely what makes Marius a powerful man outside the military sphere.

He is certainly not a statesman, and it is difficult to see him as a politician, but as a leader of the *populares*, he will be able to collect many votes in the next elections. Marius's electorate comprises lower-class plebeians, a modest share of the patriciate, and the *equites*. The soldiers adore him because, in times of war, he shared their toil and suffering; therefore, they are ready to vote for him, always and under any circumstances. Furthermore, Marius is the darling of the lower classes, especially the non-propertied, who are grateful to him for having opened the doors of the army to them. Before his reforms of the army and conscription, non-propertied men were exempted from mandatory military service and excluded from voluntary recruitment.

Marius has few friends among the patricians, but those he has include the *Iulii Caesares,* to whom he is related by marriage. He is married to Julia Major, daughter of the senator Caius Julius Caesar (the grandfather of the famous future consul, conqueror of Gaul, triumphator, and dictator for life, who will be the victim of a conspiracy of senators in 44).

The *equites*, who have considerable weight in economic and public life, are also on his side. They don't support Marius because he is "one of them" (or at least, not just for this reason) but because they trust he will get them licenses, permits, authorizations, administrative concessions, and make various intercessions on their behalf.[8] The *publicani*, in particular, depend on him to promote and protect their investments in Roman Asia. This is a constant in their political outlook. The *equites* always smile on military conquests because these enable them to share the spoils of war, hoard the natural resources of the subjugated lands, and participate in international trade with increasingly important roles.

Despite being over 70 and therefore above the age limit for public office, Marius refuses to retire from public life. Instead, he constantly fantasizes about exaggerated successes and longs to get back into the thick of things.

It's also worth noting that Marius has already been very disloyal to the Caecilii Metelli after benefiting from their electoral support. In 118, as tribune of the plebs, he promoted and obtained approval for an electoral reform bill (*lex Maria de suffragiis ferendis*). The law was approved after Marius threatened the consul Lucius Caecilius Metellus Dalmaticus with arrest after the latter intervened to help his colleague, Lucius Aurelius Cotta. When Cotta had tried to persuade the Senate to summon Marius to explain his initiative to them he was subjected to threats from Marius if he didn't withdraw his motion. In 108, Marius slandered Quintus Caecilius Metellus, later named Numidicus, in the Senate. When Metellus consequently wasn't confirmed in his command of the army fighting in North Africa against Jugurtha, king of *Numidia* (Jugurthine War, 111–105), Marius, who had been elected as consul for 107, replaced him.

Another person whom Marius has treated badly is Lucius Cornelius Sulla. Born in 138 in Rome, Sulla has ashen skin, a pockmarked face, and thick copper-blond hair. He comes from a patrician family that was once socially and economically prominent but has fallen into poverty. As such, Sulla is a self-made man. He is also Marius's brother-in-law, having married his wife's sister, Julia Minor. As quaestor in 107, he served with Marius, who was consul for the first time that year, in the Jugurthine War. That conflict effectively ended when Sulla, as Marius's deputy, captured Jugurtha following the betrayal of Bocchus I of *Mauretania*, Jugurtha's father-in-law and erstwhile ally. The

---

8   M. Bocchiola & M. Sartori, *Teutoburgo. La selva che inghiottì le legioni di Augusto* (Milan: Mondadori, 2014), 46.

deposed sovereign was taken to Rome, where he was imprisoned until he was paraded as a prisoner of war during Marius's triumphal procession, then put back in prison and left to die. *Numidia* was split in two. The eastern part was given to Gauda, a descendant of Masinissa and one of Jugurtha's predecessors, while the western part was given to Bocchus to reward him for his collaboration. After the Jugurthine War, however, relations between Marius and Sulla deteriorated due to Marius taking all the credit for the success, even for the part owed to those who helped him secure victory.

Due to his large electoral backing, Marius was able to set out on a path through the *cursus honorum* all the way to the finish line, which he has crossed not once but three times, including two times in a row. He is now able to have "his" candidates elected, those whom he has chosen to support not out of fondness, esteem, or friendship, nor because of their personal abilities, but because he knows that, once elected, they will remain bound to him, like a client to his patron, and he will be able to maneuver them however he likes. He selects his "chosen ones" principally from among the candidates for the tribuneship for the plebs because this magistracy, like the consulship, has the power of legislative initiative.

In exchange for his electoral support, Marius obtains a promise from Saturninus that, if elected, he will promote and obtain approval for a bill that aims to secure a portion of *ager publicus* for each of Marius's veterans from the Jugurthine War. The "settlement" of these veterans is very important to him because it's vital for him to keep the promise he made them upon enlistment; otherwise, he will no longer hold their esteem or enjoy their gratitude. However, he also wants to use Saturninus to launch a decisive attack on Metellus Numidicus to destroy the source of all his nightmares once and for all. Marius considers Metellus Numidicus to be his most formidable political opponent, and he is right to be afraid of him, given how he slandered him in the Senate to oust him as military commander.

It should be emphasized that Saturninus's commitment to Marius is of no little importance. The management of *ager publicus populi Romanorum* is a realm of endless controversies: between patricians and plebeians, *optimates* and *populares*, Romans and their allies, and those who own property and those who don't. Stepping into this arena, either to change the rules or to found new colonies, is very risky and could be fatal; the political history of the Gracchi is evidence enough of this.

During the electoral campaign, Saturninus sets out a Gracchan-like reform program. This is very divisive. The *optimates* fear that waving the banner of the myth of the Gracchi will have the effect of fanning the flame of "democratic revolution." So, they regard Saturninus as a seditious individual.

Besides Saturninus, Marius has decided to support several other candidates for the next set of elections: Caius Norbanus Balbus, Marcus Baebius, and Lucius Equitius. It's worth focusing on the latter.

Equitius was only conditionally admitted to the elections for the tribuneship while verifications were underway to prove there was not a shadow of a doubt over his possession of Roman citizenship. To this end, he filed a request for judicial recognition of paternity, asserting that he was born from the extra-marital relationship of Tiberius Sempronius Gracchus and Equitia, a free Roman woman from a good (albeit humble) family. He also claimed that Tiberius's wife, Cornelia Africana, entrusted him to a pair of servants, who then sold him as a slave to a wealthy married couple from *Firmum Picenum* (Fermo in the Marche, about 250km northeast of Rome). Equitius says after he gained his master's favor, he allowed him an education, freed him, and made him the couple's sole heir, inheriting lots of real estate, all located in Firmum and its environs. Later, he increased his assets and moved to Rome.[9]

Metellus Numidicus, one of the two censors, denies that Equitius can be registered in the census lists and, therefore, whether he can be recognized as a Roman citizen because, he argues, he isn't Gracchus's son[10] but a lower-class plebeian trying to win favor with the deception and complicity of his friend Saturninus. Indeed, it's well known that Gracchus had three sons, none of

---

9   On Equitius's name, birthplace, and origins: Val. Max. III.2.18; III.8.6; IX.7.1; IX.15.1; *De vir. ill.* 62.1, 73,3; Flor. II.4.I.e, IX.15.1. The *Liber de viris illustribus* calls Equitius *Quintum*, or *Quintium*, rather than Lucius. This is perhaps a transcription error. Valerius Maximus claims to know nothing of Equitius's origins, while the anonymous author of the *Liber de viris illustribus* calls him a *"libertini ordinis"* (73.3). This means that "our man belonged to the category of freed slaves," with the caveat that "he could not be considered a freedman, unless one thinks he was the freedman of a non-Roman." P. Floris, 2009, *Lucius Equitius Insitivus Gracchus* (Cagliari: Edizioni AV, 2009). Florus says Equitius was *"hominem sine tribu, sine notore, sine nomine"*. Cicero (*Rab. Perd.* VII.20) scornfully calls him *"ille ex compedibus atque ergastulo Gracchus"* and considers him a runaway slave, as does App. *B Civ.* I.141. When speaking "Of those who have falsely thrust themselves into families where they do not belong," Valerius Maximus writes: "I must not omit Equitius, the monster from *Firmum* in *Picenum*, who was mentioned in an earlier part of this book. His manifest lie in pretending that he was the son of Tiberius Gracchus was defended by the turbulent mistake of the populace and by the power of the tribunes" (IX.15.1).

10   A. Passerini, *Caio Mario come uomo politico* (Pavia: Amministrazione dell'Athenaeum, 1934), 258. On Metellus Numidicus's refusal to add Equitius to the census rolls and his motivation: E. Gabba, *Appiani Bellorum civilium liber primus* (Florence, 1967), 98–126. On the date of the incident: T. R. S. Broughton, *The Magistrates of the Roman Republic* (New York: American Philological Association, 1951–60), 567 (it is believed it can be dated to 102 or 101). According to McDonnell, Metellus's censure lasted until the autumn of 101. M. McDonnell, *Roman Manliness: Virtus and the Roman Republic* (Cambridge: Cambridge University Press, 2006), 286.

whom are still alive. Furthermore, Numidicus observes, Equitius is a member of the *Suburana*, one of the four urban tribes; if his property is in Firmum, he should have been enrolled in the *tribus rustica Fabia*.[11] Numidicus is right. Equitius is in the midst of a deceitful affair, certainly in agreement with Saturninus, perhaps even with Marius. His aim is clear and evident. If he were recognized as Gracchus's son, he would become the owner of his deceased father's rights and obligations, hold the patronage of important clientele,[12] and obtain full Roman citizenship and could thus claim to be the heir of the Gracchi's legacy of ideals and run for election.

The truth emerges when Equitius's case is debated publicly and Sempronia, Scipio Aemilianus's widow and the last living member of the Gracchi family,[13] is called to testify. She says that Equitius isn't her nephew, thereby denying that Equitius is who he says he is.[14] The consequences are immediate. As official duty requires, Marius has Equitius arrested and imprisoned awaiting trial on the charge of having made untruthful statements aimed at misleading the judgment of a public authority.

However, although it's evident that Equitius is an imposter, his candidacy is put to the vote, and once all the votes are counted, Saturninus, Norbanus, Baebius, and Equitius are all proclaimed victors. In fact, Saturninus garners more votes than he expected. At the same time, Marius is re-elected to the consulship. Once again, the electorate has faith in his ability and fortune.[15]

Therefore, four of the 10 candidates elected to the plebeian tribuneship for 103 are Marius's men. Of the six other elected officials, three—Lucius Aurelius Cotta, Lucius Antistius Reginus, and Titus Didius—are "loyal to the Senate." Their point of political reference is Scaurus.

---

11 Enrollment in the census lists took place for the purposes of tax collection and military conscription. To be enrolled, you had to be of free status, aged 17 or over, and be the recipient of an income above the propertyless threshold (1,500 asses). It was equivalent to recognition as a Roman citizen (Cic. *Arch.* 11) and was accompanied by enrollment in a *tribus*, to be understood here as an electoral district. Registration allowed an applicant to exercise the right to vote actively and passively, and they were enrolled with the tribe where most of the applicant's assets were registered. There were 35 tribes, of which 31 were rural and four were urban (*Collina, Esquilina, Palatina, Suburana*). Those enrolled in the census lists were registered with rural tribes; the propertyless were registered with urban tribes.

12 Floris, *Lucius Equitius Insitivus Gracchus,* 10, esp. n. 32. On the provincial clients of Tiberius Sempronius Gracchus, see E. Badian, *Foreign Clientelae, 264–70 BC* (Oxford: Clarendon, 1958), 193–220.

13 Floris, *Lucius Equitius Insitivus Gracchus,* 14 with n. 46.

14 Floris, *Lucius Equitius Insitivus Gracchus,* 14 with n. 48.

15 Plut. *Mar.* 14.8.

The newly elected tribunes of the plebs enter office on 10 December 104. Each delivers a speech from the Orators' Tribune, addressing the crowd gathered in the Forum. Saturninus, in particular, takes advantage of the opportunity to announce two legal actions: one against Cnaeus Mallius Maximus and Quintus Servilius Caepio for having led the Roman army to disaster at the Battle of *Arausium* (Orange, France), one of the worst catastrophes in Rome's military history, and the other against Caepio for stealing the Gold of *Tolosa* (Toulouse, France).

To explain these stories, which are intertwined, we must introduce a new character: Quintus Sertorius, the son of Marius's cousin.

Sertorius was born in *Nursia* (Norcia), a town in Umbria. When he was very young, he lost his father and moved to Rome. Thanks to Marius, he could study and gain a good education. Later, he made a reputation for himself as a jurist and judicial orator. When Marius was elected to the consulship for the first time and raised an army, he would lead it to North Africa to fight against Jugurtha, king of *Numidia*. Sertorius hurried to enlist, and in 106, he fought in *Gallia Transalpina* during the Cimbrian War (113–101).

The Battle of *Arausium* was fought in 105 between Rome and a multitude of migrants originally from Northern Europe (Cimbri, Teutons, Ambrones). The migrants were entire peoples: Germanics (the Cimbri and Teutons, originally from Jutland), Celto-Germanics (Ambrones, from the coast adjacent to Jutland to the west and from the Frisian Islands opposite), and Helvetians (Tigurini, originally from the Helvetian plateau). The first of these—the Germanics and Celto-Germanics—began moving in 120 and had already crossed half of Europe. In 113, in *Noricum* (southern Austria and western Slovenia), they clashed with the army of the consul Cnaeus Papirius Carbo at the Battle of Noreia, inflicting heavy losses. Then they moved to *Gallia Transalpina* (France, Belgium, the Netherlands) over the Swiss plateau and descended through the Rhone Valley toward *Gallia Narbonensis* (central-southern France), the Roman province in *Gallia Transalpina*. They penetrated deep into *Gallia Narbonensis*, and there was a risk of other Roman provinces—*Hispania Citerior* and *Hispania Ulterior*—being invaded as well. Numerous legions that were sent against the invading migrants to destroy them were overwhelmed. In 107, they annihilated the four legions of the proconsul Marcus Junius Silanus. In 105, they inflicted the same fate on two entire legionary armies, commanded by consul Maximus and proconsul Caepio at *Arausium*. Meanwhile, in 106, the Gold of *Tolosa* had been stolen by unknown assailants, its escort massacred, while it was being transported to *Massilia* (Marseille, France) ahead of being shipped to Italy.

The Gold of *Tolosa* was a priceless treasure, accumulated during the sacking of a Celtic sanctuary near *Tolosa* by Caepio's army. It had been loaded onto a convoy of wagons to be transferred to Rome and paid into the public treasury. En route, it was violently seized, and the soldiers driving the wagons and acting as escorts were massacred. Caepio was named by a reliable witness as the instigator of the robbery and charged with aggravated robbery, multiple aggravated homicides for depriving Rome of the lives of numerous soldiers, and larceny against the citizenry. However, no evidence was found against him, and the case was closed. In 105, the Roman army was again defeated by the migrants at *Arausium*, principally because Caepio, now proconsul, disobeyed Maximus's command to coordinate his actions with him, even after the Senate dispatched emissaries urging him to obey the consul.

The Roman people judged that Marius was the military commander who offered the best guarantees of knowing how to defend Roman lands from the barbarian onslaught and elected him to the consulship for 104. Given the army was lost at *Arausium*, Marius recruited another. Again, Sertorius raced to sign up. Marius was subsequently elected to the consulship another three times (serving consecutive terms from 104–101) to ensure the necessary continuity in overseeing military operations in the Cimbrian War.

Throughout that period, before the theater of war moved from *Gallia Transalpina* to *Gallia Cisalpina*, Sertorius worked as a secret agent behind enemy lines. Disguised as a Gaul, he mingled with the Transalpine Gauls, took note of everything he saw, listening to the conversations of others, and returned to report to Marius. His service reports were so highly appreciated that he was decorated with a prize for valor.[16] Sometimes, Sertorius went on missions with Sulla. One of their greatest successes was the capture of Copillus, the leader of a Gallic tribe called the Tectosages in 102. Under interrogation, Copillus revealed a secret to improve his position: Caepio was the instigator of the robbery of the Gold of *Tolosa*.

Caepio and Maximus, Saturninus declares, have the blood of the 100,000 men they sent to the slaughter on their hands for behaving senselessly toward each other in a perilous situation. Because of their negligence, Saturninus continues, the Roman state is now threatened with a barbarian invasion. (There is a widespread fear that the migrants, emboldened by their victory, will cross the Alps to invade Italy.) Saturninus highlights how Caepio committed the crime he is accused of when he was proconsul of Gaul, thereby failing to fulfill his official duties, and how this detail becomes vitally important as

---

16 Plut. *Sert.* 3.

an aggravating circumstance. He underlines how Caepio is the perpetrator of crimes that are not only serious but also dishonorable and disreputable for having committed them when he held a public office of extremely high prestige and equivalent responsibility.

The group of *equites* is particularly critical in this regard, both because the legal action targets one of them (Maximus is an *eques*) and because it isn't clear where Saturninus is going with this. The doubt arises from the fact that the *populares'* tribunes of the plebs usually drag magistrates and military commanders to court not so much, or not only, because the alleged offenses are violations of the laws of civil coexistence and require their perpetrators to be punished but rather to draw inspiration from the single judicial case to indict the entire nobility and to demonstrate that they aren't above moral reproach or the law. In the present case, however, another hypothesis can be made. By striking at Maximus, Saturninus perhaps wants to send a message: to make it clear that he feels free to follow a political line that diverges from the *equites'* interests, instead leveraging the favor he enjoys with the common people. This could mean that he is intending to secure his independence from Marius now that he has been elected because he no longer needs him.

Proving Caepio's and Maximus's responsibility for the defeat at *Arausium* will be difficult. But Saturninus promotes two interconnected plebiscites that aim to reform the rules that provide for and punish the crime of *perduellio* (high treason). The first bill aims to insert *perduellio* within the scope of a broader crime known as *crimen maiestatis*, which consists of any deed or fact that harms the *dignitas* of the Roman people and offends their greatness. *Crimen maiestatis* is punishable by death, which can be commuted to voluntary exile with the accessory penalties of deprivation of citizenship and confiscation of assets. The second legislative project provides for the establishment of a court of justice called a *quaestio perpetua de maiestate*, presided over by a praetor. The purpose of this intervention is to ensure that offenders can be prosecuted for a *crimen maiestatis*. In the past, the complexity of the procedure set before the *comitia centuriata* rendered *perduellio* a crime punishable more in theory than in practice.[17]

Saturninus describes the two plebiscites at a specially convened public assembly, then submits them to the *concilia plebis* for a vote and gets them approved. The *lex Appuleia de maiestate minuta* and the *lex Appuleia de quaestione extraordinaria istituenda* thus come into force. However, it's important to

---

17   E. S. Gruen, *Roman Politics and the Criminal Courts, 149–78 B.C.* (Cambridge, MA: Harvard University Press, 1968), 168; E. Gabba, *Mario e Silla* (Berlin-New York: 1972): 779; B. Santalucia, *Diritto e processo penale nell'antica Roma* (Milan: Giuffrè, 1998), 128, n. 77.

note that the *lex Appuleia de maiestate minuta* doesn't provide a comprehensive description of *crimen maiestatis*. Consequently, this crime may be recognized in various behaviors, such as being responsible for a military defeat.

In 102, Saturninus presents an agrarian law proposal that has the aim of "settling" Marius's thousands of war veterans from the Jugurthine War and Cimbrian War through the assignment of portions of arable land in new colonies to be founded in the provinces, specifically in *Gallia Cisalpina*, Corsica, Sicily, Greece, and North Africa.[18] The project envisages that everyone involved in the colonial enterprise receives a plot of arable land.[19] A three-man commission will be set up for each foundation, selected from among the Italics associated with the affair, who will receive Roman citizenship. The move will be financed by the proceeds of the fines and sale of the assets confiscated from the perpetrators of the robbery of the Gold of *Tolosa*, thereby demonstrating that Caepio's prosecution isn't so much about bringing the robbery's instigator to justice as ensuring the financing of Saturninus's agrarian land bill.[20]

It should be noted that before Saturninus's tribuneship, agrarian laws—traditionally promoted by tribunes of the plebs from the *populares'* camp—always aimed at serving the poorest Roman citizens: *proletarii* (manual workers with dependent families), *humiliores* (unskilled workers; unemployed), and *capite censi* ("have nothings"). The agrarian laws proposed by Saturninus, however, have a different objective: ensuring a source of income for war veterans who have been discharged from service and now have the problem of making ends meet. But this isn't the main objection to Saturninus's bill when it's debated in the Senate and explained in a *contio*. The main criticism takes its cue from the nexus between the colonies' foundation and the naturalization granted by the *triumviri coloniae deducendae* (the leaders of the colonial contingent). Saturninus's proposal to create three Roman citizens in each new colony therefore brings the Italic Question back to the fore.[21]

In recent decades, we recall, the Italic Question has been one of the leading foreign policy problems of the Roman state due to the discontent it aroused among the *socii* and the tensions and conflicts it created among the allies. In 125, the situation was aggravated when the praetor Lucius Opimius bloodily repressed the popular insurrection of *Fregellae*. The rebellion broke out after

18 In North Africa, the lands to be assigned to ex-legionaries are in *Numidia*, near the border of Roman Africa and an important crossroads, while those to be assigned to ex-*auxilia* are located between Syrtis Minor, the High Steppes, and the Majardah Valley.

19 Cavaggioni, *L. Apuleio Saturnino*, 111.

20 Cic. *Balb.*, 48.8.

21 Cic. *Balb.*, 48*.

the consul Marcus Fulvius Flaccus was forced to withdraw his proposed bill on citizenship due to the insurmountable opposition of the Senate, his consular colleague Marcus Plautius Hypsaeus, and large swathes of Roman society. We have already talked about it, but it is worth summarizing what they said. In 122, Caius Sempronius Gracchus proposed extending full Roman citizenship to Latins and equating Italics with Latins regarding the right to vote, causing all hell to break loose. The Senate declared a state of emergency and instructed Lucius Opimius to do whatever was necessary to save the *res publica*. A militia dispersed a protest demonstration by the Gracchans on the Aventine by killing thousands, while Gracchus himself ordered a slave to kill him to escape an undignified death. The subsequent ferocious judicial harassment of the Gracchans claimed thousands more victims. Therefore, the discontent aroused by Gracchus's proposed land reforms fueled further resentment and tensions.

Between 120 and 112, the controversy of the Italic Question was exacerbated on other occasions, particularly when Latins serving in the army were denied the right to appeal against first-grade sentences and when a law was passed allowing Latin magistrates to become full Roman citizens, thus instituting a policy of double standards that discriminated against the Italic *socii*. The passage of time hasn't softened the attitude of those who oppose the idea of mass naturalization in the least. In 101, after the Battle of the Raudine Plain, Marius was accused of illegally conferring Roman citizenship on a cohort of auxiliaries from *Cameria* (or *Camerta*) who had distinguished themselves through acts of valor in battle. Marius replied that "the clash of arms had prevented his hearing the voice of the law."[22]

The success of Saturninus's motion is a matter of great concern to Marius. If it fails, he won't be able to give his war veterans their promised "pension" and would lose face. Therefore, he speaks up in the Senate in favor of the plebiscite. This is one of the rare occasions when Marius actively participates in a public debate, given that he is anything but a skilled orator, overcoming his reluctance to speak and exposing himself in the political arena. Getting straight to the point (rhetorical devices are alien to him), Marius points out that:

- the lands to be distributed to the settlers are located in lands where the soil and climate are less generous than in Italy;
- the settlers and their descendants will not leave the land uncultivated (as landowners sometimes do) but will look after their land, which would otherwise be left bare;

---

22 Plut. *Mar.* 28.3. This incident is also mentioned in Val. Max., 5.2.8.

- Rome and Italy are distinct but complementary entities due to being linked by geography and mutual interests;
- Rome's Italic allies fight alongside them in its wars and sacrifice their lives just like the Romans, which fully justifies the envisaged naturalizations (which, moreover, is a question of granting full Roman citizenship only to a limited number of people); and
- within the context of the new colonies, the lands will first be distributed to Roman citizens (who will therefore receive the best plots) and then to everyone else.

At the opening of the discussion following the illustration of the bill to fellow senators by the proponent, Metellus Numidicus argues that Marius is thinking and saying "unacceptable things" because he isn't a Roman but an Italic and is working with other Italics to harm Rome and the Romans; suggests that Marius won't limit himself to distributing the provincial *ager publicus* to the Italics but will also give them *ager publicus* in Italy; and points out that nobody can ensure the best lands will be distributed first. He ends with a sucker punch: Marius is using Saturninus to garner new and wider acclaim, he does so because he aspires to tyranny; he wants to be king.

The criticisms leveled at Marius reflect the long-standing resentment between the two, but they are also an indirect attempt to defend solid economic interests. The problem that needs to be resolved is always the same, the one that has already led to the failure of Tiberius Sempronius Gracchus's land reform in 133. Senatorial families have a quasi-monopoly over access to the economic exploitation of the *ager publicus*, and it is thus in their interests to prevent access to new beneficiaries.

On the expected day, the vote on the plebiscite by the *concilium plebis* takes place in the *comitium*, in the Forum, in front of the *Curia*. A tribune of the plebs loyal to the Senate claims to have heard a roll of thunder. The augurs deduce from this that the *auspicia* are unfavorable and that the vote must not proceed. A reproachful murmur arises, low at first before quickly rising to a roar. Saturninus senses the danger. He shouts in a loud voice that the augurs, complying with the intrigues of the enemies of the people, have declared a falsehood and that he doesn't accept the vote's postponement. Just then, as if answering a call, a mob emerges from the crowd and threatens the tribune who had claimed to have heard thunder. The accused flees but is caught, yanked back, showered with insults, and thrown into prison, even though he is a magistrate protected by sacrosanctity, immunity from coercion, and inviolability.

The *equites* refuse to accept that violence will have an influence in the political arena yet again. They insist that the way to voice opposition consists, at worst, of resorting to legal proceedings. Their spokesmen dissociate themselves from Saturninus and his acolytes and announce their vote against the proposed colonial law. Marius instinctively criticizes their decision. Again, a crowd of war veterans besiege the *comitium*, intending to influence the vote through intimidation. The plebiscite is put to the vote and approved in an atmosphere of confusion, arrogance, and oppression.

In the lands of the Italics, the people take to the streets to protest that they have been excluded from the field of application of the law proposed by Saturninus and to demand that full Roman citizenship be granted to them. Their spirits are more heightened than ever. Echoes of the demonstrations reach ears in Rome, but the Senate and consuls pretend not to hear them, knowing they are supported by most of the Roman people, who oppose the mass naturalization of the Italics on account of their fear of losing control of the legislature, through which the relations between the state and its citizens, as well as private interests, are regulated.

Following Saturninus's re-election as tribune, the trial for the robbery of the Gold of *Tolosa* takes place in 101.[23] Caepio was accused of being the lead instigator, and numerous others were charged with being his accomplices. Once the ritual preliminaries have been completed, the president of the court begins the debate. He is summarizing the boundaries of the matter in a particularly tense atmosphere when the tribunes of the plebs Lucius Aurelius Cotta and Caius Titus Didius veto the further development of the trial.[24] The act sparks a furious brawl.[25] Norbanus ignores both the veto and the scuffle and, amid the chaos, says that most of the stolen gold and silver came from the sacking of his sanctuary at Delphi in 279 by a barbarian horde. He deduces that the defeat at *Arausium* was a punishment inflicted on the Romans for offending Apollo. Therefore, the trial continues amid the tumult. When the verdict is pronounced, condemnations pour in. Caepio is acquitted.[26] The instigator of the robbery will remain unknown.

23 On the trial of Caepio and Maximus: *Rhet. Her.* I.24; Cic. *Balb.* 11.28; *Brut.* 35, 135; Liv. *Per.* LXVII; Strab. IV.1,13,188; Val. Max. IV.7,3; VI.9,13. For a legal proceeding relating to the events of 106 that seemingly involves various unidentified persons: Dio. *Framm. Fr.* 90 (=EV 81). A "far-reaching" investigation linked to the Gold of *Tolosa*'s disappearance is mentioned in Oros. V.15.25. A hint at the trial is also found in Cic. *Nat. D.* III.30, 74.

24 Cic. *De Or.*, II.47, 197*.

25 For the sources: MRR I 563 ff.

26 Cic. *Nat. D.* 30.74; Oros. V.15.25; J. Lengle, "Die Verurteilung der Römischen Feldherrn

In the meantime, Mithridates VI Eupator, king of *Pontus* (an Anatolian region on the Black Sea), has attempted to get Rome to grant him total freedom to expand his territory in Anatolia, the Caucasus, and Crimea, offering money and other benefits to the senators, who, in many cases, accepted gifts. Saturninus angrily denounces this underhanded dealing, publicly declaring the corruption and insulting the king. Pontic diplomats protest before the Senate for the wound inflicted on their official immunity and their king's honor and prestige. The Senate admits that their objections are well founded, then honorably dismisses them before accusing Saturninus of impiety.

Metellus Numidicus is preparing to ban Saturninus from attending Senate meetings, and the latter's reaction is unprecedented. Backed by armed individuals, he goes to Metellus Numidicus's house and attacks him (Numidicus, we recall, is one of the leaders of the *optimates*, political adversaries of the *populares*, led by Marius, who, ostensibly supporting Saturninus politically, exploits him for his own purposes). The victim is beaten, and to escape the hail of blows, he flees, bursts into the Temple of Jupiter Optimus Maximus, and barricades himself inside. But Saturninus and his friends besiege him, and it is only due to the arrival of other people—and a bloody fight—that the censor is freed. To restore order, Metellus Caprarius steps in and persuades his cousin not to go through with his plan.

The attack on Metellus Numidicus marks a dramatic turning point in Rome's public life. Evidently, Saturninus has changed his tactics. To strengthen his grip on power and enforce his own political choices, he has organized his friends, clients, and slaves into action squads.

The fact remains that Saturninus has been accused of impiety. Everything suggests that he will be convicted and sentenced to death. But Rome's political climate is now marked by violence, impertinence, and oppression, and this is due precisely to Saturninus, his friends, and his thugs.

On the day set for the hearing, Saturninus appears in the Senate flanked by men brandishing clubs. Scaurus, the *princeps senatus*, is attempting to

---

von Arausio," *Hermes* 66, no. 4 (1931): 302–316. On Caepio's involvement in and links to the *quaestio auri Tolosani*, the sentences pronounced, and Caepio's eventual acquittal: M. Segre, "Il sacco di Delfi e la leggenda dell' 'aurum tolosanum'," *Historia* 8, no. 4 (1929): 621 and 628; T. R. S. Broughton, *The Magistrates of the Roman Republic* (New York: American Philological Association, 1951–60), 566; Gruen, *Roman Politics and Criminal Courts*, 162; M. C. Alexander, *Trials in the Late Roman Republic, 149 BC to 50 BC* (Toronto, Buffalo, London: University of Toronto Press, 1990), 33, n. 30; N. S. Rosenstein, *Imperatores Victi: Military Defeat and Aristocratic Competition in the Middle and Late Republic* (Berkeley, CA: University of California Press, 1990), 200. Cicero mentions Caepio several times but never associates him with the theft of the Gold of *Tolosa*. See, e.g., *Cic. Brut.* 35.135.

mediate between Saturninus and the soldiers posted to ensure the senators' safety to avoid bloodshed. The power play is won by Saturninus; the senators, intimidated, acquit him. The tribune becomes the champion of the *populares*, enemies of the ultra-conservative aristocracy.[27]

According to Saturninus, a great brouhaha has been raised (his indictment) to divert attention to secondary and marginal aspects of a much greater issue. The kernel of the matter is that many senators took money from Mithridates VI and that the Pontic ruler, by bribing them, had a specific purpose in mind. The grain crisis, Saturninus observes, has continued even after the commission chaired by Scaurus took over the supervision of the supply framework. The manipulations of agiotage, speculation on retail prices, and raids on bakeries continue. The fear that public order problems will hamstring internal trade and Rome's entire economy is widespread. All this proves that the malfunctioning of Rome's food supply system was not down to the quaestor *ostiensis*. Everyone knows that it actually depended on the reduced grain supply from Sicily due to the Servile War.

In the meantime, Marius, now proconsul, has emerged victorious in the Cimbrian War. The fate of that conflict was decided by two pitched battles: *Aquae Sextiae* (Aix-en-Provence), won by Marius in 102, and the Raudine Plain (a site of uncertain location but known to be somewhere in the Po Valley), won—with Sulla's help—by Marius and the proconsul Quintus Lutatius Catulus in 101. In the first battle, the Romans exterminated the Teutons and Ambrones, and in the second, they slaughtered the Cimbri. Seeing as the circumstances had turned against them so drastically, the Tigurini abandoned their idea of crossing the Alps to invade Italy and returned to their starting point on the Swiss plateau.

Marius wants to ride the wave of intense emotion that has broken out among the Romans—expressed in lively displays of joy, excitement, and admiration—for his military successes. Therefore, not satisfied with having already been elected to the consulship five times, he stands as a candidate for the consulship once again. Just when he is at the peak of his success, however, Marius feels that he is weaker than in the past. In times of peace, his interactions with the Roman people are much less productive than in times of war. A belligerent man, his natural environment is the battlefield; politics doesn't interest him except to the extent that he can gain a military command. As for the voters, they voted for him in 108 for successfully ending a war that had been dragging on for too long amid a series of scandals. Later, they voted

---

27 Passerini, *Caio Mario*, 258.

for him several times due to another ongoing war that had caused many losses and seen the enemy invade *Gallia Narbonensis* and *Gallia Cisalpina*. In 101, however, peace has returned, and Marius's exceptional ability to lead Roman armies to victory no longer has the added value required. This time, he cannot expect to be an official candidate, as from 105 onward, but will have to run for office himself; he will have to campaign and be in Rome on the day of the vote. However, Marius wants to be elected to the consulship again at any cost, and to achieve this goal, he is willing to do anything, even resort to demagoguery and bribing the electorate, throwing fistfuls of money among the tribes. His electoral campaign is dominated, however, by his competition with Quintus Lutatius Catulus Caesar.

Catulus was born Sextus Julius Caesar but was then adopted by a very wealthy man, Quintus Lutatius Catulus, and accordingly changed his name. He is the first cousin of Caius Julius Caesar (the father of the future dictator for life) and married to Cornelia, Sulla's daughter. He is a fine judicial orator, an educated and cultured man, a writer and poet, and the focal point of an intellectual circle that gathers in his home to read and comment on a literary work, discuss philosophy, and exchange opinions.

Catulus was consul in 102 and proconsul of *Gallia Cisalpina* in 101, when he played a significant role—alongside Marius—at the Battle of the Raudine Plain. After that success, however, relations between him and Marius deteriorated due to Marius's habit of taking all the credit for the success, even having a temple built in which he had it written that he won the battle, without mentioning the decisive role played by Catulus. To remind his fellow citizens of his own contribution, Catulus had a temple built on the *Campus Martius* and dedicated it to *Fortuna Huiusce* Diei ("Fortune of that Day"). Furthermore, he started to write a *commentarius* titled *De consulate et de rebus gestis suis*.

The elections for the magistrates for 100 take place in October 101. Among those elected are Marius, Caius Servilius Glaucia as praetor, and Saturninus as tribune of the plebs. Marius thus becomes consul for the sixth time.[28] His term of office will begin on 1 January 100. No one before him has held the highest magistracy so many times except for Marcus Valerius Corvinus, who was consul in 348, 346, 343, 335, 300, and 299. However, the difference here is that Corvinus's consulships spanned half a century, whereas Marius, after his first consulship, was elected five consecutive times. Once again, his election was confirmed in derogation of the prohibition of retaking office before two years had elapsed. Marius's consular colleague in 100, Lucius

---

28 Plut. *Mar.* 22.1–4.

Valerius Flaccus, is the younger son of the homonymous consul of 131. He is an unexceptional man, and it will be said that he was "more a servant than a colleague" to Marius.[29]

Glaucia is a man of about 30, with blond hair, gray-green eyes, and an energetic character. He is an enriched plebeian, a talented judicial orator, specializing in criminal law, and an able drafter of judicial and legislative acts, who elicits both positive and negative feelings ("Glaucia, though the most abandoned wretch that ever existed, was very keen and artful, and excessively humorous"[30]). A close friend of Saturninus, who is a few years younger than him, he attracted the Senate's enmity as tribune of the plebs in 104 for having promoted and obtained approval for a bill that sought to modify the *lex Servilia Caepio de repetundis* (107), which had reintroduced the senators into the composition of the jury of the *quaestio perpetua de repetundis*.

The *lex Servilia Glaucia de repetundis* is the third legislative intervention on the composition of the jury for corruption trials. First, the *lex Acilia de repetundis* restricted the jury to *equites* alone. Seventeen years later, the *lex Servilia Caepio de repetundis* modified the law by decreeing that the jury should be split equally between *equites* and senators. The *lex Servilia Glaucia de repetundis* returns total control of the court to the *equites* by excluding senators from the jury. This new arrangement, Glaucia says, will render the judicial decisions more severe. This will become evident. Meanwhile, from now on, senators will no longer have a say in corruption, malfeasance, or extortion trials involving former provincial governors, i.e., their colleagues. Moreover, the *lex Servilia Glaucia de repetundis* also allows provincials to recover the sums—even from third parties—extorted from them by the magistrates and structures the hearing phase of the criminal trial into two distinct and successive parts (prosecution-defense, defense-prosecution), separated by an interval.

The election for the renewal of the tribuneship of the plebs for 100 was marred by the horrific murder of the candidate Appius (or Aulus) Nonius.[31] The fact that he had defeated Saturninus, his direct competitor, aroused the disapproval of Saturninus and his friends, who didn't hold back from expressing it. The air was thick with resentment toward Nonius, who moved away from the voting area. But he was followed by a group of hooligans, who, through

---

29 Plut. *Mar.* 28.6.

30 Cic. *Brut.* 224. On Saturninus and Glaucia: App. *B. Civ.* 1.28–33.

31 Saturninus was able to be elected because the *lex Villia annalis* didn't apply to the tribuneship of the plebs, according to a law from 122, promoted and brought to approval by Caius Sempronius Gracchus to avoid a repeat of the events of 10 years earlier when his brother Tiberius had sought to run for the tribuneship again.

their comments, attitude, and actions, unequivocally showed that they meant him harm. He hid in a tavern, or a private residence, but was tracked down, dragged into the street, and beaten to death amid a general stampede.[32]

Rome is an unsafe city, especially at night. You can be robbed and killed for little reason in a deserted alley in a rough area. But Nonius's murder took place in broad daylight and in the presence of witnesses, many of whom now swear that Saturninus led Nonius's pursuers. Other commentators paint a broader picture: Nonius was killed on Saturninus's orders with the complicity of Marius.[33]

Asking *cui prodest*[34] undoubtedly leads to Saturninus and doesn't rule out the possibility that he may have acted with Marius's involvement.[35] Indeed, at dawn the following day, before the Forum has even filled with people, the consul Manius Aquillius, one of Marius's men, reopens the polling station and declares Saturninus, who gained more votes than any of the other non-elected candidates, to the position of tribune of the plebs that had become vacant because of the holder's death. Saturninus thus becomes tribune for the fourth consecutive time (he had already been elected for 102, 101, and 100). In the end, however, no incident reports were filed for Nonius's murder. The *praetor urbanus* was thus left with no other option than to file the case as murder by unknown persons.

In 100, Saturninus obtains approval from the *concilium plebis* for a bill for a corn law that aims to ensure that the quaestors of the public treasury are authorized to purchase all the available grain in Italy and *Gallia Cisalpina* and to put it up for sale at the price of five or six asses per *modius* instead of the price of 6⅓ asses per *modius*, the price fixed by the *lex Sempronia frumentaria* in 122. The treasury quaestors in question are Quintus Caecilius Metellus (later Pius), son of Metellus Numidicus, and Quintus Servilius Caepio, son of the homonymous consul found guilty of negligence in leading his troops

---

32 On the killing of Nonius: App. *B. Civ.* 1.127–128; Plut. *Mar.* 29.1; Val. Max. 9.7.3*; Aurelio Victor, *De vir. ill.*, 73.5*; Flor. II.4.1*; Oros. V.17.3*; Liv. *Per.* 69*. The moment of death (before or after his election) and the circumstances vary in the sources. According to Valerius Maximus (IX.7.3) and Appian (*B. Civ.* I.12), Nonius was killed before the vote to eliminate a dangerous opponent. See also Plut. *Mar.* 27.1*.

33 On Marius's connivance: Liv. *Per.* 69.1*, Plut. *Mar.* 29.

34 *Cui prodest* is short for *cui prodest scelus, is fecit,* "for whom the crime advances, has done it" (Sen. *Med.* III.500–501). This question is usually asked on the assumption that the perpetrator or promoter of a fact is usually the one who thereby sought to gain an advantage.

35 Oros. V.17.3.

to disaster at the Battle of *Arausium*.[36] Saturninus's project takes its cue from the fact that the grain crisis, which began in 105, is persisting. The increase in the cost of bread has caused widespread discontent, creating problems with preserving public order. The lower-class plebeians accuse the aristocracy of being the ones truly responsible for the famine and of wanting them to die of hunger. There are fears of outbreaks of collective violence. The goal of the legislative intervention is to prevent this situation from getting out of control. The quaestor Metellus thunders against the plebiscite and is supported by his colleague Caepio, who warns the Senate that the plebiscite's approval would aggravate the imbalance in the state accounts. A tribune of the plebs vetoes the continuation of the process of passing the law. A tribunician veto cannot be ignored, but Saturninus plows on nonetheless, opening himself up to accusations of illegality. He convenes the *concilia plebis* and puts the plebiscite to the vote. Chaos ensues. Caepio, other aristocrats, and their friends and clients demolish the voting walkways[37] and overturn the electoral urns to prevent the vote from taking place. Saturninus first inveighs against Caepio, calling him a traitor, before suspending the session. Shortly thereafter, he withdraws the bill.[38]

Meanwhile, in the Senate, the praetor Servilius Augur, with the support of the *pontifex maximus* Cnaeus Domitius Ahenobarbus, accuses Lucius Licinius Lucullus, in his absence, of conducting military operations without the required dedication. Lucullus is an enriched plebeian, descended from a family belonging to a *gens* of probable Etruscan origin. He was a praetor and governor of *Hispania Citerior* in 104. In 103, having just put down one slave rebellion in Campania (a police action, aimed at reestablishing public order and security), he was charged by the Senate with facing Salvius's revolt and landed in Sicily at the head of a new Roman and allied army numbering around

---

36 S. Treggiari, *Servilia and Her Family* (Oxford: Oxford University Press, 2019), 30. Caepio died in exile in *Smyrna* (Izmir) in Roman Asia after his son Quintus was killed. The latter's death should be placed in 90.

37 These are the narrow gangways reserved for voters leading to the bench behind which are the presiding magistrate and the clerks, and on which sits the voting urn.

38 It's unclear whether the plebiscite was approved. On Saturninus's grain bill and its controversial legislative process: *Rhet. Her.* 1.12.21. In 99, Caepio was charged with high treason for having played a part in preventing the voting procedure from taking place, thus harming the sovereign majesty of the state. The trial ended with the defendant's acquittal. It seems that Caepio said in his defense that "I have not inflicted, but rather prevented, damage, for I have saved the Treasury, resisted the license of wicked men, and kept the majesty of the state from perishing utterly." For Caepio's supposed defense: *Rhet. Her.* 2.12.17. For Saturninus: 4.22.31 and 4.54.67.

17,000 men. Recently, he won a major victory at *Triokala* (Caltabellotta) in the southwest, which was followed by a slowdown in operations.

By slinging mud at Lucullus, Servilius Augur manages to delegitimize him and undermine his credibility. In the end, the Senate appoints Servilius to replace Lucullus (thus giving him what he wanted). Lucullus was shocked by the news. He maintains a composed countenance but prepares a nasty surprise for his successor. As the end of his mandate approaches, he has all traces of his work erased to prevent his successor from benefiting from it (he lost, damaged, or rendered property of the state unusable, in whole or in part, thus making himself responsible for criminal offenses), before discharging his troops on the beach at *Agrigentum* (Agrigento) and sharing with them the accumulated spoils of war and money from the treasury. After arriving in Rome, he first shelters his family from the effects of the sentence that will surely be inflicted on him. He donates the family fortune to his eldest son, Lucius, and gives his youngest son, Marcus, up for adoption to his friend Marcus Terentius Varro, a wealthy patrician. During Lucullus's subsequent trial, Servilius supports the prosecution, and Quintus Caecilius Metellus Numidicus, asked to defend the accused by praising him, refuses to do so (Metellus Numidicus is the accused's brother-in-law). The trial ends with a guilty verdict. The defendant is sentenced to exile and associated penalties (deprivation of Roman citizenship, confiscation of assets) and expelled from the Senate. He will remain in exile in *Heraclea* in *Lucania* (Scanzano Jonico, Basilicata, southern Italy), where his son Lucius has properties and business interests,[39] until his death.[40]

Meanwhile, another grisly episode of the ongoing political struggle is about to take place. In 100, the Senate decides to erect a statue in the Forum in honor of Marcus Antonius the Orator for having successfully completed a punitive expedition against the pirates of *Cilicia* (southeastern Anatolia) and authorizes him to celebrate a triumph, an exception to the norm according to which victories won over gangs of pirates, or fugitive slaves, merit at most an *ovatio*.

Shortly afterward (in the summer of 100), to exploit the favorable moment to the fullest, Antonius runs for the consulship for 99 alongside Quintus Servilius Glaucia, Caius Memmius, and Aulus Postumius Albinus.

Memmius is known among his fellow citizens as an excellent judicial orator and a crowd-puller. He served as praetor in about 104 and governor of Macedonia in 102.

---

39 Cic. *Arch.* IV.6.

40 Cic. *Arch.* 8.

In 110, Albinus had been given command of an army in North Africa by his brother, Spurius Postumius Albinus, who had to return to Rome to preside over the elections for the magistracies for 109. Antonius is Albinus's direct rival. He is the champion of the *optimates*, and forecasts on the eve of the elections predict he will secure a comfortable victory.

Memmius is Glaucia's rival. He started in a good position and has been increasing his lead with each passing day. As the electoral campaign progresses, it becomes clearer and clearer that Memmius will win. On the day of the vote, however, Memmius is beaten to death by a commoner named Publius Mettius[41] in the enclosed space on the *Campus Martius* known as the *ovilis*, where electoral procedures take place. The episode is particularly bloody and gruesome and occurs in the presence of numerous witnesses. News of what has happened passes from mouth to mouth, and bedlam breaks out. Voting is suspended. It will resume when calm has been restored and result in the election of Antonius and Albinus.

Memmius's assassination is another point on the path of the degradation of public life that no one can stop Roman society from following anymore. First Nonius and then Memmius were killed to prevent them from being elected. The perpetrators of these crimes are only the material perpetrators, however. The instigators are elsewhere, and it's widely believed that they are Saturninus and Glaucia. These magistrates, in cahoots with each other, introduced the method of violent struggle into public life, leading to explosions of savage ferocity, repeated with dramatic frequency, conditioning the free choices of the electorate, and creating problems that were not easy to solve.

The patriciate, the lower-class plebeians, the *equites*—the whole of society—believe that events have gone too far. Marius is furious: he has trusted a man (Saturninus) who has proved imprudent and impulsive and undertaken politically subversive acts. He fears this will come back to hurt him. A critical moment has arrived; Marius must decide which side he is on, clearly and transparently, abandoning all reservations, doublespeak, and pretenses. Ultimately, however, he decides not to take sides at all but to pander to and agree with everyone.

Rumor has it that Saturninus wants to unleash a social revolution, bring down the *res publica*, become king of Rome, and replace the Senate and consuls with a public safety committee to protect the restored monarchy from foreign invasions and internal rebellions. He talks about it in private homes,

---

41 Liv. *Per.* 69*. Oros. V.17.5. explicitly names Publius Mettius and provides a macabre detail, describing how Mettius committed the crime by "crushing Memmius with an unshapely bludgeon as he fled."

the Forum, and the markets, amid concern and bewilderment. The Senate is more convinced than ever that Saturninus is a tribune who foments unrest. It addresses the question in a meeting convened in the Temple of Bellona on the *Campus Martius*. It concludes that Saturninus is a serious threat to the security of the state and its citizens and must be thwarted by any means necessary. Therefore, it declares a state of emergency by adopting a special provision called the *senatus consultus ultimum* and gives Marius special powers to prevent damage being done to the *res publica*.

At that moment, Marius is consul and cannot fail to fulfill his institutional duties, not even if it involves moving against a friend like Saturninus. He withdraws his support for Saturninus, appoints Sulla as the head of a militia of approximately 1,000 volunteers, including Caepio and Metellus Pius, distributes weapons of war and military equipment, and establishes a plan of action. All this takes place on 9 December 100.

The following day, Saturninus addresses the crowd gathered in the Forum. He accuses the aristocracy and the *equites* of starving the common people to speculate on the price of grain and instigates a revolt against the profiteers. Even before he has finished speaking, Marius's militia emerges from the alley separating the Temple of Castor and Pollux from the *Basilica Sempronia* and charges at the crowd, resulting in numerous injuries and even deaths. Saturninus and his men, after a weak resistance, beat a retreat, rush up the *clivus Capitolinus*, enter the Temple of Jupiter Optimus Maximus facing the *Area Capitolina*, and barricade themselves inside. They give up only when Sulla cuts the water pipes that supply the temple to escape a horrible death from thirst. They are arrested and rounded up in a corner of the *Area Capitolina*, where a hostile crowd gathers menacingly around them. Saturninus loudly reveals his secrets, saying that Marius was behind all his ideas, projects, and actions before being locked up in the *Curia Hostilia* together with all the other prisoners.

The ending of the story is worthy of a Greek tragedy. In the dead of night, at the instigation of Caepio and Metellus Pius, a rowdy crowd clamber onto the roof of the Curia, uncover the location of the cell in which those arrested are being held, and throw the tiles they've removed down at the inmates. Saturninus collapses to the ground, where he is hit by more heavy projectiles. Equitius, Labienus,[42] and the plebeian quaestor Caius Saufeius are among the others to die. Afterward, the mob goes in search of Glaucia and kills him in the street, tearing him to pieces.[43]

---

42 Uncle of the more famous Titus Labienus, the legionary commander and Caesar's deputy during the Gallic Wars.

43 A different account is provided in Oros. V.17*. Orosius doesn't mention the hail of roof tiles

The *comitia tributa* meets as a matter of urgency and agrees on the subrogation of the tribunes of the plebs who have been killed with those who gained the most votes without being elected. Marius officially declares that the *res publica* is no longer in danger, and the Senate proclaims a general amnesty to foster the return of harmony in the city.

Simultaneously, a question arises: at the time of the assault on the *Curia*, had Marius lost control of the situation, or had he endorsed the slaughter? It's reasonable to assume that the answer must be both. Marius couldn't have opposed it without exposing himself to the charge of complicity in the attempted coup. The hostility toward Saturninus and his friends had reached a fever pitch. At that point, the "seditious" had to die.

The victors' vengeance also extends to the memory of the vanquished so as to erase any trace of Saturninus, as if he had never existed. From now on, the name of Saturninus will be execrated. Anyone who owns a portrait or bust of him could be convicted. Anyone who dares to speak well of him in public will spark a violent outcry.

Additionally, Saturninus's legislation is repealed.[44] The Senate declares that the agrarian law promoted and brought to approval by the tribune must not be observed or enforced because the vote on it occurred without consideration of an inauspicious omen and because it took place through the coercion of those who wanted to block it to avoid infringing on the *pax deorum*.

However, the provisions authorizing the foundation of colonies in North Africa are saved, given that these colonial enterprises are already in progress.[45] As a result, six permanent settlements, including *Cercina* (Kerkennah Islands),[46] will be established in North Africa for 6,000–10,000 colonists.

---

but says instead that the doors of the *Curia* were forced open and those inside were killed by members of the *equites*. He then adds that Glaucia was seized from the house of Claudius, dragged outside, and cut to pieces.

44 Opinions differ on this point. Some suggest that the Senate ordered its annulment, while others suggest it was abandoned or only partially applied. H. H. Scullard, *From the Gracchi to Nero: A History of Rome from 133 BC to AD 68*, 5th ed. (London: Routledge, 1982), 401, n. 34; E. Badian, "From the Gracchi to Sulla (1940–59)," *Historia: Zeitschrift für Alte Geschichte* 11 (1962): 197–245, esp. 219; A. W. Lintott, *Violence in Republican Rome* (Oxford: Oxford University Press, 1968), 152ff.; Passerini, *Caio Mario*, 348ff.; R. Seager ed., *The Crisis of the Roman Republic* (1969), 132ff.; Cic. *Leg.* 2.14, Cic. *Balb.* 48.

45 A. Ibba, *L'Africa Mediterranea in Età Romana (202 av. C.-442 d. C.)* (Rome: Carocci, 2012), 28.

46 It may be that this colony's establishment was decided in 103 but only realized in practice in 100.

CHAPTER VII

An Excellent Crime

In 97, the censor Lucius Valerius Flaccus is pursuing a broad-minded policy regarding granting Roman citizenship to foreigners residing in Rome. This attracts large numbers of new immigrants to the city, principally Latins and Italics, who often use fraudulent means and false oaths to be registered on the census lists and tribal registers (equivalent to formal recognition of possession of full Roman citizenship). The Senate and the consuls suspect that this policy is designed to strengthen the *populares* and, indirectly, the *populares'* leader, the six-time consul, triumphator, and victorious general Caius Marius, who is seemingly trying to relaunch his political career after his involvement in the Saturninus affair.

In 95, in order to hinder both irregular immigration and the presumed strategy of the *populares* outlined above, the consuls Quintus Mucius Scaevola Pontifex and Lucius Licinius Crassus, both patricians and *optimates*, propose and obtain approval for a bill that provides for the establishment of a *quaestio extra ordinem* to prosecute immigrants who have fraudulently claimed Roman citizenship and determines that the punishment to be exacted on those found guilty is flogging and forced removal from the city (*lex Licinia Mucia de civibus redigundis*). Pursuant to that law, the status of all those registered on the census rolls is verified, and charges are brought against those who appear on them without having the right to do so before being indicted, tried, and convicted. The result is that many people are driven out of Rome.

All this generates increased tension between Rome and the Latin *socii*.[1] In fact, the *lex Licinia Mucia* tacitly repeals, due to incompatibility, the *ius migrandi*, that is, the right of Latins to choose to settle in Rome and acquire Roman citizenship after renouncing their former citizenship.[2]

---

1   Cic. *Off.* 3.47; Cic. *Balb.* 48.8, 54.

2   It should be noted that the *ius migrandi* was based on the ancient awareness of a common lineage

But the question is more general, involving not only Latin, but also Italian people. Between 95 and 91, relations between Rome and its Latin and Italic friends and allies go from bad to worse. In 91, the tribune of the plebs Marcus Livius Drusus, speaking in the Senate, observes that, if it's true that many *socii* are dissatisfied with their relations with Rome and that there is a tendency to forget that, at the heart of their association with the *imperium*, they desire not to be treated as defeated peoples—which they are, on the whole—but to be integrated as free men into the Roman system; it is also true that such discontent is now approaching dangerous levels.

The 33-year-old Drusus is the son of the homonymous tribune who, in 123, in agreement with the Senate, littered a series of traps across the political path of his colleague in the tribuneship, Caius Sempronius Gracchus. As tribune of the plebs, he has already promoted and obtained approval for the *lex Livia iudiciaria*, which reserves the places on the jury of the *quaestio extra ordinem de repetundis* for senators alone, modifying the *lex Servilia Glaucia*, which had established that the jury be composed only of *equites*. The brother of Livia Drusa, he has married Servilia, sister of Quintus Servilius Caepio, and adopted Marcus Livius Drusus Claudianus, the biological son of his friend—Caius Claudius Pulcher(?)—and a descendant of Appius Claudius Caecus.

Drusus warns that if the *socii* insist on claiming mass naturalization and Rome continues to deny this to them, an increasingly intense political confrontation will arise between the parties, which could lead to an armed conflict, amounting to a brutal war that would be undoubtedly disastrous for all involved. He highlights how mass naturalization is the only way to avoid such a harrowing and otherwise inevitable result, underlining that the current state of relations between Rome and its Latin and Italic *socii* is a powder keg—potentially a very dangerous one: if it explodes, it will wound Roman society to its core and shatter the equilibrium currently maintaining the *imperium*.

As soon as Drusus has finished speaking, chaos erupts, with many senators loudly voicing their opposition. Caepio insults Crassus, his brother-in-law, accusing him of conspiring with his Italic friends against the state.

Some don't realize the gravity of the moment. Lucius Marcus Philippus and Quintus Lutatius Catulus lambast Crassus for having married an Italic

---

between Latins and Romans through the Trojan Aeneas. It stems from the *foedus Cassianum* (493) and survived the dissolution of the Latin League (338) before being regulated by various Roman immigration laws. It was mentioned in various bilateral association agreements (*foedera*) established between Rome and the remaining Latin cities.

woman; Marius, Quintus Pompeius Rufus,[3] and Quintus Varius Severus Hybrida Sucronensis for their Italic or provincial origin; and Cnaeus Pompeius Strabo for their vaguely Gallic somatic traits.[4] When Catulus declares that "certain people" shouldn't be sitting in the Senate, Rufus and Strabo lash out against him. Ultimately, Sextus Julius Caesar suspends the session and leaves the hall, escorted by his lictors, and followed by Lucius Aemilius Scaurus, Lucius Cornelius Sulla, and others. With Crassus's help, Marius separates Rufus and Strabo and escorts them out of the hall.

It's worth focusing on Quintus Servilius Caepio, a prominent figure among the *optimates*, for a moment. Caepio, the son of the homonymous ex-proconsul of Gaul who led the legions under his command to disaster at the Battle of *Arausium*, was a political opponent of Saturninus. In 95, Caepio was cleared of high treason after Crassus spoke persuasively in his defense. In 92, he was in court again after bringing an action against Scaurus for being bribed by Mithridates VI, and the *princeps senatus* brought a lawsuit against him in turn for slander. Ultimately, both were acquitted. Caepio's opposition to Drusus's politics perhaps has its roots in a personal conflict arising due to his divorce from Livia Drusa. The birth of two children initially brightened their marriage, but it was marred when Livia began an adulterous relationship with Marcus Porcius Cato Salonianus. Caepio discovered the affair, repudiated his wife, and threw her out of the house, together with their young children, Marcus and Servilia. Later, Livia married her lover and had more children: a son, Marcus, and a daughter, Livia. After their parents' divorce, Caepio and Livia's children were adopted by their stepfather, Cato Salonianus. Before long, however, both parents died and the orphans were welcomed into the house of their uncle, Drusus. The youngest Marcus, will become Marcus Porcius Cato Uticensis, while Servilia will get married twice: first to Marcus Junius Brutus, tribune in 83 (with whom she will have a son, Marcus Junius Brutus, one of Julius Caesar's killers) and then to Decimus Junius Silanus, with whom she will have three daughters, all called Junia: Junia Prima will marry Publius Servilius Vatia Isauricus, consul in 48; Junia Secunda will marry the triumvir

---

3   Probably a member of the *gens Pompeia* originally from Pompeii and of Oscan descent.

4   Cnaeus Pompeius Strabo would have had to be an individual with long blond hair, a beard and moustache, and of tall stature and robust build. He would have had this appearance because while he was a Roman citizen, his family was originally from the *ager Gallicus*, an area of central-eastern Italy (the Marche) peopled in part by the descendants of the Senones, a Gallic tribe, that, under the leadership of Brennus, had carried out a long-range incursion into central Italy, going so far as to sack Rome. This happened in 390–386. Afterward, the Senones were subjugated by the Romans and, by the early I century, were completely "Romanized." The Romans, we recall, called Gauls those barbarians who were called *keltoi* (Celts) by the Greeks.

Marcus Aemilius Lepidus, and Junia Tertia, or Tertulla, will be married to Caius Cassius Longinus, another of Caesar's assassins.

Drusus explains his position on the Italic Question at a *contio* on 4 September 91. Marius agrees with Drusus because he shares his political vision, and Scaurus has converted to the idea of supporting Drusus. The *contio* is underway when the consul Philippus orders Drusus to dissolve the meeting, arguing that it is an illegal gathering. Drusus and the crowd resist, and a fight breaks out. Drusus, in pain, adjourns the meeting.

A few days later, at another *contio*, Drusus stresses the advantages Rome would obtain from the mass naturalization of the Latins and Italics. Subsequently, Scaurus, Crassus, Marcus Antonius, and Scaevola Pontifex all speak in support of him. It should be noted that, in 95, Crassus and Scaevola hectored the Latins and Italics to harm Marius. In 91, however, they support them because Drusus's success would score a point in favor of their political bloc.

The Senate meets again on 19 September. After the usual preliminaries, the meeting begins with Philippus asking for the first of the laws that Drusus promoted and brought to approval to be struck from the legal system. Rising to speak in response is Crassus, who has returned to Rome with great haste specifically to participate in the session. He's tired, sweating, and has a slight cough. While waiting to join the debate, his cough has become more persistent, and he feels a burning sensation in his eyes. Still, he doesn't give it much thought. Little does he know that he's incubating pneumonia.

Crassus's speech is a prime example of oratory. Once he's finished, he receives many compliments and thanks everyone but declines to stay and discuss the session with colleagues. Having become pale, he is accompanied home while sweating profusely and struggling to breathe. Crassus's pneumonia is serious, and unfortunately, the outcome will be fatal. After being in agony for six days in his bed, Crassus takes his last breath.

Crassus was the greatest and most celebrated judicial orator of his time and one of the most prominent and authoritative figures in Roman public life. His death at the age of 49, at the peak of his success, leaves a huge void for his family, his friends, and the entire city.

But not everyone mourns him. Philippus and Caepio rub their hands in satisfaction because Crassus was one of Drusus's main supporters. After Crassus's funeral, they enact a strategy aimed at accelerating Drusus's political decline. They bend over backward to convince their fellow senators that the gods oppose the Drusian legislation, proof of which—they claim—is that the key milestones in Drusus's politics have coincided with strange events occurring in Rome and the rest of Italy, interpreted by the augurs as omens of calamities, perhaps even of an impending war.

But other, more significant events are on the horizon. The screw tightens on the *nonae* of October 91 (7 October), when 10,000 Marsi, organized into two legions, march along the *Via Tiburtina Valeria*, heading for Rome, led by Quintus Poppaedius Silo, a notable figure from *Milonia* (Ortona dei Marsi, Abruzzo, central-eastern Italy). They threaten to unleash hell if the Senate doesn't address the Italic Question. Cnaeus Domitius Ahenobarbus meets them on the *Campus Martius* and manages to convince them not to enter the city. He assures them—falsely—that the Senate will drop its opposition to the requested naturalization.[5]

The Senate discusses the incident at its very next meeting. Many consider what happened as a sign of the seriousness of the moment. Many others play it down as a sign of irritability but acknowledge that it would be a good thing for the Marsi to calm down. Someone asks Philippus to report on an uncontrolled rumor going around the city according to which the Marsi have sworn to identify their friends and enemies with those whom Drusus currently considers his friends and enemies. Philippus confirms that the Marsi have sworn allegiance to Drusus and reads out the formula of their oath.

The *optimates* kick off. The political debate very quickly becomes fiery, and the subject of all the criticism changes: it's no longer Drusus's legislation but the tribune himself. When the attack arrives, it's deadly: Drusus has betrayed Rome for his own political and economic interests. In short, he aspires to tyranny and wants to become king. On hearing these words, Drusus is overcome and temporarily loses consciousness.

The next day, Drusus returns to the Senate and, with great courage, reiterates that he will support the cause of the mass naturalization of the Latins and Italics and moves from words to deeds, presenting a *plebiscitum de civitate sociis*, which aims to extend *civitas* to the Italics indiscriminately. This development is heatedly discussed both within and outside Rome. Before long, a vast movement opposing Drusus's legislative initiative forms. All those who cannot imagine extending full Roman citizenship to Latins and Italics cling to it for fear that the Roman people might lose control of the legislature.[6] The landowners contest Drusus's legislative proposal because the more those who can participate in the economic exploitation of the *ager publicus* increase in

---

5   Diod. Sic. XXXVII.13. 2.

6   On the root causes of the Social War: E. Gabba, "Rome and Italy: The Social War," in *Cambridge Ancient History*, vol. IX: *The Last Age of the Roman Republic, 146–43 B.C.*, 2nd ed. (Cambridge: Cambridge University Press, 1994), 104–128.

number, the less space is left for them. But not all those who stand to benefit from the bills proposed by Drusus favor their approval. The ruling elites of *Etruria* and Umbria, for example, fear that mass naturalization could destroy the social order in which they currently enjoy a favorable standing.

The atmosphere surrounding Drusus gradually cools until it becomes freezing. The considerable support and sympathy that the tribune enjoys with people in authority melts like snow in the sun. Only Poppaedius Silo sticks by Drusus at the moment of greatest danger to his political career—and his own life—both because he sees in him an ex-comrade-in-arms and a friend and because Drusus is the only chance the Marsi have of obtaining naturalization through legal channels. Rallied by Silo, a crowd of Marsi gathers in front of Drusus's house to express their solidarity with the magistrate.

Drusus, prudently, surrounds himself with an armed escort and reduces the number of his public appearances. However, he maintains his habit of receiving clients and friends at home. This proves fatal. One clear, cold evening in January 90, he is dismissing a small crowd when he is stabbed by a stranger, who immediately takes advantage of the confusion to escape. Drusus is in agony. His demise is imminent. After his brother Mamercus gives him a kiss to collect his last living breath,[7] Drusus loses consciousness and dies.

News of Drusus's murder spreads in a flash, prompting the victim's friends and supporters to lose heart, while his opponents are euphoric. It's widely believed among commentators that Drusus's assassination is a political murder, and, naturally, the strongest suspicions about the identity of the instigators fall on Quintus Servilius Caepio and Quintus Varius Severus Hybrida Sucronensis. Indeed, they are the staunchest opponents of any suggestion of the mass naturalization of Latins and Italics. Furthermore, Caepio harbored a personal grudge against Drusus, while Hybrida is a close friend of Caepio and is a seditious, violent man.

Drusus's death results in the *plebiscitum de civitate sociis* being blocked. In its next session, the Senate postpones discussion of the project indefinitely. Not one of Drusus's nine colleagues in the tribuneship asks for a vote on the plebiscite to be entered on the agenda of the *concilium plebis*. No one files a complaint about the tribune's murder.

---

7   *Aen.* 4.684.

CHAPTER VIII

The Social War

The Italic *socii* interpret Drusus's assassination as definitive proof that the Senate, the consuls, and large swathes of Roman society will never legally equate them with Roman citizens. They convince themselves that it's useless to hope they will get what they are asking for through legal channels and decide to break the pact of friendship and alliance that binds them to Rome. But not everyone does so for the same reason. Some want to compel Rome to naturalize them—by force, if necessary. Others—those with a more marked, collective awareness of their individuality and personality—want to separate themselves from Rome to fully recover their identity and independence. The situation rapidly descends toward a point of no return. The *socii* who have decided to rebel, unbeknownst to the Romans, join together and give life to a federal state called the Social League, or the Italic League. These are the Picentes, Marsi, Peligni, Vestini, and Marrucini from central Italy and the Frentani, three of the four Samnite tribes (Carricini, Irpini, and Pentri; the fourth tribe is the Caudicini), Apulians, Lucanians, and Bruttians from southern Italy.

The League is organized in imitation of the *res publica*: it has a senate with 500 members, two consuls, and 12 praetors. Its capital is *Corfinium*, which the League renames *Italica*. *Corfinium/Italica* is a city in Marsica, between the Valle Peligna and Lake Fucino, in the middle of a region inhabited mainly by the Peligni but also by Marsi, Marrucini, Vestini, and Samnites. The League also establishes a treasury, some military warehouses and weapons caches, and a mint in the city. Some coins issued by the mint depict a bull killing a she-wolf underneath the Latin word *Italia* (this is the first time this name appears officially). In the future, other coins will bear the inscription *Viteliu* in the Oscan language, which means the land of young cattle.

The consuls of the League are the Marsian Quintus Poppaedius Silo and the Samnite Caius Papius Mutilus. We have already met the former; after the murder of Drusus, with whom he had been close friends, he was convinced that the Marsi had no choice but to split from Rome. The latter comes from a family that played a prominent role during the Samnite Wars (IV century). The League's praetors form two groups of six. Among them, we should mention the praetor of the Picentes, Titus Lafrenius; the praetor of the Vestini, Caius Pontidius; the praetor of the Marrucini, Herius Asinius; the praetor of the Peligni, Publius Vettius Scato; and the praetor of the Lucanians, Marcus Lamponius. The League's army is under the command of the consuls, each of whom leads about 50,000 men. Poppaedius Silo's army is in *Picenum* (central-eastern Italy) in the land of the Italics, while Papius Mutilus's army has taken up a position in Campania and the rest of *Samnium* (the heart of central-southern Italy).

The event preventing a return to the *status quo ante* is a horrendous massacre. The Senate, wanting to ascertain the truth of an unchecked rumor that the Italics were preparing for war against Rome, charged two praetors to go into the Italics' lands to investigate and then report back.

During this mission, the praetor Quintus Servilius Caepio (not the same Caepio indicted for the robbery of the Gold of *Tolosa*) went to the city of *Asculum Picenum* (Ascoli Piceno). *Asculum Picenum* is the capital of the Picentes, a people of Sabine origin who, following a mass emigration, settled permanently on the Adriatic coast between the Foglia and Aterno rivers. Rome first came into contact with *Asculum Picenum* due to the trade along the *Via Salaria*. In 268, this city became a *civitas foederata*.

Caepio, feeling that he has been offended by the local community, threatens them. The Ascolani riot and slaughter Caepio, his escort, and any other Roman present in the city, whether they are residents or only passing through. Then the defenders, led by Caius Vidacilius, bar the city gates and prepare to resist the inevitable siege.

News of the massacre in *Asculum* reaches Rome at the same time as a formal declaration of war by the Marsi. The Senate and the consuls announce a draft and conscript 10 legions to be added to the 20 existing legions. In this way, the Roman army grows to 100,000 men. The consuls for 90 are Publius Rutilius Lupus and Lucius Julius Caesar. The former deploys his legions on the northern front and the latter on the southern front.[1]

The forces of the League and Rome are numerically equivalent. There is a similar equivalence regarding their organizational profiles, armaments, equipment, technology, tactics, and strategy. Nor should we forget that the

---

1 Lucius Julius Caesar, consul in 90, is erroneously cited as Sextus Julius Caesar in App. *B. Civ.*, who is confusing him with Sextus Julius Caesar, consul in 91.

members of the League fought in Rome's wars until only recently, reinforcing the legions and fighting shoulder to shoulder with them against common enemies.

The Roman people are divided about what is unfolding. The *optimates* are against any suggestion of a concession to the Italics in matters of citizenship, while the *populares* are in favor. When the political discussions of the *populares* degenerate into a popular insurrection against the Senate and the consuls, the aristocrats react by criminalizing those who, with words and deeds, have induced the *socii* to take up arms against Rome. But the *quaestio Appuleia de maiestate*—the court ordinarily competent for cases of *maiestas*—has suspended its activity because the praetor who presided over it has been mobilized for war. To remedy this setback, the tribune Quintus Varius Severus Hybrida Sucronensis promotes and obtains approval for the *lex Varia de maiestate*, establishing a temporary court of justice—the *quaestio extra ordinem Variana*—that will carry out the duties of the *quaestio Appuleia de maiestate*. During one of its sessions, Varius "begins the dance" by declaring Scaurus to be one of the agitators. The *princeps senatus* replies, addressing the crowd: "Varius Sucronensis says that Aemilius Scaurus has incited the Italic allies to arms, Scaurus denies it; which of the two do you believe?" The crowd responds as one: "Scaurus!"[2]

Marcus Antonius Orator is indicted but acquitted. Among those found guilty and exiled are Caius Aurelius Cotta and Lucius Mummius Achaicus.[3] In 92, Cotta went to court to defend his uncle Publius Rutilius Rufus, accused of extortion on false evidence, but failed to prevent him from being sentenced to exile. Rufus was indicted in September 91, a few days after Crassus Orator's death, but was poorly defended by Lucius Aelius Stilo Praeconinus and exiled. He will return to Rome with Sulla in 82. Mummius is an enriched plebeian whose father was the first member of his family to become a senator. As consul in 146, his father won a decisive victory over the Achaean League at the Battle of Leucopetra, abandoning *Corinthus* to pillage and destroying its foundations.

In the meantime, hostilities have begun. The Italics attack Roman strongholds, and their guerilla warfare on both fronts is frequent and successful. Before long, there will also be pitched battles. Rutilius Lupus has seven legions and personally leads two. Perperna, one of his legates, is defeated trying break the siege of *Alba Fucens*, the urban heart of a colony of Latin law located in

---

2   Asc. *Sc.* 22C.

3   It's uncertain whether the crime provided for by the *lex Varia* was punishable with exile or death, but it seems to have been inclined toward exile. Cnaeus Pompeius Strabo was also tried under the *lex Varia* in 88.

central Italy on the slopes of Monte Velino. Another of Lupus's legates, Cnaeus Pompeius Strabo, is so rich that he can recruit and maintain a private army of three or four legions, perfectly trained, armed, and equipped, at his own expense.

Strabo descends from Quintus Pompeius, the consul of 141 and a *homo novus*, and is married to Lucilia, the daughter of a senator, with whom he has a son, Cnaeus (born in 106), and a daughter, Pompeia. Cnaeus Pompeius (the son) isn't particularly handsome but is serious and firm in his resolve. His hair is pushed back, and his gaze is lively, constantly shifting. He is fond of physical exercise, is a lover of women, is particularly interested in solving the basic problems of life, and has the gift of eloquence (he has a clear, resonant voice). Growing up in an environment colored by politics, he has a propensity for weapons and war.[4] We'll meet him again in Chapter XI.

Lucius Julius Caesar has seven legions and has established his headquarters in *Capua* (Santa Maria Capua Vetere), the main Roman stronghold in Campania. Another Roman stronghold in Campania is *Venafrum* (Venafro), the main center of the Volturno valley on the slopes of Monte Santa Croce.

Aesernia (Isernia) is another Roman stronghold in Campania, located in a basin between the Apennines at about 450m above sea level on a major transhumance route. The urban area of *Aesernia* is enclosed within a polygonal wall and, on its long sides, overlooks deep valleys. It therefore has a peculiar topography: narrow and elongated. From the V century, it was inhabited by Samnites. Due to its strategic importance, it was bitterly contested during the Samnite Wars (343–341, 326–304, 298–290). It fell into the Romans' hands in 295, and in 209, unlike other *socii* who defected and passed under Hannibal's banners, it remained loyal to Rome.

In 91, *Aesernia* is defended by five cohorts, led by two young officers of senatorial rank: Lucius Cornelius Scipio Asiaticus and Lucius Acilius Glabrio. When the League's consul Caius Papius Mutilus and the League's praetor Publius Vettius Scato arrive at the head of one legion of Samnites and another legion of Marsi, Scipio and Acilius desert. Disguised as servants, they sneak out of the fortress and disappear into the darkness of a moonless night.

When he learns that *Aesernia* has been besieged and the commanders of the local military garrison have deserted, Marcus Claudius Marcellus, commander of the garrison at *Venafrum*, rushes to its rescue with six cohorts. Mutilus's Samnites and Scato's Marsi take advantage of this and *Venafrum* falls to treachery; the Romans surrender but are killed. Marcellus could seek safety

---

4   Plut. *Pomp.* 2.1–2, 5–12; Cic. *Brut.* 239; Sen. *Ep.* 11.4; Tac. *Dial.* 37.2–3; Veg. *Epit.* I.9.8.

in *Nuvla* but insists on carrying out his plan; at night he crosses enemy lines, enters *Aesernia*, and takes charge of the settlement's defense.

The defenders and the people are beleaguered; once the food supplies run out, they are forced to eat anything just to feed themselves: dogs, cats, mules, donkeys, horses, goats, wild herbs, and even shoe soles. In the winter of 91/90, Marcellus, unable to hold out any longer, hands the city over to the besiegers, at which point he disappears. His death will only be discovered later.

After taking *Aesernia*, Mutilus also takes possession of *Nuvla*, *Pompeii*, *Herculaneum*, and other settlements. *Nuvla* is taken by treachery. Mutilus kills Postumius, welcomes the soldiers who decided to defect under his banners, then lets their commanders—who had refused to switch sides—starve to death. Next, Mutilus conquers the Campanian towns of *Stabiae*, *Minervum*, and *Salernum* and enlists the prisoners of war and slaves. Later, he devastates the lands of *Nuceria Alfaterna* (Nocera), one of the main cities in Campania, and adds the nearby towns to his list of allies, who supply him with 10,000 infantry and 1,000 cavalry. Finally, he besieges the Campanian town of *Acerrae* (Acerra).

Caesar rushes to the aid of the people of *Acerrae* with 10,000 Gallic infantry, as well as cavalry and infantry from *Numidia* and *Mauretania*. Oxyntas, son of the deceased Jugurtha, the deposed king of *Numidia*, is being held by the Romans in the Lucanian town of *Venusia* (Venosa). Mutilus has him brought to *Acerrae* and parades him repeatedly, dressed in regal purple, before Caesar's Numidians. Some of the Numidians recognize Oxyntas as their king and defect. Caesar sends the other Numidians back to Africa, fearing they might betray him. Mutilus attacks Caesar's fortified camp, but the latter makes a sortie with his cavalry and kills 6,000 of the enemy in battle before falling back to *Acerrae*. He ought to return to Rome to preside over the elections for the next set of magistracies (September—October 90), but he cannot. *Venusia*, *Canusium*, and other towns in Puglia, including, perhaps, *Salapia* (near Canosa di Puglia) and *Cannae* (Canne della Battaglia), defect from their alliance with Rome and join the enemy. Vidacilius massacres the most prominent Romans found in these settlements and conscripts the plebeians and slaves.[5] At the same time, the city of *Grumentum* (Grumento Nova) falls into Lamponius's hands. Later, it will be retaken by the Romans and besieged by the Lucanians.

When Caesar falls ill and is being transported in a litter through a narrow, steep valley in Campania with 30,000 infantry and 5,000 cavalry, he is attacked by the Italic praetor Marius Egnatius's Samnites. He is driven back with the

---

5   App. *B. Civ.* 1.185–190.

loss of most of his army and weapons and retreats to *Teanum Sicidinum* (Teano), where he organizes further resistance. He receives reinforcements and heads for *Aesernia*.

In the meantime, Lupus and his legate, Caius Marius, have each built a bridge over the Liris River, not far from one another. On 11 June 90, when Lupus is crossing his bridge, Scato launches an ambush and kills many of his men, some of whom are drowned in the river. Lupus himself loses his life (Battle of the Tolenus River). After seeing the bodies floating past him down the river and realizing what has happened, Marius crosses his bridge and attacks Scato's camp, which is only guarded by a handful of men, and captures it. The Senate, needing to replace Lupus, appoints Caepio to assist Marius in leading the operations on the northern front. Attracted by his own greed for riches, Caepio falls into a trap laid for him by the Italic consul Poppaedius Silo and is killed in battle together with many of his men. Now alone in charge of operations, Marius repels the Marsi after being attacked, probably in an area south of Lake Fucino. Then, alongside Lucius Cornelius Sulla, he kills more than 6,000 enemies, including the Italic praetor Asinius, and captures a large amount of weaponry.

Sulla, we recall, as legionary legate responsible for logistics, fought in the Cimbrian War, first under Marius and later under Quintus Lutatius Catulus, and participated in the definitive victory over the Cimbri at the Battle of the Raudine Plain (101). In 97, he was elected as urban praetor, though not without aspersions being cast on the proceedings' regularity (he was accused of electoral fraud). In 96, he was *propraetor* and governor of *Cilicia*. In that capacity, he conducted a demonstrative action (an attack or show of force on a front where a decision is not sought, made with the aim of deceiving the enemy) against the king of Armenia, during which he met the plenipotentiary ambassador of Mithridates II of *Parthia* on the banks of the Euphrates in the presence of the king of *Cappadocia*. The meeting served to delineate spheres of influence and trade relations between Rome and the Parthian Empire. At the end of 96, Sulla returned to Rome and joined the *optimates*, thus becoming part of the opposite faction to that of Marius. Upon the outbreak of the Social War, he made himself available to fight against the Italic League.

In the meantime, Strabo is heading to *Asculum* to retake it when he is attacked by a large force of Picentes, Vestini, and Marsi near Mount Falernus, led by the Italic praetors Lafrenius and Ventidius. The outcome of the battle is inconclusive, but Strabo, outnumbered, retreats and is pursued to Firmum, where he is besieged by Lafrenius's Marsi.

In 89, Marius suffers a stroke and is taken to Rome for treatment. The Senate removes him from his command and replaces him with the consul Lucius Porcius Cato, the son of Marcus Porcius Cato Salonianus and Livia Drusa. Cato was praetor in 92. In 90, he defeated an Etruscan army that had joined the Italics in revolt and, together with Strabo, was elected to the consulship for 89. Despite his undisciplined and mutinous troops, he manages to defeat the enemy. However, when Cato faces the Marsi of Poppaedius Silo at the Battle of the Fucine Lake, he dies in obscure circumstances. On closer examination, it emerges that the consul didn't die at enemy hands, nor due to an accident, but in an altercation with his deputy, Caius Marius the Younger, Marius's son. A legionary commander, the 46-year-old patrician Lucius Cornelius Cinna, is charged with ascertaining the facts and determining who was responsible. Cinna was a praetor in 90 and is known to his superiors and subordinates to be a very capable man. Cato's death occurred in the presence of a witness. However, he died suddenly and quickly, and it can't be determined whether it was accidental or provoked. Thus, the accusation against the only suspect, Marius the Younger, is dropped. It seems that before dismissing the case as a homicide at the hands of unknown persons, Cinna receives a note from Marius, who, although ill, is nevertheless alert and aware of ongoing events.

In the meantime, Caesar has won a great victory and ceded command of operations on the southern front to Sulla before going to the aid of Strabo, who is under siege in Firmum. Before November 90, with Caesar's help, Strabo breaks the siege (Lafrenius falls in battle and is succeeded by Fraucus). Next, Strabo lays siege to *Asculum*. Vidacilius, the commander of the Picentes, returns from northern *Apulia* with eight cohorts and manages to evade the enemy lines and enter the city, but after losing hope of the city holding out, he deems it honorable to die for it and commits suicide by taking poison.[6]

When the Etruscans, Umbrians, and other peoples closely tied to them defected from the alliance with Rome, the Senate and Caesar fear Rome may lose the war. To strengthen their bond of friendship and alliance with the Latin and Italic *socii* who remained faithful after the outbreak of war and to divide their enemies, Caesar, in agreement with the Senate, promotes and obtains approval for the *lex Julia de civitate latinis et sociis danda* (90). This intervention extends Roman citizenship to the Italian *socii* who upheld their allegiance to Rome and those who laid down their arms after fighting against Rome. Furthermore, it recognizes that military commanders have the authority to grant Roman citizenship to all Italic *auxilia* and, in certain circumstances,

---

6   App. *B. Civ.* 1.207–210.

to non-Italic *auxilia* who have fought under them. However, during the law's implementation, the new citizens aren't enrolled in the 35 existing tribes but in 10 newly instituted tribes.

The motivations and aims of this escamotage are clear, and it prevents these new citizens from determining the outcomes of votes, considering that they are in a clear minority compared to the 35 existing tribes. Intense disputes arise from this, and these will become increasingly heated over time. The quaestors of the public treasury are given the task of supervising the registrations, in addition to other duties, including working with the censors to maintain and update the census lists. This law pushes the Etruscans to return to the bosom of their alliance with Rome. But the Italics fighting on the northern front don't learn about it before sending 15,000 armed men to *Etruria* to help their allies. These 15,000 men are attacked by the consul Cnaeus Pompeius Strabo, who kills 5,000 of them. The 10,000 survivors try to return to their homes but, having to traverse impervious country in the middle of a harsh winter and having nothing but acorns to eat, only 5,000 reach their final destination.

In January–February 89, Strabo takes *Asculum* after the besieged defenders attempt a desperate sortie in which 18,000 fell, including their commander, and 3,000 were captured (another 4,000 will die of exposure, wandering in the mountains). Following this, Strabo is acclaimed *imperator* by his soldiers[7] (this is one of the preconditions required to celebrate a triumph). He treats the city ferociously, slaughtering all males capable of wielding a weapon (5,000 victims), enslaves the remainder of the population, and sets the entire settlement ablaze. Then he defeats the Vestini and Peligni once and for all and, later, the Marsi. He conquers *Italica*, among other places, and, on 25 December 89, he celebrates a triumph in Rome. Lined up in the triumphal parade, behind his father, is the young Pompey.

With the fall of *Italica*, the League's capital is transferred to *Bovianum* (Bojano), the administrative center of the Samnite tribe known as the Pentri, located in northern *Samnium* on the ridge of Monte Caraceno, an isolated hill at the foot of the Matese mountains. *Bovianum* is a rich, populous, strongly fortified city and a critical road junction on the road from *Beneventum* in Campania to *Gerunium* in the Molise region. It played a vital role in the Samnite Wars and garrisoned Roman legions during the Hannibalic War. However, Caesar has died of illness while preparing to face the Marsi, while Hybrida Sucronensis has been sentenced to exile, perhaps because he

---

7   Oros. V.18.20. Vell. Pat. II.21.1 speaks of a battle near *Asculum* in which 75,000 Romans and 60,000 Italics perish.

disregarded a veto and forcefully imposed his law or because he bore the moral responsibility for the conflict.[8]

The stronghold of *Nuvla* in Campania (today Nola) is 35km northeast of *Neapolis* (Naples) at the foot of Vesuvius. Located in a basin between plains, mountains, and hills in a strategic position compared to the other major centers of the region, on the outbreak of the Social War, it broke its alliance with Rome and joined the Samnites in the Italic League, led by Papius Mutilus. In 90, a garrison of 2,000 men was established there under the command of Lucius Postumius, praetor of the Italic League. Currently, *Nuvla* is besieged by Lucius Cornelius Sulla and proudly resists every attack.

While Sulla besieges *Nuvla*, the Italic leader Lucius Cluentius helps the besieged, but a haruspex (a class of minor priests who practiced divination), Postumius, foretells that Sulla will be victorious. Since Sulla is very mindful of any sign that could constitute a warning or caution about what is about to happen, Postumius's words encourage him to face the enemy. Cluentius dies, with thousands of his men, below the city walls. Sulla is acclaimed *imperator* and receives the *corona obsidionalis*, "blockade crown" (also known as the *corona graminea*, "grass crown"), the most resounding honor of which a Roman soldier can be proud. It is an extremely rare honor and therefore highly coveted; in 400 years of military history, it had only previously been awarded six times. Many aspire to the grass crown even though it has no material value. It is formed of intertwined grasses from the battlefield, and its recipient is honored by his soldiers.[9]

Sulla records numerous other victories in Campania, Basilicata, and *Apulia*, increasing his reputation as a skilled strategist and ruthless fighter. Among other things, he manages to recover the Lucanian city of *Venusia* and many Campanian settlements. One of his most notorious feats is his capture of the town of *Aeclanum* (Mirabella Eclano) in Irpinia, which takes place amid immense slaughter. *Aeclanum* will be utterly destroyed following a raging fire.[10]

The same year (89) also sees the approval of the *lex Plautia-Papiria de civitate sociis danda*, commonly considered as a way to implement the *lex Julia de civitate latinis et sociis danda*. The intervention attributes the status of *municipium optimo iure* ("local community able to participate with full voting rights in the elections for the renewal of magistracies in Rome") to all the already federated cities, Roman colonies, and colonies of Latin law,

---

8   Cic. *De natura deorum*, III.82*.

9   App. *B. Civ.* 1.216–221.

10 App. *B. Civ.* 1.222–226.

regardless of location in *Italia Propria* or *Gallia Cisalpina*, south of the Po, and establishes that whoever is registered in the population lists of the said *municipia* will be able to apply for full Roman citizenship within 60 days and be registered with the tribes. After this becomes law, most of the Italic soldiers lay down their arms, though some continue to fight.

The Social War ends in 88 with a death toll of 300,000 and immeasurable destruction. It was the most useless of wars. Ultimately, Rome, having endured immense losses and risked succumbing, prevailed on the military level but lost on the political level because it approved two laws on citizenship that, in practice, gave the enemy what it had asked for. It was also somewhat paradoxical because most of Rome's enemies hadn't been fighting it to sever ties with it forever but to become part of the Roman state by obtaining Roman citizenship. However, some cities in the south of the peninsula, still in the Italics' hands, still resist. These are pockets of isolated resistance where a private war continues.

In this respect, what happens under the walls of *Nuvla* is significant as it continues to resist even after the Social War has ended. In 88, *Nuvla* is surrounded by a large group of legionaries: 35,000 men, of whom 2,000 are on horseback. But what is being fought under its walls is a forgotten war because capturing *Nuvla* is no longer a priority for Rome. Instead, the Senate and consuls' attention has been drawn to a more serious and urgent matter—the war against Mithridates VI Eupator Dionysus, king of Pontus.

CHAPTER IX

Sulpicius's Tribuneship

From about 110, Mithridates VI, who is fantastically rich and powerful, has been practicing a policy of territorial expansion. He has conquered almost all the regions bordering the Black Sea (the northern coast of Anatolia, from the ancient *Sinope* eastward; Caucasian Georgia; part of Russia; Ukraine; and Romania, up to the mouth of the Danube), but he has also been looking with interest at the rest of Anatolia, that is, at the Roman provinces of *Asia* and *Cilicia* and the kingdoms of *Bithynia*, *Galatia*, and *Cappadocia*, all client states of Rome.

In 89, a Roman army, reinforced by contingents of *auxilia* supplied by these client states, invades Pontus. This is the brainchild of the consular legate in Roman Asia, Manius Aquilius, who had been consul in 101 alongside Marius and who agreed in 89 with the king of *Bithynia* that their lust for plunder needed to be satiated. The Pontics counterattack and rout the invaders. Mithridates VI doesn't just drive back the invaders; he chases them into *Bithynia* and Roman Asia, leading to the occupation of *Bithynia* and Roman Asia by the Pontic army and the outbreak of war between Rome and Pontus.

During this war, a horrendous pogrom took place: 80,000 Romans and their slaves, totaling 150,000 people, are killed in a single day. The massacre is carried out by the Greek communities of Roman Asia, executing an unavoidable order from Mithridates VI. Defeated in battle near *Protopachium*, a fortress in eastern *Bithynia*, in late 89/early 88, Aquilius flees first to *Pergamum*, then to Mytilene/Lesbos. Eventually, he is captured and handed over to Mithridates VI. The king of Pontus, after publicly shaming Aquilius, gives him a terrible death by pouring molten gold down his throat. Subsequently, the theater of war moves to Greece when Delos is captured and looted amid immense slaughter; the treasure of Apollo's sanctuary is transferred to Athens, where a puppet government is installed.

Subsequently, an Athenian philosopher called Aristion, who had lived in Asia Minor for a long time and placed himself in the service of Mithridates VI, enters Athens escorted by 2,000 Pontic soldiers under the pretense that he wants to deposit the treasure stolen from Delos. Instead, he uses those troops to seize power in the city and massacre any Roman or Italic present. Immediately afterward, he denounces the treaty of friendship and alliance between Athens and Rome, making himself hated among his fellow citizens for his cruelty. Meanwhile, Mithridates VI has formed new alliances with the Achaeans, Lacedaemonians, and Boeotians; Archelaus occupies Attica, Boeotia, and Phocis; another Pontic general, Metrophanes, ravages Euboea; and Arcathias (Ariarathes IX), son of Mithridates VI, enters Macedonia from Thrace and occupies it, making it into a province.

Rome has been slow to react because it was engaged in the Social War. Now that the conflict is essentially over, it can think of settling the scores with the Pontic sovereign. Five of the six legions encamped under the walls of *Nuvla* are ordered to prepare to leave for the East. But their marching orders are late in arriving as the Senate hasn't yet appointed a new governor of the province of Asia. This is an essential step because, concomitantly, it carries the appointment of supreme command of the army that will leave for war. The natural candidate is Sulla, who is supported by the political majority, comprising senatorial and consular families from the *optimates*. Quintus Pompeius Rufus, Sulla's consular colleague, isn't interested in obtaining riches and glory by participating in that conflict. Instead, he is aiming to continue his *cursus honorum* as proconsul for *Gallia Cisalpina*.

However, another candidate has stepped forward. He currently doesn't hold any public office, but it cannot be said that he is just any Roman. This candidate is Caius Marius, who we know has served as consul six times—an unprecedented record in the history of Rome—led the Roman army to victory in two wars, celebrated a triumph, been highly praised, and hailed as the "savior of the fatherland" and the "first man in Rome." Nevertheless, Marius still isn't satisfied. He is always looking for further confirmation, even if he no longer has to prove his worth to anyone.

Marius wants to improve his public image and prestige, which had become compromised due to his involvement in Saturninus's attempt at political subversion. Despite being more than 70 years old, he refuses to step back from public life. However, there is something more profound that energizes him. Marius has a spectacularly high opinion of himself and his abilities; he is self-centered, conceited, insensitive, and egotistic to the nth degree, as well as wildly ambitious, consumed by envy, crude, and arrogant. All this causes him to demand attention, constant approval, and admiration from others. In short, he considers his neighbors, and the laws, as mere tools for his own use. Since he is totally absorbed in himself, he believes the only possible and entirely valid ways of living, thinking, and feeling are his own. He is one of those people who cannot give anyone else credit for their achievements but rather grabs all the glory for himself.

Many *optimates* recognize that Marius is a living national monument but point out that he is old and is yet to fully recover from his *ictus* and they underline that a second stroke is a distinct possibility. They state that the ideal candidate to direct military operations is a man whose military abilities and experience are equal to Marius's but who is younger and in the prime of life, i.e., a man like Sulla.

Marius has a strong character and doesn't let himself be disheartened by these arguments. He insists on presenting himself as a candidate, boasts of his many laudable awards acquired for service to the state, and doesn't hesitate to throw all his political weight onto the scales. To demonstrate that he is in good physical shape, he works out and practices fighting on the *Campus Martius* in full view of everyone.

Appointing Sulla is also difficult because the provincial governor of Roman Asia is a praetor of consular rank and is identified by the drawing of lots, as stipulated by the *lex provinciae Asiae*. However, this problem can be easily resolved for the following reasons: the *lex provinciae Asiae* isn't a law approved by the people gathered in assembly but a consular degree, endorsed by the Senate; the *optimates*, who support Sulla, have a majority in the Senate; and Sulla and his consular colleague, Quintus Pompeius Rufus, form a close-knit pair, so it's unthinkable that Rufus would want to block Sulla's path by using his veto.

Shortly afterwards, the *lex provinciae Asiae* is partially modified by establishing that the governor of the province of Asia is a proconsul appointed by the Senate *intuitu personae*. The Senate could therefore, at its sole discretion, appoint Sulla to the office of proconsul of Asia when his term as consul has expired.

Most senators of equestrian extraction and some senators of patrician rank support Marius's appointment, including the Iulii Caesares. However, none of the other senators want to hear even a mention of Marius, and they reproach him for having only distanced himself from Saturninus at the last moment. There's no question that their candidate is Sulla. Those who work hardest on Sulla's behalf are the Caecilii Metelli, particularly Quintus Caecilius Metellus Pius, the son of Metellus Numidicus.

The debate on the choice of candidate concludes as it logically ought to have done, that is, in the *optimates'* favor. Thus, Sulla is appointed proconsul of Asia, effective from 1 January 87, and he will be the one to direct operations in the Mithridatic War. However, the new consuls taking office on the same day are Lucius Cornelius Cinna and Cnaeus Octavius. Sulla trusts neither of them, so much so that he forces them to swear that they will do nothing that deviates from the political course he has set out in his absence.

Marius, who has ended up empty-handed, finds this a bitter pill to swallow. But he doesn't let adversity overpower him. He has never resigned himself to defeat and never will. Therefore, he doesn't give up on his goal. Furthermore, he wants revenge on the Senate for the personal affront. Marius knows that many of his fellow citizens don't love him, but he also knows that many others are grateful to him for having saved Rome from the Germans who invaded Italy and admire him for his *virtus* (courage and valor in battle, authority in the Senate, and prestige among the people), for never having faltered, not even when fortune had abandoned him.

As usual, he doesn't act himself but sends his most faithful followers into action on his behalf. In this case, he uses Publius Sulpicius Rufus, who is especially devoted to him because he owes his election as tribune to him so he would do anything for him.[1] Therefore, as with Saturninus, Marius again maneuvers a tribune to get him to promote a bill that favors Marius personally.

Sulpicius was elected in October 89, entered office on 10 December 89, and will remain in office until 9 December 88. First, he takes legal action against Caius Norbanus Balbus, who, as tribune of the plebs, had accused Quintus Servilius Caepio of *crimen maiestatis* following Rome's defeat at the Battle of *Arausio*. Sulpicius accuses Norbanus of not having taken into account the veto that other tribunes of the plebs had used to have Caepio judged by the *concilium plebis* rather than by the *quaestio perpetua de maiestate*, uniquely qualified to judge cases of high treason.[2] One wonders if it wasn't Caepio himself who encouraged Sulpicius to commence legal proceedings with the promise of financing his electoral campaign in exchange for doing it. This hypothesis is supported by the fact that Caepio took ownership of the Smyrna bank deposit from his father and is therefore very rich, even if he maintains

---

1   On Publius Sulpicius Rufus: J. G. F. Powell, "The tribune Sulpicius," *Historia* 39 (1990): 446ff.; A. Keaveney, "Sulla, Sulpicius and Caesar Strabo," *Latomus* 38 (1979): 451ff.; A. W. Lintott, "The tribunate of P. Sulpicius Rufus," *Classical Quarterly* 21 (1971): 442ff.

2   A law passed in 90 (*lex Varia de maiestate*) authorized the prosecution of those who had betrayed Rome by inducing the *socii* to take up arms against Rome (*crimen maiestatis*) and set up a new court (*quaestio extra ordinem Variana*) specifically to prosecute those indicted.

a modest standard of living so as not to arouse suspicion. The attempt fails because, using exceptional oratorical skill, Marcus Antonius manages to convince the jury of Norbanus's innocence.[3]

Most of the Senate and the consuls Cinna and Octavius consider Sulpicius a dangerous subversive. Nevertheless, they also fear him because Sulpicius will maintain strong support from the common people instead. Yet Sulpicius is also aware he's playing with fire. Therefore, he asks Marius for help, and Marius not only confirms his political backing but also puts significant resources at his disposal: 600 young *equites* activists, all educated and cultured and all animated by idealistic and political zeal, whom Sulpicius will call the "Anti-Senate," and 3,000 ex-gladiators, freedmen, and urban underclass, all shady figures with grubby pasts.

Sulpicius will be able to make use of Marius's men both as a personal escort and to intimidate political opponents, dissidents, and ordinary citizens who don't vote for him. Moreover, he can count on the connivance of other magistrates, whose strings are pulled by Marius, who will be able to favor him and his men in any way, even by surreptitiously supplying them with weapons of war and military equipment.

Heartened and objectively strengthened, Sulpicius presents four plebiscites simultaneously and convenes a public meeting in the Forum to explain them to the people, respond to observations, and provide clarifications. The first plebiscite aims to ensure that the enrollment of new citizens no longer takes place among 8–10 tribes, drawn by lot from the 35 tribes, but in all 35 tribes, and this reflects a promise Sulpicius made during the electoral campaign. The matter is not superficially trivial. Many Roman citizens are against the mass naturalization of Latins and Italics. The reason for this is well known: following mass naturalization, there would be so many new citizens that if they were enrolled in all 35 tribes, they would become the majority. Deciding how to enroll new citizens among the tribes has become a critical part of the political debate. The atmosphere of tension that hovers over discussions on this issue is why the census procedures for new citizens, a prerequisite for their registration in the lists, are moving so slowly. The second plebiscite authorizes the expulsion of those with debts greater than a stipulated amount from the senatorial rolls. Again, the stakes are very high. If the law passes, almost every senator will find themselves in breach of it. Expelling them all would mean the absence of a quorum until the creation of an equivalent number of new senators. In effect, it would paralyze the Senate. The third plebiscite extends

3   Cic. *Off.* II.14. On the accusation made against Norbanus and the content of Antonius's speech: Passerini, *Caio Mario*, 42, n. 1.

Roman citizenship to Roman freedmen, while the fourth provides for all those exiled under the *lex Varia de maiestate* to be recalled to their homeland.

In an already white-hot political climate, Sulpicius's political activity throws yet more fuel on the fire. Sulla asks the *pontifex maximus* Quintus Mucius Scaevola, his colleague Pompeius Rufus, and Lucius Cornelius Merula, *flamen dialis*, to help him find a suitable technical, operative, and legal expedient to ensure that the people gathered in assembly don't vote on Sulpicius's plebiscites. An escamotage is found. Shortly afterward, Sulla convenes the Senate and announces that the consuls, in agreement with the College of Pontiffs, have decreed the *feriae imperativae*, the days on which all private and public activities, both civic and religious, including legal cases and elections, are suspended by the authorities under penalty of sanctions and people must visit the temples of the gods and offer prayers and sacrifices. The consuls and *pontifices* announce these days at their discretion by issuing a decree called an *institium*. Generally, the suspension of activities doesn't exceed nine days.[4] In the case of the *institium* of Sulla and Rufus, however, it's much longer: it ends on 15 December, shortly after the end of Sulpicius's term as tribune of the plebs. Their *institium*, therefore, effectively prevents Sulpicius from carrying out any political activity until the expiry of his mandate, which would cause his legislative initiatives to founder.

Sulpicius refuses to accept this and forcefully demands the revocation of the *institium*. When the consuls resist, Sulpicius confirms the convocation of the public meeting to describe his four plebiscites, thus demonstrating that he is openly willing to oppose the Senate and the consuls.

As thousands upon thousands of people crowd into the Forum, Sulpicius prepares to address the crowd from the raised platform of the Orators' Tribune. He is surrounded by bodyguards, clients, and friends, the Anti-Senate, and the 3,000 ex-gladiators, freedmen, and urban underclass. All the tribune's men hide a weapon in the folds of their robes. Many of Sulpicius's political opponents have also come to listen to him. The consuls and many senators watch what's happening in the Forum from the foot of the Temple of Saturn.

Unexpectedly, a thousand young people emerge from the alleys that lead into the Forum. They are all between 17 and 30 years old, and all are armed. Instinctively, Sulpicius's men draw their weapons and close ranks, creating a tight-knit formation in which they stand shoulder to shoulder. In turn, the crowd massed in the Forum, is assailed by fear, and clusters closer together. Bodies are pressed against each other, pushed this way and that. Someone falls

---

4   The *feriae imperativae* differed from the *feriae publicae* due to their greater solemnity.

and is trampled. The thousand newcomers take their orders from Quintus Pompeius Rufus, son of the consul Rufus. This young man didn't warn his father of what he was about to do, so when the consul sees what unfolds, it comes straight out of the blue.

With a gesture from Rufus (the son), the thousand youths rush at Sulpicius's men, screaming and swinging their blades, which glint in the sunlight. A gigantic brawl thus breaks out, sparking cries and invocations for help, followed by groaning, crying, moaning, and guttural choking sounds. Young Rufus is about to launch himself against Sulpicius, running up the steps of the *comitium*, when a *lictor* blocks his way and throws him down from the Tribune. The Anti-Senate immediately surrounds the young man and beat him to death. Rufus's father, the consul, witnesses his son being lynched with his own eyes, and is powerless to help him due to the wall of people between them.

The crowd is in a panic. It swells, moving this way and that, spilling out of the Forum, swarming up the stairways and podiums of the temples and adjacent buildings. The consuls and senators are sucked in too. Sulla flees breathlessly in the direction of the slope leading up the Capitoline.

Just as he starts the climb, he is struck by a sudden idea and does something no one was expecting: he pounds on Marius's front door with his fists, shouting his name loudly and calling for someone to let him in. The door opens a fraction, and Sulla slips inside. He asks the slave who opened the door for him to announce him to Marius.

The host receives his unexpected guest in his office. Although Marius can rid himself of his enemy, doing so doesn't occur to him. The two were comrades in arms and even friends. In fact, they are even related because Sulla married Marius's wife's sister. Furthermore, no one can conceive of killing a duly elected consul in cold blood. The two talk for a few minutes, and then Sulla, escorted by Marius's men, goes back out into the Forum, where, together with Rufus and the *pontifices*, he officially announces the *institium* has been annulled.[5]

Sulla has publicly stated that his life is in danger. He is no less agitated than his colleague, who is distraught after the killing of his son, but he controls himself better. In the hours immediately after the tumult, he and Rufus jump into the saddle, leave the capital, and head for *Nuvla*. First one and then the other emerges from the *Porta Capena*, the *Circus Maximus* at their backs, where the Celian, Palatine, and Aventine Hills meet and the *Via Appia* and

---

5 Plut. *Mar.* 35. No one knows what Marius and Sulla said to each other. Plutarch cites Sulla's memoirs, in which it is said that Sulla didn't take refuge in Marius's house but went there under coercion, at the point of Sulpicius's henchmen's swords, to discuss some issues with Marius as Sulpicius wanted to force him to approve them against his wishes.

Via Latina begin. Each of the consuls is escorted by a cavalry squadron of 30 men, arranged in lines of four.

On its initial stretch, the *Via Latina* runs alongside the *Via Appia*. On this section, riders must proceed at a walk, making their way through a crowd of men on foot or on horseback, as well as wagons and carts pulled by beasts of burden, passing each other without stopping. Having emerged from this scrum, they urge their horses into a full gallop. They speed through the *Ager Romanus* and then the Roman Campagna, passing through *Tusculum* (Tuscolo), *Toleria* (Valmontone), and the landscape beyond without stopping.

Meanwhile, Sulpicius takes advantage of the absence of the consuls from Rome to achieve his goal. He urgently convenes the *concilium plebis*, and not only does he put all four of his plebiscites to the vote but he also adds a fifth, which he presents on the spot in violation of the current law that regulates discussions of new bills and obliges those proposing them to submit them to a vote only after three *nundinae* (market days), i.e., 21 days (*lex Caecilia Didia de modo legum promulgandarum*). The fifth plebiscite aims to deprive Sulla of his military command in the Mithridatic War, appoint Marius in his place, and prevent Rufus from becoming proconsul of *Gallia Cisalpina*.

Sulpicius's henchmen, all armed, are crowded at the fringes of the meeting place.[6] The assembly passes all five bills in an atmosphere of intimidation and fear, under undue pressure exerted through violence and threats, altering the formative process of the voters' will, limiting their power of self-determination, and inducing them to vote in a different way than they probably would have. The *lex Sulpicia de bello mithridatico C. Mario decernendo* (the fifth bill) in particular is illegal for several other reasons: it is conditioned by a procedural defect (non-compliance with the timeframe of three *nundinae*); it deprives a consul of his province and his war when nothing and no one can do so except the Senate and the *comitia centuriata*;[7] and the *concilium plebis* infringed upon the sphere of competence of the Senate, the only constitutional body with the power to decide on the assignment of magistrates to their provinces.

---

6   Plut. *Mar.* 35. Plut. *Sulla*, 8. App. B. Civ. 1.56; Diod. Sic. 37.29.2; Flor. *Mithr.* 3.21.6; Liv. *Per.* 77; Val. Max. 9.7. On the legislation put forward by Sulpicius: R. G. Lewis, "P. Sulpicius law to recall the exiles, 88 BC," *Classical Quarterly* 48 (1998): 195–199; E. Valgiglio, "Sulla legislazione di P. Sulpicio Rufo (88 a.C.)," *RSCI* 15 (1967): 163ff.

7   J. Carcopino, *Silla* (Milan: Bompiani, 1977), 197, n. 43.

CHAPTER X

The Outbreak of Civil War

As in any Roman military camp, there is a large open space in front of the tent of the commander-in-chief of the six legions currently besieging the city of *Nuvla*. It is intended for multiple purposes: to administer military justice, to make speeches to the troops, to host musterings of troops for inspections, and to measure the degree of combat training.

In 88, Sulla delivers a speech to the troops lined up in battle array in that space. He speaks from a platform, so he is visible to everyone. Sulla summarizes what has happened in Rome, highlights how he was wronged, and underlines that he cannot overlook what has occurred. What has happened, in his opinion, is a *coup de main*, a breach of the legal system and the constitution. Sulla is indignant both at the offenses committed and at the personal insult he has suffered. He can't tolerate them; therefore, he prepares to react, leading troops to take Rome and punish those responsible. He doesn't ask the legions to follow him in what he is about to do to obtain redress, but he encourages them to be ready.

The answer is immediate, but its content varies according to whether it comes from the lower ranks (rank-and-file, junior officers, centurions) or the higher officers (tribunes, prefects, legates). The rank-and-file feels it suits them to be led by Sulla, both because they fear that Marius may dismiss them and replace them with others recruited for the occasion and because Sulla is widely renowned for his commitment to his soldiers. Many senior officers refuse to follow Sulla, partly because they abhor the idea of taking up arms against other Romans and partly because they are closely tied to Marius and, therefore, to the political party to which Sulla is opposed.

Consequently, after Sulla has finished speaking, some senior officers leave the camp. The quaestor Lucius Licinius Lucullus remains by Sulla's side for both personal and family reasons. Firstly, he has already served under Sulla during the Social War as a military tribune. When Sulla was elected to the consulship, he asked that as soon as Lucullus was elected as a quaestor he be assigned to him to manage the military purse, starting with the payment of wages, in view of the military campaign he was about to undertake. Secondly, both family ties and bonds of *amicitia* link the Luculli to Sulla and the Metelli, Sulla's supporters. Lucullus's mother, Caecilia Metella Calva, is the sister of Quintus Caecilius Metellus Numidicus and Lucius Caecilius Metellus Dalmaticus, Sulla's political sponsors, and the aunt of Metella Dalmatica, Sulla's third wife.

Born in Rome in 117, Lucius Licinius Lucullus is now 29.[1] He is handsome, with straight hair and a slender, lean body. He is perceptive, has a prodigious memory, is an excellent judicial orator, and loves studying history. He has one brother, Marcus Terentius Varro Lucullus. The Lucullus brothers are very fond of each other. They descend from a family of enriched plebeians and were aediles together. Their father—Lucius Licinius Lucullus—was sentenced to exile for having lost, damaged, or rendered property of the state unusable, in whole or in part, while serving as praetor in Sicily in 104. Accordingly, their father's successor in command in Sicily, Caius Servilius Augur, took him to court. As soon as the brothers had the opportunity (perhaps in 91), they in turn took Servilius Augur to court for having taken possession of movable property owned by the state to make a personal profit for himself or others.[2] However, Servilius Augur was acquitted amid chaotic scenes.[3]

Meanwhile, the political process initiated by Sulpicius subverts the rules governing the functioning of the republic's institutions and puts the constitutional bodies involved, i.e., the *concilium plebis* and the Senate, into conflict. The situation evolves quickly. In the summer of 88, shortly after the approval of the *lex Sulpicia de bello mithridatico C. Mario decernendo*, two military tribunes arrive in Sulla's camp, charged with taking over the legions and making them swear allegiance to Marius, their new commander-in-chief.

They are soldiers who don't answer to the Senate and the consuls (Sulla and Rufus) but to a tribune of the plebs (Sulpicius) whose political point of reference is an ordinary citizen (Marius), who is pursuing his own private, very personal interests.[4] Sulla ensures the handover of the insignia of command

---

1   The principal source for Lucius Licinius Lucullus is Plut. *Luc.* See also A. Keaveney, *Lucullus: A Life* (London: Routledge, 1992); G. Antonelli, *Lucullo* (Rome: Newton Compton, 1989); J. Ooteghem (Van), *Lucius Licinius Lucullus* (Brussels, 1959).

2   Diod. Sic. 36.8.1–8; 36.8.5; 9.1; Flor. 2.7.10–11; Plut. *Luc.* 1.

3   On Lucullus's trial and the subsequent trial of Servilius: Alexander, *Trials in the Late Roman Republic*, 35–36, n. 69; 37–38, n. 71.

4   Plut. *Sulla* 8 doesn't specify whether they are *tribuni militum* or tribunes of the plebs, merely

takes place in public. One of the tribunes is delivering a speech in front of the arrayed legions when a stone is thrown violently at him, hitting him on the temple and killing him instantly. Not a moment later, his colleague is also hit by a stone and falls to the ground, lifeless.

News of what has happened spreads like wildfire. The killing of two military tribunes in peacetime is an almost unique rather than a rare event, and it isn't easy to understand what caused it. No one would have imagined that a consul would rebel against the state. But that's exactly what's happening. We're looking at a situation of enormous gravity, without precedent in the political and military history of the *res publica*, except, perhaps, for the story of Coriolanus (491).[5]

Aware that the killing of the tribunes marks a point of no return but comforted by the fact that most of the Senate and the army are on his side, Sulla makes a virtue of necessity. First, he fills the gaps that have opened in his chain of command. He knows that the circumstances require him to march on Rome and he is tempted to order the legions to depart immediately, but he hesitates. As such, he struggles with the dilemma. But then two events occur that share the element of divine providence: after examining the entrails of a sacrificial offering, Postumius predicts his victory (Postumius is the same seer who predicted Sulla's victory over Cluentius during the Social War), and Sulla dreams that Ma,[6] the Cappadocian goddess of war, is standing next to him, puts a thunderbolt in his hand, and makes him name his enemies, one by one, and as they are named, each falls to the ground, dead.

Postumius's prophecy and Ma's appearance in a dream appear to Sulla to be divine signs, which prompts him to act. Therefore, he orders the legions to prepare to march on Rome.

When the defenders of *Nuvla* see a squadron of cavalry, a column of infantry, a few squadrons on horseback, and a long train of pack animals and wagons leave the camp, all the emotional tension of the siege comes to the fore. The entire garrison and the whole population take to the streets and shout joyfully that their resistance has paid off and that the city is safe. But their joy is short

---

speaking generally about tribunes, but the most plausible interpretation is that they are *tribuni militum*.

5   Eutr. I.15; Liv. II.39–40.

6   Plut. *Sulla* 9.3. Plutarch doesn't explicitly name Ma but "a goddess whom the Romans learned to worship from the Cappadocians, whether she is Luna, or Minerva, or Bellona." This goddess can be identified as Ma if we consider that, after the First Mithridatic War, it was Sulla himself who introduced the cult of Ma to Rome after his army had encountered it in *Cappadocia*.

lived. One legion, led by Appius Claudius Pulcher, remains in place, tasked with maintaining the siege.

Sulla is leading his soldiers' departure, surrounded by a unit of horse. The consul Rufus rides on Sulla's right, with Lucullus behind them and a mounted escort around them. Behind them marches a column of soldiers, 20km long. Once in *Capua*, Sulla and his soldiers continue along the Via Latina, which leads to Rome. In answer to the many locals who ask him why on earth he has decided to wage war on his homeland, Sulla responds: "To free it from those who tyrannize it." In his eyes, what's happening isn't a *coup d'état* but a direct intervention to restore public order and the regular functioning of the political institutions.

Marius and Sulpicius grasp the precise scope of the ongoing political process and react angrily. That day, many of Sulla's friends are murdered, the victims' houses are looted and burned, and Sulla's *domus* is ransacked, ruined and set on fire. Sulla learns of the massacre and devastation from some refugees when he and his army are approaching Rome.

Marius has a clear idea of what must be done. Intending to instill courage in his fellow citizens, he places himself at the head of the civilian population and implements all those measures, arrangements, and procedures necessary to forcefully oppose the "invaders". He proclaims that those who have been mobilized must consider it their duty and sacred right to contribute to the community resistance, as a fighter or worker, for the security of the homeland is in danger. He declares that all free and able men aged between 17 and 65 must go to the places of assembly and take up a position as and where they are ordered to do so, starting with those who have been judged fit for military service, while those who are unable to fight replace the enlisted in their civilian tasks and duties. He establishes fighting corps and units, appoints commanders, assigns their duties…

Marius arbitrarily replaces the Senate and the consuls to take these initiatives. Not only has the Senate not involved him, but it has not even declared a national state of emergency, the prerequisite for mass mobilization. Therefore, how can Marius's behavior best be described? It seems to be that of a revolutionary or a putschist, but actually it is simply that of a private citizen who, for personal reasons, is rebelling against his legitimate government and calling citizens to arms in defense of his own arrogance and pride. The main purpose of Marius's general mobilization is to oppose the consuls after having wronged one of them and who is now marching on Rome to reassert his rights.

The call for mass mobilization falls on deaf ears. Only the magistrates who are politically obligated to Marius, their friends, clients, freedmen, and slaves, the 3,600 men placed at Sulpicius's disposal, and some of the propertyless heed the call. Almost all the patricians are aligned with the *optimates*, who support Sulla. Lower-class plebeians have nothing to gain from getting involved in an institutional conflict that has nothing to do with them, and the policy of the *equites* has always been, and is currently, to enjoy the spectacle of the fighting, see how it ends, and rush to the aid of the victor.

Marius sees defeat on the horizon. But he doesn't give up and tries a desperate gambit: he makes a public appeal to the slaves of Rome, promising them that if they enlist in his army, they will obtain their freedom, despite knowing that, to the Romans, promising freedom to slaves is as ignoble as declaring war on the state. The slaves are tempted by the offer but fear that Marius won't be able to keep his promise. Therefore, few of them accept it.[7]

While the legions are inexorably advancing on Rome, the Senate sends three delegations to Sulla, one after another.[8] The first representation is made by the *praetor peregrinus* Publius Servilius and the *praetor urbanus* Marcus Junius Brutus. Each of the two praetors is escorted by his lictors. The former is an *eques*, and the latter is a descendant of Lucius Junius Brutus, one of the founders of the *res publica*. The arrogance dripping from the tone of these two magistrates as they address Sulla infuriates the legionaries. Some soldiers rush at the lictors, breaking their curule chairs and tearing the praetors' *toga*, before they insult them harshly, manhandle them, and chase them away with stones. The second deputation manages to parley with Sulla but doesn't convince him to stop. The third deputation meets Sulla at *Ad Pictas* in the Roman Campagna.[9] Sulla says he is willing to negotiate and orders the legions to halt on the stop as he waits for a response.

But he only wants to buy time. In fact, once the messengers have left, he orders his legates, Lucius Basilius and Caius Mummius, to go to Rome and take control of some strategically important locations, all near the Esquiline. Then he commands the other two legions to resume the march toward Rome,

---

7 Plut. *Mar.* 35 claims that only three slaves presented themselves.

8 Since the Senate is composed of conservative men, who previously supported Sulla, one might ask why they would want to negotiate to stop Sulla's march, thus acting in a way that would benefit Marius? The response is to be found in the fact that Sulla is now doing something unprecedented, and to them, this is even worse than an old man seizing military command out of vanity. Most of the Senate share Sulla's grievances (the Metelli, leaders of the *optimates*, support Sulla against Marius). However, they cannot tolerate anybody assaulting the city to occupy it by force. In view of an inveterate tradition, if not the law, no one can enter the city bearing weapons. During the Republican Period, the urban space is demilitarized.

9 Plut. *Sulla* 9.5. App. *B. Civ.* 1.57. On the location of Ad Pictas: A. G. Thein, "The via Latina, the via Labicana and the Location of Ad Pictas," *PBSR* 73 (2005): 131–155.

to camp between the *Porta Esquilina* and the *Porta Collina*. He will join them later, together with the V Legion and 2,000 cavalry.

Basilius's and Mummius's legions push on as far as the *Porta Esquilina*, which opens on the east side of the Servian Walls between the *Porta Capena* and *Porta Collina*. They break through the heavy gates, to the dismay of the defenders, and push on toward the area of the Forum, raising their banners amid the din of shouts and trumpet blasts. As the centuries pass by, the city streets empty in a general stampede. This is a military invasion, an unprecedented and—until recently—inconceivable event. No enemy has invaded the city for more than 200 years since Brennus's Gauls, who occupied Rome for six months and sacked it in 390/386, retreating only after having been paid a ransom.

Sulla enters the city by force through the *Porta Capena*, overwhelming all resistance. When he learns that Basilius and his legion are being blocked by a hail of tiles and stones being showered down on them from the rooftops by unarmed commoners, he reaches Basilius at a gallop and yells at him to set fire to the houses by shooting clouds of incendiary arrows at the roofs. Sulla's order achieves its goal. The hailstorm from the roofs ceases when the first volleys of fire arrows hit their targets and lighted torches are thrown into the houses through doors and windows because the inhabitants are now scrambling to pour water on the flames to save their homes.[10]

The heavily armed, well-equipped legionaries, supported by archers and slingers, press on and engage Marius's ragtag militia in the Forum; the latter suddenly give in, throw down their weapons, and flee in disarray. Sulla's cavalry charges after the fugitives. Many men are cut down. Many others surrender, begging for mercy. The battle is over. Sulla's victory is clear. The legions complete the occupation of the city as night falls. Sulla has forbidden his men, under pain of death, from pillaging to prevent them from behaving as enemies of Rome. Some soldiers disobey and loot the dead, aided by the darkness of the night. But sentries during their patrols catch them in the act and execute them on the spot.

The following day, Sulla convenes the Senate and explains that he has used his *imperium* in defense of the *res public*. He brands the approval of the law that removed his military command and handed it to Marius as an unprecedented illegality, he accuses Marius and his friends of having incited the citizens and slaves to revolt and of having taken up arms against the consuls, and condemns the persecution of his family, relatives, and friends. He also says that he dreamed that the goddess of war authorized him to punish his

---

10 Plut. *Sulla* 9.6–7.

enemies and names 12 people who he claims are primarily responsible for the political upheaval: Caius Marius, Publius Sulpicius Rufus, Caius Marius the Younger, Marcus Junius Brutus, Quintus Granius and his brother Cnaeus, Publius Cornelius Cethegus, Publius Albinovanus, Marcus Laetorius, Quintus Rubrius Varro. Cnaeus Papirius Carbo, and Lucius Decimius.[11]

Sulla puts a motion to the vote among the senators to brand the 12 individuals as *hostes publici* and put a bounty on their heads.[12] The motion is approved,[13] with the only vote against coming from Scaevola Augur, who justifies his choice by saying that he will never accept that a man like Marius should be shown such dishonor. Scaevola defends Marius because he thinks he deserves gratitude for saving Rome from the Cimbri. However, Marius the Younger is married to Licinia, Scaevola's granddaughter, which may have influenced his judgment.

The following night, the *hostes publici*, after saving what could be saved, meet in secret in the Temple of Jupiter Stator on the *Campus Martius*. Albinovanus, Cethegus, Brutus, Laetorius, and the Granius brothers are missing. They agree to leave the city, separately and quickly, and to meet again on 1 December in Aenaria, a port town on *Pithekoussai* (Ischia), an island in the Gulf of Naples,[14] after which they will go to Sicily to ask the provincial governor, Caius Norbanus Balbus, a *popularis* and a client of Marius, for refuge. When Sulla leaves for the East, they will return to Rome and take revenge on the Sullans remaining in the city.

After saying their farewells and embracing each other, those present wish each other good luck, then disappear into the darkness, each following his own path. Marius and his son separate too, though they shrug off the idea that the state will search for them and that their assets will be confiscated.[15]

---

11   According to Vell. Pat. II.9, Sulla targeted *"XII auctores novarum pessimarunque rerum."* Plut. *Sulla* 10.1 is less precise, limiting himself to saying, "Sulla now called together the senate, and had a sentence of death passed on Marius himself and a few others, among whom was Sulpicius." App. *Bell. Civ.* I.60 says that there were 12 public enemies and names nine: Marius (father and son), Sulpicius, Cethegus, Brutus, the Granius brothers, Albinovanus, and Laetorius. Cic. *Brut.* 168 also mentions Quintus Rubrius Varro.

12   Vell. Pat. II.19; Plut. *Mar.* 43; Cic. *Brut.* 168; Val. Max. III 8.5; Diod. Sic. XXXVII 29.3. See also F. Sini, *Bellum Nefandum. Virgilio e il problema del "diritto internazionale antico* (Sassari: Dessì, 1991), 304.

13   On Sulla's declaration of public enemies: R. A. Bauman, "The hostis declarations of 88 and 87 B.C.," *Athenaeum* 51 (1973): 270–293.

14   Marius chooses this as a meeting place because it is remote and away from prying eyes. At the same time, it isn't far from *Puteolis*, where he still has many supporters.

15   The Roman state will make no attempt to bring Marius and the other public enemies of 89

Sulpicius travels along the Tiber by boat, wrapped in a cloak with the hood over his eyes and hoping to proceed unnoticed. When the river flows into the sea at *Ostia*, he sails north and reaches *Lavinium* (Pratica di Mare), where he pushes the boat ashore. Numerous wealthy individuals from the capital have villas in *Lavinium*. One of these villas belongs to Sulpicius, and it's there that he takes refuge for the night. He plans to resume his escape the next day but is betrayed by a slave, captured by Sulla's assassins, and beheaded on the spot, despite the fact he is a tribune of the plebs and, as such, inviolable. His head is brought to Sulla, who will order it to be publicly displayed on the Orators' Tribune.

Sextus Lucilius, a cousin of Strabo, is a candidate in the elections for the plebeian tribuneship. He believes that if he can bring the *publicus hostis* Marius to justice, he could get more votes, so he hires cutthroats to kill him. Lucilius's assassins find Marius in a vast, turbid swamp near *Minturnae* (Minturno) in lower *Latium* and drag Marius into the town square for a public execution. However, the *duumviri* claim jurisdiction for the prisoner's execution, put Marius in prison, and send a giant Cimbrian slave to kill him. But the slave can't handle the emotion of finding himself in the presence of the (super)man who annihilated his people and runs away. At this point, the town's entire population obtains Marius's release because he is a national hero, and this gives Marius the means to continue his escape.

Marius is thus able to reunite with his son and the other refugees in Aenaria. The group then goes to Sicily but doesn't receive the requested asylum because the provincial governor doesn't want to put himself on a collision course with Sulla. As a result, they go to Roman Africa. Among the ruins of *Carthago*, however, Marius learns that the provincial governor, another formerly good acquaintance of his, is refusing to give him shelter and protection. The group thus sets off again and ends up on the Kerkennah Islands, a handful of low, almost flat islands in the Gulf of Gabès (off the coast of Sfax in Tunisia). In *Cercina*, they find one of the colonies founded in North Africa within the framework of Saturninus's colonial legislation.

Marius then learns that the whereabouts of his son and Cethegus, who was with him, are currently unknown. They had passed through *Cercina* but left before Marius's arrival, heading for *Rusicade*, the port of *Cirta* (Costantina, Algeria). The young men intended to request hospitality from Hiempsal II, king of *Numidia*, relying on the fact that Marius had helped his father Gauda I (r. 106–88) succeed Jugurtha on the throne. However, Hiempsal II

---

to justice, nor will it initiate any proceedings to confiscate their property. In all likelihood, all Sulla is concerned with is driving Marius and his friends as far away from Rome as possible.

(r. 88–60) detains his Roman guests, making various excuses. He has every interest in maintaining good relations with Rome, so he wants to wait and see who will win the clash between Marius and Sulla. But one of the king's concubines falls in love with the young Marius (some say that Caius Marius the Younger is the most handsome young man in Rome) and helps him and his companion escape. The two return to *Cercina*, where they find Marius and their other companions.

In the meantime, Sulla has two new consuls elected for 87: Lucius Cornelius Cinna and Cnaeus Octavius. We have already met the former. The latter is about 42 years old. In 100, he sided with the Senate against Saturninus (he was among those who took weapons from the public armory when the Senate reacted to Saturninus's latest wrongdoing by ordering his arrest). Since then, he has run unsuccessfully for the *aedileship* but was elected to the praetorship (he held this office before 90). Furthermore, Sulla has seen to it that Rufus becomes proconsul for Roman Gaul and entrusts him with implementing his governmental program, which mainly aims at achieving the following objectives: limiting the powers of the tribunes of the plebs, doubling the number of senators, and obliging anyone presenting a bill to submit it to the Senate before discussing it in public and having it voted on by the people gathered in assembly. As his final act before leaving for the Mithridatic War, Sulla forces Cinna and Octavius to solemnly swear—in public—that they will do nothing to hinder or prevent his program's implementation.

CHAPTER XI

Marius and Cinna Capture Rome

In 97, Quintus Sertorius was a military tribune in the army of the praetor Titus Didius in *Hispania* and was decorated with the grass crown for distinguishing himself in the repression of a popular uprising. At the same time, he was wounded in the face and lost his left eye; since then, he has worn a black bandage over his scarred eye. When he returned to Rome, he was elected to the quaestorship and collected armaments and supplies from the *socii* in *Gallia Cisalpina* in view of the imminent outbreak of the Social War. In 88, he stood for election as tribune of the plebs but failed due to Sulla's opposition. He and Sulla quarreled, and each went their own way.

We've already met Sertorius, a Roman citizen of Italic origin. He fought under the orders of Marius, his relative, in the Jugurthine War and, later, in the Cimbrian War, on the battlefield as well as behind enemy lines as a spy. Sertorius has now aligned himself with Lucius Cornelius Cinna, who has been elected as consul for 87 and is trying to revive the *populares* faction, which has been weakened since Marius's stroke.

Cinna's consular colleague, we recall, is the plebeian Cnaeus Octavius. After Sulla's departure for the Mithridatic War, Cinna supported the plebeian tribune Caius Papirius Carbo Arvina's plebiscite, which sought to ensure that new Roman citizens and freedmen be enrolled in the 35 historical tribes (it is rumored he was corrupted by the payment of a staggering bribe of 300 talents). Some tribunes of the plebs vetoed the continuation of this controversial bill's legislative path, but during a protest organized by Cinna in the city center, attended not only by many Latins and Italics but also by many of Octavius's friends, a riot broke out that left 10,000 people on the ground. During the tumult, Cinna called on the city slaves for help, promising them their freedom in return, but his appeal fell on deaf ears.

The Senate consulted the Sibylline Books in public, something that had never happened before, and it emerged that Rome could never have peace and security until Cinna and his friends among the tribunes were banished from Rome. Therefore, it dismissed Cinna, Carbo Arvina, Minutius Magius, Caius Milonius, and Marcus Vergilius from office and declared them *hostes publici*. The public enemies fled Rome, together with Marcus Marius Gratidianus and Sertorius, and reached the camp of the besiegers of *Nuvla*.

Gratidianus is Marius's nephew on his mother's side (he is the son of Marcus Gratidius and Maria, Marius's sister). He was adopted by Marius's brother Marcus after his father died fighting against the Cilician pirates during the expedition led by Marcus Antonius Orator (102–101). His sister, Gratidia, married Lucius Sergius Catalina, whom we will meet again later. In 109, Gratidianus was defended in court by Lucius Licinius Crassus following a dispute with Caius Sergius Orata, an oyster farmer and real estate speculator, regarding the sale of a property on the Lucrine Lake.[1]

In 87, the only military unit still maintaining the siege of *Nuvla* is a contingent of Gallic *auxilia*. Originally, there were six units, but Sulla removed five of them to march on Rome and reclaim control of war operations in the East, which he had been deprived of by the *lex Sulpicia de bello mithridatico C. Mario decernendo*. The besiegers' commander-in-chief is Appius Claudius Pulcher, the homonymous son of the consul of 143, censor of 136, Salian priest, augur, and *princeps senatus*, who died in 130. His father was the father-in-law of Tiberius Sempronius Gracchus and shared his political vision. He was a land reform commissioner, a skilled, persuasive speaker, and unfailingly proud.

Conversely, Pulcher, who served as praetor in 89, is a brooding, distant man afflicted by family problems. His soldiers detest him. Therefore, they are the first to be re-energized when Cinna swoops into their camp and enjoins Pulcher to hand command to him. Indeed, they are bursting with joy when they learn that Sertorius will be their new commander-in-chief because he was the one who enlisted them in *Gallia Cisalpina*. Pulcher leaves the field and goes to join Metellus Pius, who is besieging the city of *Aesernia*, another remnant of the Social War.

Carbo, Magius, Milonius, and Vergilius visit all the *municipia* along the *Via Latina* in lower *Latium* on Cinna's behalf. They stir up the local authorities, landholders, and the people. They say that the consul Octavius, to oust Cinna from power, had 10,000 unarmed citizens massacred, and they rally the locals around Cinna. They raise funds to restore Cinna to power, pass

---

1   Cic. *Off.* 3.

Carbo's plebiscite, and enlist fresh recruits and enfranchised slaves (freedmen), to whom they distribute weapons of war and military equipment taken from the army's storehouses at Alba Fucens.

Sertorius lifts the siege of *Nuvla* and marches his forces to rejoin Cinna, whom he finds in *Labicum* (a site of uncertain location). On the way, he is joined by volunteers and slaves enlisted by Carbo, Magius, Milonius, and Vergilius. Sertorius supplies them with weapons, helmets, breastplates, shields, and greaves. Subsequently, Sertorius's ranks are swelled further by a large group of gladiators, fugitive slaves, and a large group of Samnites. On their arrival in *Labicum*, Sertorius delivers 30,000 well-armed, well-equipped men to Cinna. Cinna organizes this force into three legions. He keeps command of one legion for himself, places the two remaining legions under the command of Carbo and Sertorius, and puts the cavalry under Milonius's command.

In the meantime, Cinna has invited Marius to join his attempt to regain power in Rome, and the invitation is accepted. Marius is arriving at the port of *Talamo* (Talamone) when Cinna instructs Sertorius to welcome him and deliver the proconsular insignias and *lictoral fasces* in Cinna's name to him. Evidently, despite being dismissed as consul, Cinna is continuing to behave as if he were in full possession of his consular powers. He even goes beyond the competences of the consuls because, without any mandate or authorization to do so, he appoints Marius to the office of proconsul, thus replacing the Senate, which is the only organ of the Roman state authorized to assign extraordinary magistracies (*proconsulships*, dictatorships).

Marius reaches *Talamo* with numerous ships, having set sail from *Cercina* and probably arriving via *Lilybaeum* (Marsala, Sicily), *Caralis* (Cagliari, Sardinia), Sari-Solenzara (Corsica), Montecristo (an island in the Tyrrhenian Sea and part of the Tuscan Archipelago), and *Incitaria* and *Portus Herculis*, the ports of Argentario (a promontory in Tuscany). He is accompanied by some of the public enemies of 88, 1,000 mounted Numidian soldiers, and about 500 other armed men.[2] Among the latter, there are, perhaps, some Gaetuli, war veterans from *Cercina*, and Etruscan merchants who had been in North Africa on business.[3]

Marius isn't depressed but vexed by his reversal of fortune. He refuses the proconsular insignias and *lictoral fasces* that Sertorius offers him because—he says—they don't suit his current, wretched position. He confides to Sertorius that he intends to be elected consul for a seventh time (he has already been

---

2   Plut. *Mar.* 41; Gran. Lic. XXXV.6 Crin.

3   App. I.67, 305; Gran. Lic. XVI.4 Fl.; Passerini, "Epigrafia Mariana," in *Athenaeum* 17 (1939): 69–69.

consul in 107 and consecutively each year from 104 to 100). The last five times, he was a candidate *ex officio* and was always absent on election day. He adds that this will certainly happen because it has been prophesied to him by Martha, a fortune teller whom Sertorius knows (Marius places a lot of trust in soothsayers).

The prophetess Martha arrived in Rome in 105 and comes from the coastal region of the eastern Mediterranean (Syria/Lebanon), currently divided between the Seleucid Empire, the Kingdom of *Commagene*, the city-state of *Palmyra*, the Kingdom of Judea (Hasmonean dynasty), and the Nabataean Kingdom. Initially, she offered—without success—to predict the outcome of the Cimbrian War in the Senate. Later, she was able to mix with a group of ladies from Roman high society. In 102, at a gladiatorial bout, Martha was sitting at the feet of Julia Major, Marius's wife, and divined precisely who would win a duel. Julia, struck by Martha's talent, introduced her to her husband. Marius agreed that Martha should join him on the front line in *Gallia Transalpina* and asked her to help him keep the soldiers' morale up ahead of the Battle of *Aquae Sextiae*. Since then, Martha has followed Marius like a shadow and oversees his sacrifices to the gods.[4] Sertorius first met Martha in *Gallia Transalpina* when he was fighting under Marius.

Marius also confides in Sertorius that he landed in *Etruria* because he wants to try to rile up the small farmers, workers of the land, free Roman citizens, and slaves against the Senate and the consul Cnaeus Octavius. He says that he wants to take revenge on those who have "disrespected" him, first by preferring Sulla to him to lead operations in the war against Mithridates VI, then by branding him a public enemy. In particular, he says he wants to take revenge on those who said they were his friends but instead turned their backs on him, starting with Sulla and his family, relatives, friends, and clients. And the more he talks about them, the more he burns with indignation and fury.[5]

Marius has changed a lot in both his physique and his character since his stroke. His face is deformed by a grimace, and he's more irritable, irascible, self-centered, haughty, proud, touchy, and nasty than ever. Sertorius doesn't recognize his old commander in him, only a man who has aged badly, blinded by inordinate ambition and prey to an irrepressible desire for revenge.

Marius and his companions head for *Labicum* to meet Cinna. During the march, they are joined by a group of people who had been exiled after being found guilty of high treason under the *quaestio Varia de maiestate* and who

---

4   Plut. *Mar.* 17.

5   On Marius's disembarkation at *Talamo*: App. *B. Civ.* I.305–306; Gran. Lic. 35.16–17.

have come from *Hispania*, where they found refuge. One of these individuals is Marcus Junius Brutus, who was military tribune in 88. They also pass through the lands Marius owns in *Etruria*, which should have been confiscated but are nonetheless still fully available to him.

The column marches on in an orderly manner, like a regular army unit. Local people from urban settlements and the countryside who see the parade are particularly struck by Marius's run-down appearance. Nevertheless, Marius boasts to everyone he meets of his military victories, the decorations he has been awarded, and his six consulships, and he promises his intercession in the matter of new citizens' enrolment in the tribes. He inspires confidence in his interlocutors, so much so that he manages to recruit 4,000 volunteers and free 500 slaves on the condition that they fight for him. Most of the latter are Illyrians. Specifically, they originate from an area south of the Narenta River (in the hinterland of Croatia and Bosnia-Herzegovina) and belong to the Ardiaei tribe, which is made up of peasants and occasionally pirates. The Romans call them Bardiaei, so we will also call them that from now on.[6]

Sertorius notes with regret that Marius is a different man from the one he knew and for whom he fought in North Africa and *Gallia Transalpina* and considers that an alliance with Marius isn't beneficial to Cinna's cause but, on the contrary, will damage it, so he decides to go ahead of Marius to be able to talk about it with Cinna. Spurring his horse into a gallop, he arrives in *Labicum* and warns Cinna that Marius has gone mad due to his illness and exile, and advises him not to embrace his arrival because Marius's extremism would make Cinna lose the support of the moderates, which he needs. However, Cinna cannot reject Marius because he was the one who sent the invitation, so he doesn't accept the suggestion. Instead, he goes to meet Marius, together with Sertorius, the four former tribunes of the plebs, and his three legions.

Marius's and Cinna's columns meet on the *Via Aurelia*, 35km from Rome, in a marshy, insalubrious part of the coast between the mouth of the Tiber and the ancient Etruscan city of *Alsium*, located between Pyrgi and Fregenae. Marius and Cinna exchange warm greetings, then, together with Sertorius and the other senior officers, sketch out a strategy to conquer Rome. Marius will attack *Ostia* and the nearby localities to cut off the grain supplies and force it to surrender. Cinna, Carbo, and Sertorius will go upriver to Rome, where Cinna will occupy the northern slopes of the Janiculum, Carbo the nearby Vatican Plain, and Sertorius the *Campus Martius*.

---

6   For a summary of the origins of the Bardiaei: N. Criniti, "Ludovico Antonio Muratori e i Bardiaei," *Aevum* 53, no. 1 (1979): 162–164.

At this point, it's justifiable to wonder how to frame what's happening. It isn't a *coup d'état* because none of the protagonists is a magistrate, even though Cinna is acting as if he were. Nor is it an organized, violent movement with which a new social or political order is to be established (social revolution). Rather, it is an attempt by two private individuals—Marius and Cinna—to seize the constituted power by force, placing themselves in name and deed as public enemies. In short, it's armed sedition.

At the news that Marius and Cinna are marching on Rome at the head of no fewer than 35,000 men, all well armed and well equipped, the Senate and the consuls are briefly bewildered. When they recover, they prepare a plan for defense: they solicit military aid from the *municipia*, mobilize all able-bodied men between the ages of 17 and 65, urge a multitude of repairmen, workers, and laborers to complete the expansion and consolidation works on the city walls, which have been underway since before the Social War; and ask Cnaeus Strabo, who is in his lands between *Picenum* and Umbria, to come to Rome to assume command of the defense of the city.

Strabo has the merit of turning the fate of the Social War in Rome's favor for his victories over the Marsi, Peligni, Picentes, and Vestini. Acclaimed *imperator* by his soldiers, he has celebrated a triumph in Rome. Then, in 89, as consul, he promoted and obtained approval for a bill that aimed to extend Latin law to *Gallia Cisalpina* and organize this "province" into urban districts, the *lex Pompeia de Transpadanis*.

Strabo doesn't need to be asked twice. He leads his personal army to Rome, made up of three well-armed, well-equipped, and well-trained legions, and camps on the *Campus Martius*, near the *Porta Collina*. As always, his son is with him, the 19-year-old Cnaeus, who, despite his innocent face and boyish features, is an angel of death. This Cnaeus Pompeius will become one of the key players on Rome's political and military scene over the coming decades (until his death in 48) and will be nicknamed *magnus*, "the Great."

Strabo isn't as interested in defending Rome as he is in proving himself worthy of the *res publica* to cash in his credit in the next elections when he intends to run for the consulship. Consequently, he doesn't want to present himself as a contender but as an arbiter in the dispute. He wants to wage war by offering terms of peace. Proof of this is that in agreement with the Senate and the consuls, he immediately sends envoys to Marius and Cinna. However, negotiations don't get off the ground, and the envoys return to Rome.

Meanwhile, Marius has taken possession of *Ostia* without a fight, thanks to the betrayal of Valerius, the commander of the local cavalry garrison. He abandons the city to pillage, then cuts Rome's food supply lines. Marius also blocks and requisitions all incoming shipments of grain as well as cargo that has already been transferred onto other boats that are preparing to sail up to Rome. He has a pontoon bridge thrown across the Tiber to impede navigation and roughs up some towns near *Ostia*: *Antium* (Anzio), *Aricia* (Ariccia), and *Lavinium* (Pratica di Mare).[7] Finally, he goes up the Tiber and reunites with Cinna at the foot of the Janiculum while Sertorius is on the *Campus Martius*.

The city is surrounded on three sides by 6,000 men belonging to Marius and Cinna's three legions and is defended by a militia and Strabo's three legions. Fighting soon breaks out on the Pincian Hill. It will end without winners or losers and a death toll of 600 on each side. A brutal clash is also raging on the Janiculum, where Marius has managed to break into the fortress thanks to the betrayal of a military tribune who was once one of his soldiers. He is about to let Cinna in when Octavius, leading six cohorts of reinforcements from Strabo's army, attacks them. Octavius has raced up the road that climbs the hill after crossing the Tiber and defeating the enemy cavalry (Milonius was killed in the fighting) and manages to repel Marius and Cinna, inflicting losses of 7,000 men. Meanwhile, Sertorius has attacked Strabo's cohorts to ease the pressure on Marius. Octavius's victory would have been clearer if Strabo—insisting on his fence-sitting politics (although he has responsibility for the defense of Rome, he is incongruously collaborating, openly, with the enemy, favoring the latter's aims)—hadn't detained him and recalled one of his legates, Publius Licinius Crassus. Octavius therefore confers command of the fortress to Crassus and his son.

A pause in the fighting follows, which will last until the elections for the renewal of the magistracies for 86. The people of Rome soon feel the effects of the food blockade, and goods have become scarce and expensive. But the emergencies arising in the city and the surrounding camps don't only concern collective security and finding food. In fact, another enemy, more furtive and insidious, has joined the twin threats of the army at the gates and famine.

The concentration on the outskirts of the city of tens of thousands of men in camps without adequate sanitation has caused a severe form of water pollution and the onset of an epidemic. Under the watch of Strabo, solid waste from cesspools and latrines and fecal pollutants from animal excrement and food waste are allowed to be discharged into the waters of the Tiber. Due to the contaminated water, increasing numbers of besiegers contract intestinal diseases. The sanitary emergency also affects the besieged city because the defenders and the civilian population use the waters of the Tiber, wells, and

---

7   App. I.69, 313. Liv. *per.* 80. Oros. 5.19.19.

springs for domestic, industrial, artisanal, agricultural, and zootechnical purposes. Roman doctors don't know the causes of the infectious diseases and, attributing the contagion to bad air, do nothing to address the cause. This attitude leaves the field free for an epidemic, which spreads rapidly and unchecked, claiming many victims. Men on both sides get sick and fall like flies. Before long, Strabo loses 11,000 men, while Octavius loses 6,000.[8] There are thousands of victims among the civilian population too.

Mortality due to the epidemic reduced Strabo's forces to such an extent that they were reduced to a state of numerical inferiority compared to the enemy. For Strabo, this was yet another reason to remain inert. He gives one excuse after another to the Senate and the consuls to justify his reluctance to attack the enemy. The Senate is initially patient before ordering him to hand over his command to Quintus Pompeius Rufus, proconsul of *Gallia Cisalpina* and commander-in-chief of two legions, one of which is quartered in *Placentia* (Piacenza) and the other in *Aquileia*, both in northern Italy.

Rufus was consul with Sulla in 88, then joined him in the fight against Marius and Sulpicius, during which he lost his son, Quintus, Sulla's son-in-law. He was supposed to ensure that the consuls Cinna and Octavius didn't deviate from Sulla's political reform program after the latter left for the Mithridatic War, but he failed to prevent Cinna from drifting toward the *populares*, resulting in the massacre of 10,000 people.

Strabo steps aside, but it's evident that he's foaming with rage. But just when Rufus goes to him to receive the insignia of command, a military revolt breaks out, and Rufus himself is killed. The Senate and the consuls struggle to understand what happened: it's possible that Strabo incited the troops against Rufus, but the incident remains unclear both in terms of the motivations and purposes and in terms of how it all unfolded. Either way, they are careful not to insist that Strabo relinquish control of his legions.

Strabo is an odious, cruel, greedy, perfidious man. He has a reputation as a butcher for the cruelty to the point of ferocity with which he treated the defenders and civilian population of Asculum after they had surrendered.[9] His men can no longer tolerate him, and word of this reaches Cinna, who leverages the state of latent tension in the enemy camp to hatch a conspiracy. Some of his most trusted men enter the enemy camp without the authorization or the right to do so and they bribe some soldiers to kill Strabo and his son.

---

8   Gran. Lic. 21.11 Fl.; Oros. V.19.18.

9   Cic. *Brut.* 47.

Cnaeus Pompeius (the son) is informed of the conspiracy, joins his father in the officers' quarters, alerts the guards, and awaits the night's events with them. The attempt on Cnaeus's life fails, but a revolt inflames the camp. A mass of soldiers, weapons in hand, head toward the gap in the palisade that separates the officers' quarters from the troops' quarters.[10] Cnaeus materializes at the palisade entrance and challenges those who want to enter to pass over his body. The rioters change their minds and later reconcile with Strabo, except for 800, who desert.

In addition to Strabo's three legions, the Senate and the consuls can count on other legions: the two of Quintus Caecilius Metellus Pius, which are engaged in the siege of *Aesernia*, and the two of the proconsul Publius Servilius Vatia, who took over the defense of *Gallia Cisalpina* from the murdered Pompeius Rufus. They send a delegation to each of them to recommend to Metellus Pius that he leads most of his troops to Rome and lets the remainder continue the siege. Subsequently, Metellus Pius and one of his two legates, Appius Claudius Pulcher (the other is Mamercus Aemilius Lepidus Livianus[11]), lead a delegation to the Samnite Caius Papius Mutilus, the leader of the besieged city's defenders, to try and strike a deal. Pulcher is the same legate who had to cede command of his legion to Cinna during the siege of *Nuvla*.

Mutilus says he will sign a peace agreement if Rome naturalizes the Samnites en masse, allows them to keep all the booty they have accumulated in four years of war, returns to them all the spoils of war it has accumulated in the same period at the Samnites' expense, frees all its Samnite prisoners, and hands over all the Samnite deserters. Metellus Pius deems the conditions unacceptable, and negotiations collapse. Metellus Pius leaves for Rome with his legates and 15 cohorts, leaving five cohorts behind, led by Marcus Plautius Silvanus.

---

10   See Plut. *Pomp.* 3. The details of the account suggest Strabo's quarters were beyond the palisade, outside the camp, which was accessed by four entrances. However, it may be that inside the camp, the troops' quarters and the *praetorium* (the commander's headquarters) were separated by a palisade, which itself had a door to provide entry. Cnaeus Pompey apparently lay down on the threshold of this entrance.

11   Born Mamercus Livius Drusus, Livianus is the brother of Marcus Livius Drusus, the tribune of the plebs assassinated in 91 for proposing the extension of full Roman citizenship to the Italic *socii* and whose murder upset the precarious balance between Rome and the *socii*, quickly leading to the outbreak of the Social War. He married Cornelia, Sulla's daughter, after she was widowed by Quintus Pompeius Rufus, killed in a public riot in 88. After the death of his brother Marcus, he replaced him in the College of Pontiffs. He was a legionary legate in the Social War, serving under Metellus Pius, and it was he who killed Quintus Poppaedius Silo, the leader of the Marsi, in the assault on the walls of *Venusia*. Later, he tried unsuccessfully to be elected to the praetorship.

By the time Metellus Pius arrives in Rome, news has reached him that Mutilus has made a sortie, overwhelmed Plautius and his cohorts, and descended into the Campanian plain, where he has sacked and burned *Abella*, a town near *Nuvla* on the road between *Capua* and *Abellinum* (Avellino). However, these diehard Samnites are as interested in making peace as the Romans. Indeed, Mutilus suggests resuming peace talks and addresses his offer to Marius. The reason is intuitive. Rome is exhausted from the long siege. If it falls, any agreement reached with Metellus Pius would no longer be valid. Marius instructs the military tribune Caius Flavius Fimbria, serving in Sertorius's legion, to see negotiations through at any cost. Fimbria and Mutilus meet in the Gole della Melfa (between the Liri Valley and the Comino Valley in lower *Latium*) and come to an accord. Among other things, the agreement provides for the mass naturalization of the Samnites. Marius and Cinna will approve it.

Vatia responds promptly to the call to help the Senate and the consuls. He orders Caius Caelius, commander of the legion in *Placentia* (appointed by the consul Octavius), to set out for Rome immediately. He will depart from *Aquileia* with his own legion and join him in Rome. Caelius sets out on the *Via Aemilia*. In turn, Vatia heads for *Ariminum* (Rimini). Marius and Cinna order the military tribune Gratidianus to block Vatia's path. He leads numerous cohorts along the *Via Flaminia*, reaches *Fanum Fortunae* (Fano), and heads up the Adriatic coastline, passing through *Pisaurum* (Pesaro), where he intercepts Vatia and defeats him in battle. On hearing of Vatia's defeat, Caelius takes his legion back to *Placentia*. Ultimately, Rome will receive no military aid from *Gallia Cisalpina*.

In the meantime, Strabo has announced he is standing for the consulship, but shortly afterward, he falls ill and suffers for three days before breathing his last in a field hospital.[12] Thus does "cross-eyed" Pompeius, the butcher of Asculum, die.[13] During his funeral, the inhabitants of the Quirinal and Viminal districts, who are the hardest hit by the epidemic, take their revenge. The hot-headed crowd pounces on the bier, wrecks it, seizes the body, and drags it down the street on the end of a hook until the militia intervenes, snatching the body and hiding it.

---

12 The cause of Strabo's death is uncertain. According to App. *B. Civ.* I.312–313, it was disease. According to others (Gran Licin. 22.3 Fl; Oros. l. c.; Vell. Pat. II.21.4; Obseq. 56 a; Plut. *Pomp.* 1.2), it was a thunderbolt (Strabo was said to have been struck by lightning, together with many other nobles, while a storm raged).

13 In Latin, *strabo* means "squinty" or "cross-eyed."

Rome is exhausted by hunger and disease, the defenders are in disarray, no one has faith in the city's government anymore, and there is a constant stream of desertions. Crassus and his son abandon the Janiculum and return to the city, where the hunger is unbearable and there are even reports of cannibalism.

It is widely believed among the besieged that the battle for Rome has been lost, so anyone who has reason to fear the victors' revenge disappears. A delegation of civilians and soldiers goes to Metellus Pius to ask him to take over the leadership of the city's defense in Octavius's place. But Metellus Pius refuses, seeing no other solution than to negotiate a surrender. He sends the soldiers back to Octavius, but they desert. In turn, the legions of the late Pompeius Strabo refuse to follow to fight for a lost cause, so they retreat to the Alban Hills. Even Merula says that his office of suffect consul is incompatible with his role as *flamen dialis* and resigns, though he must have known this from the beginning when he accepted the position.

The Senate and Octavius ask to negotiate a surrender. Cinna agrees to receive a delegation of the besieged, formed by Metellus Pius, Lucius Julius Caesar, and his brother, Caius Julius Caesar Strabo Vopiscus (Caesar Strabo). But the attempt is short lived. When Octavius disdainfully states that he would never agree to surrender to a public enemy (Cinna), Metellus Pius attempts to make him understand that it's impossible not to negotiate with Cinna because the alternative would be unconditional surrender. In the end, Octavius authorizes Metellus Pius to have another conversation with Cinna.

On 5 September 87, Metellus Pius goes to the enemy camp for a second time, this time accompanied by Quintus Lutatius Catulus. This time, the talks end positively. The terms agreed can be summarized as follows:

- Cinna and all the other public enemies of 88, starting with Marius and his son, as well as all those exiled previously under the *lex Varia de maiestate*, will be recalled to their homeland, destigmatized, and reinstated in their positions; Cinna, in particular, will be reinstated as consul, Octavius's colleague once more;
- there will be no retaliation, revenge, reprisals, trials, convictions, or proscriptions against anyone who sided with Cinna during the civil war;
- the 10 newly established tribes will be abolished, and new citizens will be authorized to enroll in the 35 historical tribes;
- any slave who responded to Cinna's or Marius's calls to arms to fight under their banners, starting with the Bardiaei, and was therefore freed, thus becoming a freedman, will obtain full Roman citizenship;

- Sulla (who is fighting in the East) will be dismissed from the proconsulship and his command of the Mithridatic War, declared a public enemy, stripped of Roman citizenship, and have his assets confiscated, and anyone can kill him without fear of legal reprisals;
- Marius will be elected to the consulship for 86 and will replace Sulla in his military post;
- all the laws Sulla promoted and obtained approval for as consul will be repealed; the *lex Caecilia Didia*, which regulates the formulation of laws, will also be revoked; and
- the Sulpician laws, abrogated by Sulla, will be brought back into force.

The terms are shared and endorsed by the Senate and the consuls, then approved by the people gathered in assembly. Sulla is thus deposed and declared a public enemy; Cinna, Carbo, Magius, Milonius, and Vergilius are destigmatized; and Brutus and the other exiles are officially recalled to their homeland. Cinna is reinstated as consul, while Marius, waiting to be elected to the consulship, is appointed proconsul for *Gallia Cisalpina*.

Immediately afterward, the censors Lucius Marcius Philippus and Marcus Perperna start enrolling the new citizens, who number around 500,000, in the historical tribes. Metellus Pius and his 15 cohorts leave for Roman Africa, and Catulus also leaves the city. Pulcher, Lepidus Livianus, and Catulus remain in Rome, as does Octavius. The latter retires to the fortress on the Janiculum—which has remained abandoned and deserted since the departure of the *Crassi*—together with his 12 lictors and some other eminent citizens.

Cinna, dressed as a consul, preceded by his lictors and the bearers of the consular insignia and surrounded by an escort, passes under the high archway of *Porta Collina*, and flanked on both sides by the crowds, heads toward the Forum.

Marius, the Bardiaei, Sertorius and his legion, and the bulk of Cinna's army remain in their camps outside the city. Marius wants the pronouncement declaring him to be *hostis publicus* withdrawn to safeguard himself against the risk of Cinna agreeing with the Senate and Octavius that they should get rid of him. While the victors celebrate, the markets of Rome are restocked and open their doors once more. City life thus starts to resume its normal course.

In that atmosphere of apparently renewed serenity, a squad of cavalry, led by the military tribune Caius Martius Censorinus, enters the fortress of the Janiculum, and stops his horse in front of Octavius, who is surrounded by a small crowd. Censorinus dismounts, slowly draws his sword, and approaches the consul. Octavius remains seated, deaf to the crowd's urges to flee. He doesn't make a move other than to motion to his lictors not to intervene. Without saying a word, Censorinus grabs him by the hair and shoves him to his knees. Octavius doesn't resist. On the contrary, he offers his neck to his executioner. Shortly after, Marius will receive Octavius's head and orders it to be displayed on the Orators' Tribune.

It isn't clear who ordered Octavius's execution. The peace agreement said there would be no vendettas or reprisals. But it was Octavius who prompted the Senate to vote to declare Cinna a public enemy, and Cinna isn't a man of his word. One must wonder, however, whether Cinna is in control of the situation. Marius's position has a hidden implication that perhaps not even Cinna has noticed. After being aggregated as a *privatus* to Cinna's army, Marius became its de facto commander-in-chief. Thus, the strongman in the situation isn't Cinna but Marius. Cinna is, in fact, Marius's hostage.

Octavius's execution starts a chain of reprisals. One of the victims is Varius Hybrida Sucronensis,[14] targeted because of the *lex Varia de maiestate*, which he promoted and had passed, probably in 90, in accordance with the aristocracy's interests. In all probability, he is accused of forcibly enacting this law despite the imposition of a veto and of causing the Social War. He is killed in unknown circumstances while trying to save himself.

---

14   Cic. *Brut.* 305.

CHAPTER XII

Marius's Reign of Terror

By the time Marius enters the city, escorted by the Bardiaei and passing between crowds on both sides, the Senate has revoked the pronouncement declaring him a public enemy. Marius and Cinna immediately stand for the consulship for 86. Both will be elected. This will be Cinna's second consulship, having already held the office in 87. For Marius, on the other hand, it will be the seventh time. Thus, what a soothsayer predicted to Marius in North Africa at the end of the Jugurthine War comes to pass.

Marius celebrates his election in an unusual way: he accuses Sextus Lucilius—the man who, in 88, hired assassins to kill him and very nearly managed to do so—of high treason (against himself, as Lucilius thinks Marius is embodying the state), judges him to be guilty, and sentences him to death with all haste. The condemned is thrown off the Tarpeian Rock.

Marius then dismisses his personal army, except for the 5,000 Bardiaei and Sertorius's legion. On 1 January 86, he delivers a speech in the Forum, which is packed with people and guarded by the Bardiaei. He has just finished speaking and is receiving praise and congratulations from a swarm of flatterers when a gruesome incident occurs. Marius stiffens, slowly raises his right arm, then lowers it to point his finger at someone he has noticed in the crowd and curtly orders for him to be killed. The designated victim is an elderly senator who previously argued with Marius over trivial matters. The Bardiaei immediately kill the man and cut off his head amid cries of horror from the bystanders.

The senator's summary execution is a predetermined signal. It triggers multiple acts of violence and hostility against anyone who supported Sulla or accepted him as *dominus* of the situation in the days immediately following the capture of Rome (88). The plan about to be implemented consists of the willful and grave deprivation of the Sullans' rights, starting with their right to life, for reasons related to their political identity. Thus begins the violent persecution of Marius's political opponents; the notoriety of this persecution will last for a long time and will go down in history as his reign of terror.[1] Marius has been waiting for this moment ever since his enforced distancing from his homeland, when the spirit of revenge gave him strength and he foresaw the moment in which he could retaliate against those who had withdrawn his citizenship from him and cast him out, making him an outlaw.

First the Bardiaei bar the city gates, then they throw themselves on the trail of the Sullans like packs of ravenous dogs, intent on unleashing their ferocity and greed on their prey. Every street is quickly filled with men pursuing other men, driving them out of their hiding places, killing them, and, if they are senators, beheading them. Many of the designated victims seek refuge and protection in sacred areas, which have always been places of asylum, but they are dragged outside and slaughtered. Those who cling to altars in statues in terror, raising their hands to the heavens, invoking one of the gods, have their hands cut off. In the whirlwind of killings and bloodshed, those who lose their lives include Caius Atilius Serranus, Publius Lentulus, Caius Nemetorius, Marcus Pletorius, and Marcus Baebius.[2] The latter's body is pierced in the throat by a hook and dragged through the streets to the Forum, where a crowd tears it to pieces with their bare hands.

Fimbria was a military tribune during the most recent elections (in 87 for 86). Marius showed his trust in him when he sent him to ensure negotiations with Mutilus, leader of the Samnites, were concluded. Now Fimbria's mental imbalance and extreme malice solely for the purpose of causing harm and suffering to others are shown in several savage episodes. He has a haunted gaze and is highly agitated as he leads a group of cavalrymen around the *Palatium* district, catching Publius Licinius Crassus and his son Lucius by surprise in an alley near their home.[3] During the siege of Rome, the two attempted (unsuccessfully) to negotiate a compromise agreement with Marius and Cinna.

---

1   The main primary source for the Marian terror is Plut. *Mar.* A few details are provided in App. *B. Civ.* I.73. See also Gruen, *Roman Politics and Criminal Courts,* 231ff.; C. M. Bulst, "'Cinnanum Tempus: A Reassessment of the 'Dominatio Cinnae,'" *Historia* 13, no. 3 (1964): 313ff.; T. F. Carney, "A biography of Marius," *JRS* 54, no. 1–2 (1964): 65ff.; H. Bennett, *Cinna and his Times: A Critical and Interpretative Study of Roman History During the Period 87–84 B.C.*" (Menasha, WI: George Banta, 1923), 20ff.

2   App. *B. Civ.* I.72.

3   Publius Licinius Crassus, an incredibly rich man, was born from the marriage of Marcus Licinius Crassus Agelastus and Tertula. His paternal grandfather was Publius Licinius Crassus Dives Marcianus, consul and *pontifex maximus.* Crassus's own marriage to Venuleia, an Etruscan woman, produced three sons: Publius (who was killed during the Social War), Lucius, and Marcus (the future "banker of Rome").

Crassus realizes there is no way out and, feeling all is lost, rejects the prospect of dying under torture and decides to beat the executioner to his task. He quickly draws a dagger from the folds of his robe and fatally stabs his son before turning the weapon on himself, causing a mortal wound, and falling heavily on his son's body. Their bodies are beheaded.

The situation quickly spirals out of control. When the Bardiaei have killed all the Sullans they've managed to track down, they start targeting other citizens who aren't politically aligned but have been subjected to false accusations out of envy, revenge, or other unspeakable reasons. They raid houses in search of money, jewels, silverware, bronzes, weapons, clothes, and fine fabrics. They plunder the items of greatest value and spoil, damage, or destroy everything else. They disfigure funerary masks and damage altars to the Lares. They kill anyone who resists while they rape and torture, showing no respect or mercy for anyone. They exterminate entire families, even slaughtering their pets.[4] As they retreat, they set fire to everything. The acrid smoke of the fires taints the air. The inferno spreads from one house to another. Before long, entire neighborhoods are lost to the flames and end up as ashes. Predictably, the district targeted most frequently is the *Palatium*, where the majority of Rome's most distinguished individuals are concentrated.

Attempts are made to salvage what can be saved. The senator Mamercus Aemilius Lepidus Livianus manages to recover the valuables contained in the house of the Drusii and, at the request of Quintus Lutatius Catulus, with the help of some slaves supervised by the freedman Lucius Cornelius Chrysogonus,[5] Sulla's secretary, some items of value in Sulla's residence and a house belonging to Caecilia Dalmatica, Sulla's wife.[6] They are only just in time. Shortly afterward, the beautiful house that Sulla has recently occupied with his wife, her children Marcus and Aemilia, born from her previous marriage, and their daughter Cornelia is ransacked, set on fire, and, when it is no more than a blackened shell, demolished piece by piece.

In 87, Catulus is 63 years old and is closely tied to Mamercus, a much younger man, for reasons of friendship and political alliance. Unlike Mamercus,

---

4 App. *B. Civ.* I.73.

5 Chrysogonus was originally one of Sulla's slaves, brought to him by Caecilia Dalmatica, before he was freed and combined Sulla's name with his own, which in Greek means "golden birth." He is an ignoble, abject individual, a rotten lowlife, who deserves profound contempt. He will demonstrate this during the Sullan proscriptions, when he will amass an immense fortune and then flaunt it without restraint.

6 Not the house where Caecilia Dalmatica went to live after marrying Sulla but the one she inherited from her first husband, the *princeps senatus* Marcus Aemilius Scaurus.

who is preparing to flee, Catulus has decided to stay in the city, even though he knows he is at the top of the wanted list. Marius wants to take revenge on him not so much because he is an aristocrat, an *optimas*, and Sulla's son-in-law, but above all because he played a role in the events that led to the expulsion of Marius and 11 other *hostes publici* from the city. Some friends of Marius interceded on Catulus's behalf, but Marius replied with a snarl: "*moriatur*" ("he must die").[7] Mamercus is leaving Rome when Catulus hands him his *commentarius*, urging him to keep it safe and publish it in better times. Then Mamercus leaves the city clandestinely with his wife, their children, the pregnant Caecilia Dalmatica, and her children.

Shortly after his departure, Catulus commits suicide, convinced that this is the only way left for him to avoid an undignified death at the hands of his enemies. He locks himself in a room in his house, deliberately lets it fill with smoke, and inhales the fumes from a brazier he had lit for warmth. Before long, due to the lack of ventilation, the room becomes thick with carbon monoxide.[8]

Death at his own hand also awaits Lucius Cornelius Merula, *flamen dialis* and suffect consul (he replaced Cinna after he was dismissed from office and declared a public enemy), who resigned during the siege of Rome. Merula didn't take up the post because he aspired to the consulship but only agreed, at the request of the Senate and after much insistence, to hold onto the office previously occupied by Cinna. Therefore, he is innocent of the faults attributed to him by those who want him dead. Nonetheless, he is actively hunted. Like Catulus, Merula prefers to kill himself rather than die indecorously at the hands of his enemies. He goes to the temple of Jupiter Optimus Maximus and enters the cella containing the god's cult statue. Taking off the *apex* (headdress) of the *flamen dialis*, which mustn't be worn at the time of death, he kneels with his toes pointing backward, and, cursing Marius and his followers, cuts his belly open with a bone-handled knife.[9]

Families who have barricaded themselves in their own homes as a precaution learn of people whose bodies have been cut to pieces and scattered through the streets, of wanted people who have committed suicide out of fear, shame, or despair after seeing their wives or children violated, their possessions robbed or destroyed, and of people who have managed to escape death but have

---

7   Plut. *Mar.* 44.5.

8   Plut. *Mar.* 44.5.

9   For the Romans, the belly is where the soul is, and therefore the symbolic meaning of inflicting a deep wound in the stomach of such severity as to cause death is to bare one's soul, freeing it from guilt in all its purity.

lost everything (family, servants, property, money). They also hear of slaves who, to take revenge for their mistreatment at the hands of their masters, put the Bardiaei on their trail in the hope of collecting a bounty, obtaining their freedom, and committing violence in turn, and of other slaves who, after their masters were killed, seized their possessions, raped their families, had sex and defecated in the house's atrium, raided the pantry, and drank themselves into a stupor.

Still other slaves let their masters be discovered through naivety. A lower-class plebeian agrees to hide Marcus Antonius, the famous orator, in his house. Confused by the great honor of having such a distinguished individual as a guest, he sends a slave to get some wine from a nearby tavern. The slave asks the innkeeper for his most expensive wine. Intrigued, the landlord questions the slave and learns that his master has an important guest. In fact, he discovers who the guest is because the slave simply tells him. The innkeeper is a snake: as soon as the slave has gone, he runs to inform Marius. At the news, the latter sends the quaestor Publius Annius to bring him the orator's head. When he sees himself surrounded by the Bardiaei, Antonius begs to be allowed to live, winning over all those present with his eloquence. Everyone except Annius. He steps forward decisively, scolds his subordinates, and kills and beheads Antonius with his own hands. Marius is having dinner when Annius, triumphant, brings him the orator's head. He gets up from the table and kisses the killer on the forehead. The head will be displayed on the Orators' Tribune.[10]

Still, not all the news circulating in the city in that dark time is bad. There are reports that some slaves have saved their masters with clever tricks. The servants of a certain Cornutus, who had hidden their master in his house, hung one of the many dead bodies lying in the street by the neck, put a gold ring on his finger, and showed it to the Bardiaei before dressing it and giving him funerary rites in the usual way. The Bardiaei suspected nothing, and Cornutus was thus able to find refuge in Gaul.[11]

What happens in Rome in the first weeks of January 86 is a crescendo of horror and brutality, ceaselessly encouraged by Marius, eager to inflict as much material and psychological damage on his political opponents as possible to balance out the hurt and insults he has suffered. He is a madman whose spirit burns with hate and thirsts for more blood every day, sparing none of those who have fallen under suspicion for any reason.

---

10   On the death of Marcus Antonius Orator: Plut. *Mar.* 44.

11   The incident is narrated in App. *B. Civ.* I.73 and, with more details, in Plut. *Mar.* 43.6.

At that time, the senator Quintus Ancarius, a former praetor and a highly respected man, is killed by the Bardiaei solely because he hadn't been greeted by Marius after approaching him. From now on, anyone whose greeting isn't reciprocated by Marius will be cut down on the spot. Therefore, even Marius's friends become ridden with anxiety and tremble with fear whenever they approach him to greet him. Nor do all those on Marius's side approve of the atrocities that he has instigated or for which he is, at least, morally responsible. Sertorius, for one, refuses to participate in the massacre, and he and his legion remain camped on the *Campus Martius*.

Finally, on about 10 January 82, Marius is satisfied with the slaughter and orders the Bardiaei to stop; the carnage decreases in intensity, although without stopping entirely. It's time to take stock. The terror only lasted five days and nights, but to many, it seemed like an eternity. About 1,000 people have been killed in those few days, including at least 50 senators.[12] The city is littered with corpses, left outside, decomposing, for the birds and the dogs. (Marius has forbidden their removal, and no one dares to disobey as the reprisals would be terrible.[13]) In many places, the cobblestones of the streets and the walls of houses are covered with blood, with spatters everywhere. The stench of death is suffocating. Dozens of severed heads are placed on the rostrums that adorn the Orators' Tribune in the Forum as macabre trophies. One of these is Catulus.

The news of Catulus's death has led Marius to consider that his father-in-law's cousin has preceded him on the path to the Underworld, and a shadow darkens his face because, even for him, the showdown is no longer very distant. Now more than 70 years old, Marius still has a robust temperament but is in very poor health both physically and spiritually. He has had brushes with death in battle several times, leaving him with numerous scars, which he loves to show off as if they were medals of valor. In 89, he came close to death again after suffering a stroke. He recovered, but only slowly and with difficulty. A grimace has marked his face ever since. His body is run down and tired. He might be said to be a wreck, but if so, the ruins were once great and mighty.[14]

---

12 For an estimate of the victims of the Marian terror: R. Warner, *Il giovane Cesare* (Rome: Castelvecchi, 2012), 84. Bennett, *Cinna and His Times*, 20ff., tends to play down the extent of the massacre, defining it as compromised by anti-Marian prejudice in the historiographical tradition. In his view, after the initial atrocities, the killings decreased. Badian disputes Bennett's suggestion that some of the victims were former friends of Marius who betrayed him; see E. Badian, "Caepio and Norbanus," *Historia* 6, no. 3 (1957): 339, n. 177.

13 App. *B. Civ.* I.73.

14 R. Warner, *Il giovane Cesare* (Roma: Castelvecchi, 2012): 87.

Furthermore, Marius has been suffering from insomnia for some time and is assailed by nightmares and worries. This is partly why he drinks a lot of wine. In fact, he's rarely sober.

In a moment of lucidity, Marius thinks about the future of his wife's nephew Caius, the son of Caius Julius Caesar and Aurelia Cotta. It is then that Marius stops thinging about nothing other than the extermination of his enemies and instead concentrates on the foreseeable future of his nephew Caius, not so much because he is particularly interested in his fate but for another, unspeakable reason.

Before revealing what this reason is, we need to introduce Caius. To do so, we must take a step back to the legend of Rome's foundation because Caius belongs to one of the most prominent families of the Roman ruling class and descends from the mythical Aeneas.

The Caesares are a group of families of ancient nobility and great social prestige and belong to the *gens Julia*, claiming lineage from Iulus, Aeneas's son, the founder and first king of *Alba Longa*, the city from which the Iulii came to Rome. The narrative of this myth begins well before Rome was born in a place far from *Latium*: Troy.

Troy was a city-state of ancient tradition in northwestern Anatolia near Mount Ida. Its last king was Priam, son of Laomedon, husband of Arisbe and then Hecuba, and father of some 20 legitimate sons and daughters, including Hector (his first-born), Paris, Deiphobus, Helen, Polites, Polydorus, Troilus, Laodice, Creusa, Cassandra, and Polyxena, as well as about 50 others with various concubines. He was a just and temperate ruler, though perhaps a weak one.

The connection between the fall of Troy and the birth of Rome is Aeneas, son of Anchises and brother of Lyrus. Anchises, young and handsome, was one of Priam's cousins, both being descended from Dardanus, like Tros, who gave his name to the *Troad* (Turkey) and founded Troy. One day, Anchises was grazing sheep on the slopes of Mount Ida when he was seduced by Aphrodite, the Greek goddess of love (known as Venus to the Romans). The fruits of that union were Aeneas and Lyrus.

All of the above were alive when an Achaean-Mycenaean army took Troy after a siege and, amid immense slaughter, sacked and destroyed it. On the last night in the city, eerily illuminated by the light of the fires, Aeneas gathered around him a group of refugees, including his young son Iulus, or Ascanius, and the elderly Anchises, now in poor health. Creusa, daughter of Priam and Hecuba and wife of Aeneas, was missing. Aeneas went back to look for her, and she appeared to him as a ghost, prophesying that he would wander for a long time before reaching a distant land, where he would find a kingdom and remarry. For her, there was no need to worry: she wouldn't become a slave because, as a cult priestess, she had been taken up into the heavens by the goddess Cybele, the Great Mother of the Gods. Finally, Creusa pleaded with her husband to take care of her son and to preserve his affection for her.[15]

After a long sea voyage with many stops, Aeneas's group landed on the coast of *Latium* at the mouth of the Tiber. By then, Anchises had died and been buried in Erice (Sicily). Well-received by a local ruler named Latinus, Aeneas married his daughter, Lavinia. Later, he founded an *oppidum* and called it *Lavinium*. After Aeneas's death, Iulus became ruler of *Lavinium* but, after ruling for several years, abdicated in favor of Silvius, the posthumous son of Aeneas and Lavinia, and founded another *oppidum* in *Latium*, *Alba Longa*, becoming its first king.[16] Iulus's numerous successors are today called "the Alban kings." The 16th was called Numitor. His daughter, Rhea Silvia, was impregnated by Mars, the god of war, and gave birth to twins: Remus and Romulus. In 753, Remus was killed by his brother, who founded a city on the Palatine, *Roma Quadrata*.[17]

In 673, during the reign of Tullus Hostilius, Romulus's second successor, a sword duel between the champions of Rome (the *Horatii* triplets) and the champions of *Alba Longa* (the three *Curiatii* brothers), proposed by Caius Cluilius, king of *Alba Longa*, decided the fate of a conflict between the two cities, which had arisen following border disputes. The Horatii won, but Cluilius didn't see his men vanquished as he had died suddenly before the duel. The Albans elected a dictator as Cluilius's successor, Lucius Mettius Fufetius, a dishonest man who wouldn't accept defeat and betrayed the Roman army at the Battle of Fidenae.

Tullus Hostilius was an irascible, merciless man, even more so than Romulus. In revenge, he had Fufetius killed, and *Alba Longa* razed to the ground. Fufetius was stripped naked and whipped, then rent asunder (his hands and feet were tied to four chariots, and the horses then galloped in opposite directions).[18] The

---

15 Aeneas's encounter with Creusa's ghost is narrated in *Aen.* 2.771–794.

16 *Alba Longa* is a site of uncertain location. It is probably in the Alban Hills, a group of hills in the countryside around Rome, on the slopes of *Monte Albano* (Monte Cavo), perhaps Castel Gandolfo.

17 The Roman historian Titus Livius reported the legend of the foundation of Rome in the first book of his *Ab Urbe Condita*. Dionysius of Halicarnassus, Plutarch and Varro drew inspiration from it.

18 For Mettius Fufetius: Dionysius of Halicarnassus, *Roman Antiquities*, III, 5, 3; Florus, *Epitoma*

city was systematically demolished, except for its sacred places. The homeless were allowed to retain ownership of the land and were welcomed in Rome, settling on the Celian Hill, which was then called the Mons Querquetulanus ("mountain of oaks") and was a wooded, uncultivated place. The heads of its aristocratic families were admitted to the Senate. One of the family clans who arrived in Rome from *Alba Longa* in 673 were the Iulii, who have various *cognomina: Caesar, Iulus, Mento, and Libo.*

At this point, we need to turn our attention to the Caesares. The Caesares have often held the office of *rex sacrorum.* But it would be mistaken to believe that the Caesares are a respected and revered family just because they have often held this office. Various Caesares have been high-ranking magistrates. Worth mentioning among them are four consuls (who held the office in 267, 157, 102, and 91) and three praetors (208, 123, 92?).

The Caesar who was consul in 102 was also born Sextus Julius Caesar but was adopted by the patrician Quintus Lutatius Catulus and, in compliance with the rules of Roman onomastics, changed his name to Quintus Lutatius Catulus. In early 86, we recall, in the days of Marius's reign of terror, Catulus preferred to kill himself rather than fall into the hands of Marius's henchmen and suffer an undignified death at their hands.

Caius Julius Caesar—son of Caius Julius Caesar and Marcia Regia—was praetor in 92(?) and proconsul of Asia in 91(?). Caius has a brother named Sextus, more commonly known as Lucius, and three sisters: Julia Major, who married Caius Marius; Julia, who married Marcus Atius Balbus; and Julia Minor, Sulla's first wife.

Some personal details regarding Caius Julius Caesar should also be mentioned here. After marrying Aurelia Cotta, the couple had two daughters and a son. In 86, their son, Caius, is 14–15 years old (he was born in 101 or 100). He has lively black eyes and a light complexion. He is quite thin but tall for his age, well-proportioned, and in excellent health. He resembles his cousin Caius, Marius's son, who is a few years his elder. As for the young Caesar, it is said that he is precocious in everything and has something unique about him. He has developed an athletic physique, actively participating in gymnastics, sports (swordplay, horse riding, swimming), and wrestling and combat training on the *Campus Martius*. He wears his hair short and neatly styled, with a lock hanging low over his forehead.

Like all young scions of the great Roman families, he was educated at home by one or more tutors of good standing (one of his grammarians was

de Tito Livio bellorum omnium annorum DCC, I, 3.3–5 and 3.6–7; Titus Livy, *Ab Urbe Condita*, I, 28 and 29.

Marcus Antonius Gnipho). Among other things, he studied Latin language and literature, Greek language and literature, philosophy, oratory, and rhetoric and became perfectly bilingual and skilled in the art of public speaking. He is drawn to politics and war and has become familiar with various literary works that formed the basis of his military education, including: *De re militari* by Marcus Porcius Cato the Elder; *On the Cavalry Commander* by Xenophon; the memoirs of Lucius Cornelius Sulla; *De consulatu et de rebus gestis suis* by Quintus Lutatius Catulus; a didactic work for military commanders by Lucius Papirius Paetus, a Latin author who was a contemporary of Caesar and a friend of the orator Marcus Tullius Cicero; and various works by Hellenistic authors, including treatises on siege techniques and the conquest of cities and fortifications.

The young Caesar not only loves reading but also writing. He has composed some orations, a tragedy, *Oedipus*, the short poem *Laudes Herculis*, and a collection of maxims.[19] He is a lover of antiquity, antiques, and works of art. He is interested in philosophy and religion, especially traditional Roman religion. His idol is Alexander III of Macedon (356–323), architect of an epic military campaign and founder of a universal empire that encompassed the eastern Balkans, western and central Asia up to the Indus River, and Egypt.

Caesar possesses a quick, perceptive intelligence, psychological and judicial maturity, willpower, and a quickness of mind that many of his peers do not. This can all be seen in how he speaks, evaluates, considers, and chooses. He is keen to project himself as marked by *dignitas* and a moderate lifestyle that reflects both his aristocratic standing and his instinctive propensity for stoicism. Caesar is aware that military commands and important operational assignments are the means and opportunities by which, if well carried out, and with the help of the goddess Fortuna, he will secure a place in history. Nevertheless, he doesn't aspire to command because he knows that it would be difficult for him to obtain it, given that his family isn't so much a family of military commanders as one of priests. Therefore, he focuses more attention on his literary career instead.[20]

---

19 Caesar's early works haven't survived, and only their titles are known. However, at some point after 28—when the great bilingual library was established on the Palatine—Octavian forbade the chief librarian, Pompeius Macer, from circulating them (Suet. *Iul.* 56). This probably wasn't because they weren't masterpieces but for political and moral reasons. L. Canfora, "Cesare scrittore," in *Giulio Cesare. L'uomo, le imprese, il mito. Catalogo della mostra* (*Roma, 23 ottobre 2008–3 maggio 2009*), ed. G. Gentili (Milan: Silvana Editore, 2008), 33.

20 R. Warner, *Il giovane Cesare* (Roma: Castelvecchi, 2012): 89–90.

The young Caesar is talented, educated, cultured, and good-looking and presents himself admirably. He is capable of sharp observations, his thoughts can be very profound, and he can appreciate people, facts, and situations appropriately. In addition, he is very self-aware and entirely free from inhibitions; for example, he has no reverential fear of the older generation, not even his uncle Marius, for whom, however, he has the greatest respect.

Anyone who meets the young Caesar for the first time gains the impression that he's destined for a brilliant future. In fact, despite what we've just said about Caesar's aspiration to become a writer, his future will be stellar: he will be *pontifex maximus*, consul five times, proconsul and conqueror of Gaul, and dictator for life. After he dies in 44, aged 56/57, the victim of a senatorial conspiracy, he will go down in history as one of Rome's most famous sons.

Caesar (Aurelia Cotta's husband) is exceptionally proud of his son and thinks he is now old enough to marry, so he arranges to marry him to the daughter of a rich *eques*, a girl called Cossutia. The marriage is planned in the usual way for family-arranged matrimonies. Instead of the betrothed, their families make the decisions based on evaluations of mutual convenience, reciprocally assuming a solemn and religious commitment. Cossutia will bring Caius a substantial matrimonial dowry, while Caius will confer on her the status of a noblewoman (the *Caesares* are a senatorial and consular family and, therefore, aristocratic). The engagement will take place in the presence of family friends as witnesses after the consultation of the auguries. The rite will involve the exchange of rings and the signing of a promise of marriage, which specifies the nature and amount of the dowry and the timeframe within which the marriage must take place (if this term elapses, the betrothed will be free to marry someone else).[21]

Unfortunately, a tragic, unexpected event knocks these well-laid plans off course. In the autumn of 87, Caesar (the father) dies of a heart attack. His is the first of the deaths that have recently deprived the Caesares of their pillars, preceding the deaths of Catulus and the brothers Lucius Julius Caesar (consul in 90) and Caius Julius Caesar Strabo Vopiscus,[22] all prominent, esteemed, and respected individuals, both for the glory of the *gens Julia* reflected in them, for the magistracies they occupied, for the military commands they had successfully held, and for their talent at maintaining and extending their clientele. As we have seen, Catulus committed suicide. Caesar Strabo Vopiscus was an orator

---

21 P. Grimal, *La civiltà dell'antica Roma* (Rome: Newton Compton, 2012), 91.

22 Lucius Julius Caesar and Caesar Strabo Vopiscus were sons of Lucius Julius Caesar and Popillia and cousins of Caius Julius Caesar (Aurelia Cotta's husband), Julia Major (Marius's wife), and Sextus Julius Caesar.

famed for his intelligence and sense of humor and was the author of at least three Greek tragedies. At just 44 years old, he and his brother Lucius were killed on the streets by Caius Flavius Fimbria. Drunk with fury and bloodlust, Fimbria, after beheading Publius Licinius Crassus and his son Lucius, went in search of the Caesares brothers. He finds them at home, kills them, beheads them, and then drags the headless body of Strabo Vopiscus to the tomb of Quintus Varius Hybrida Sucronensis, an old friend of Fimbria. There, he tears the corpse apart, breaking its limps and gouging out its eyes, before the brothers' heads are displayed on the Orators' Tribune.[23]

Marius is fond of his nephew Caius because he was by his side during his long convalescence after his stroke. Caius did so, on the one hand, because he is driven by a sense of generosity and, on the other, because his mother never tired of repeating that *pietas* was one of his duties. For the Romans, one of the meanings of *pietas* is having respect for one's family and the intrinsic and hierarchical values it represents.

The good relations between Marius and Caius, however, aren't based purely on affection. Marius respects his nephew both because he possesses many admirable qualities and, as paradoxical as this may seem, he fears him. To understand this aspect of Marius's psychology, we need to return to Martha's prophecy. The Syrian fortune teller predicted that Marius would become consul seven times, but she also foresaw that he wouldn't be Rome's greatest son because this status was reserved for his nephew.

The probability that the second part of the omen will also come true keeps Marius on edge. He doesn't want to risk being overshadowed, so he seeks to make this impossible. The simplest and most direct way of preventing the prophecy from coming true would be to physically put an end to Caius. However, Marius prefers a different path, more difficult to follow but equally effective. He will deprive his nephew of the possibility of becoming consul (thereby making him unable to snatch his primacy from him). How? By making him Merula's successor as *flamen dialis*, the priest of Jupiter. The *flamen dialis* is a lifetime assignment of considerable importance, but it also requires great sacrifices, such as not being able to leave Rome. This makes it incompatible with the consulship, which cannot abide by such restrictions.

The appointment of the highest-ranking priests is regulated by the *lex Domitia de sacerdotiis*, promoted and brought to approval in 104 by the tribune of the plebs Cnaeus Domitius Ahenobarbus, who later became *pontifex*

---

23 Plin. 30.12.

maximus (103), consul (96), and censor (92).[24] This stipulates that the 12 minor *flamines*, *pontifices*, augurs, and the *decemviri sacrorum* (a college of ten members, five patricians and five plebeians, who exercise religious functions) are elected by an *ad hoc* popular assembly, formed by 17 of the 35 historical tribes, drawn by lot; in the case of the *pontifices*, augurs, and *decemviri*, the assembly must choose from among the candidates designated by the relevant colleges. Meanwhile, the three major *flamines*—those established by Numa Pompilius, Romulus's direct successor on the throne of Rome, one of which is the priest of Jupiter—are "elected" by the *pontifex maximus*.[25]

Marius, if he wants to ensure Caesar becomes the new *flamen dialis*, will therefore have to convince Quintus Mucius Scaevola, *pontifex maximus* since 89, that Caesar is the best possible candidate because he possesses the essential requirements prescribed: he is the legitimate male son of patrician parents who married with the archaic Roman wedding rite (*confarreatio*), creating an indissoluble bond. Furthermore, he is a member of a family that has held religious offices since time immemorial, possesses great resources of intellect and spirit, and shows considerable potential.

Marius's plan will come to fruition after his death, fulfilled by Cinna, Marius's successor as the leader of the *populares*. Although Caesar will be nominated for the office while Cinna is consul (87–84), he will never assume the role—Metellus Pius will deprive him of it for having resisted Sulla's order to repudiate his wife Cornelia, Cinna's daughter.[26]

---

24 On the *lex Domitia de sacerdotiis*: J. Rupke, *Religion in Republican Rome: Rationalization and Ritual Change* (University of Pennsylvania Press, 2012); J. Scheid, *Religion et piété à Rome* (Paris: Albin Michel, 2001).

25 G. Dumezil, *La religione arcaica romana. Miti, leggende, realtà*, 3rd ed. (Milan: Rizzoli, 2011), 497. This hypothesis clashes with the fact that the major *flamines* were hierarchically superordinate to the *pontifex maximus*. It's possible that they were encompassed within the applicational scope of the *lex Domitia de sacerdotiis*. If this were the case, after this law entered into force, they would have been nominated by the *pontifex maximus* or the College of Pontiffs and elected by a tribal assembly.

26 Caesar married Cornelia after his plans to marry Cossutia were disrupted by Caesar's father's heart attack.

CHAPTER XIII

The Death of Marius

As Marius is telling some friends that the days when he could safely rely on Fortuna have passed (Marius is widely considered very lucky, a view he shares),[1] he starts to feel unwell. Physicians rush to him and, after a quick consultation, agree on a diagnosis: pleurisy.[2] The illustrious invalid will spend the next few days in bed with a high fever, feeling increasingly ill.

One of the few visitors admitted to Marius's bedside in those days is Posidonius of Rhodes (135–50), a Greek philosopher, scholar, and researcher. A repository of encyclopedic and universal knowledge, he is the author of geographic, ethnographic, historical, and scientific works on the observation and measurement of celestial bodies and the influence of the moon on the tides. In January 86, he found himself in Rome for the first time on a diplomatic mission alongside other eminent Rhodians, one of whom was Apollonius Molon, an orator, founder of the so-called Rhodian school of oratory, and rhetorician. During his stay, he is impressed by the *optimates* and critical of the *equites*, condemns slavery,[3] and becomes friends with two promising

---

1 Plut. *Mar*. 43.4. In *The Jugurthine War*, Sallust puts particular emphasis on *Fortuna*, understood both as good fortune and as opportunity, and highlights how Marius believed in divine providence. For an analysis of these concepts, with reference to their use in relation to Marius both by Sallust and by an older tradition, see C. D. Gilbert, "Marius and Fortuna," *Classical Quarterly* 23 (1973): 104–107.

2 Plut. *Mar*. 45.4: "as Poseidonius the philosopher relates," Marius suffered from a pleurisy. On Posidonius: H. Strasburger, "Poseidonios on Problems of the Roman-Empire," *JRS* 55, no. 1–2 (1965); I. G. Kidd, "Posidonius as Philosopher-Historian," in *Philosophia togata*, vol. I: *Essays on Philosophy and Roman Society*, eds. M. Griffin & J. Barnes (Oxford: Oxford University Press, 1989).

3 This refers to Posidonius's account of the Second Servile War, summarized by Diodorus Siculus. In those tragic events, Posidonius found confirmation of his belief that violence wouldn't eradicate violence, and that the liberation of the oppressed couldn't come from the oppressed themselves. See L. Canfora, *La rivolta degli schiavi in Sicilia* (Palermo: Sellerio, 1983).

young men: Marcus Tullius Cicero, the future consul, great judicial orator, and philosopher, and Cnaeus Pompeius, the future Pompey the Great, warlord and statesman. In the past, he has been in contact with Scipio Aemilianus and the Greek historian Polybius.[4]

Marius continues to have a high fever. When this exceeds 40°C, he falls into a state of mental confusion. His illness will be fatal. In the last hours of his life, he is in pain and breathing with difficulty. Then, exhausted, he loses consciousness. Early in the morning of 17 January 86, he dies.

For a quarter of a century, Marius was, for better or worse, a major part of Roman public life. He was consul seven times (an unmatched achievement), won the Jugurthine War and the Cimbrian War, celebrated a triumph twice, and was acclaimed as the savior of the fatherland and the third founder of Rome by the Senate and the Roman people, after which he also fought in the Social War and against Sulla. He reformed the military service and the army. He was politically compromised by the adventurism of Saturninus, whom he had supported. Later, his personal conflict with Sulla degenerated into a factional struggle and then civil war. He was a man devoted to war, with an impetuous and strong-willed character and unbridled ambition, who was behind actions both for and against Rome.

Male Romans exercise such authority over women that they can disavow them simply by telling them to collect their things and leave, especially if they are very important people. Marius was no exception. He dismissed his first wife, Grania, in a flash to be able to marry Julia Major, thereby giving him a chance of becoming consul that, otherwise, he would never have had. Upon resolving his marriage situation, he gave Grania ownership of a luxurious seaside villa in Capo Miseno in Campania, near the villa of Cornelia Africana, mother of the Gracchi.

Julia was at Marius's side for 22 years, a loyal and devoted companion, even though she sometimes criticized his decisions and that the Terror he unleashed claimed some of her relatives. She decides that her husband will receive a private funeral in the presence of only family and close friends. The body will be cremated according to Roman tradition. The remains of the burned bones and the ashes will be enclosed in a pyx, which will be buried in his tomb. Marius's "eternal home" will be a mausoleum near the Aniene, a major tributary of the Tiber, joining it near the *Pons Salarius*, the bridge over which

---

4   A Greek historian and writer who fought in the Achaean War on the side of the League. Later, he was tutor to Scipio Aemilianus and then his advisor and friend, as well as a scholar of the *res publica* and its admirer. He died a few years before 120 after falling from a horse.

the Salaria road crosses the Tiber, outside the city limits, 3km north of the *Porta Collina*.[5] (The reason for the quotation marks will become clear later.)

During Marius's funeral, a serious episode occurs when Fimbria makes an attempt on the life of Quintus Mucius Scaevola Pontifex, cousin of Scaevola Augur and famous jurist and jurisconsult in his turn, but only manages to wound him. The incident can be explained by the fact that the Marian faction, after Scaevola created the necessary conditions sufficient to declare Marius a public enemy, considers him an enemy and has kept him in their sights.

After Marius's burial, Fimbria—yes, him again—proposes that a ritual human sacrifice be performed on Marius's tomb, and everyone approves, even though the practice of human sacrifices is illegal in Late Republican Rome. The nominated victim is Scaevola Augur. Jurist, jurisconsult, and esteemed teacher of rhetoric, Scaevola Augur, despite being very old (in 86, he is 73), his interest in the law and public life remains undiminished. He established and, despite his age, oversees an apprenticeship in law, mentoring the likes of Cicero, Titus Pomponius Atticus, Pompey Magnus, and Varro Lucullus.

Scaevola Augur is sentenced to death by decapitation with the sword, and the execution is a gruesome affair. The executioner fails to kill him, only succeeding in mortally wounding him. As Scaevola dies, Fimbria, the madman, berates him for not having facilitated the executioner's work!

It's difficult to explain why Marius's friends targeted a doddery, white-haired man in poor health, a man honest to the bone and of whom no one had a bad word to say. Not even Marius ever dared to touch him, not to mention that Scaevola Augur was the only senator to defend Marius before Sulla in 88. Perhaps he was the victim of transversal revenge (he was harmed instead of his cousin Scaevola Pontifex), or perhaps he was the target of those who wanted to prevent the pacification of the warring factions, something Scaevola Augur was working toward. In any case, his grisly execution effectively concludes the Marian Terror.

In the past, Cinna felt he had to please Marius, but his disgust for the Bardiaei becomes evident following Marius's death. In view of their felonies and crimes, as well as their internal squabbling, he thinks the time has come to restore a state of normality, partly also to prevent his fellow citizens from identifying him with their wrongdoings. Therefore, he decides to rid himself of them and uses Sertorius's legion for this purpose. Accordingly, Sertorius sends a centurion to the Bardiaei to announce they will be paid early the next day, in the *Villa Publica*, and encourage them to get there with all haste.

---

5   Cic. *Leg.* II.56. Marius's tomb has been (erroneously?) identified with a mausoleum datable to the I century on the *Via Salaria*, close to the *Pons Salarius*.

The Villa Publica is in part of the *Campus Martius* that also encompasses a fenced-off area reserved for holding votes for the renewal of the magistracies called an *ovilis* (in the future, it will be renovated and called a *septa*), the *Circus Flaminius* (a rectangular area of a few hundred meters in length used for horse and chariot races and for holding meetings of the *comitia centuriata* and *comitia tributa*), and the Temple of Bellona, the Roman goddess of war, who symbolizes the warrior's ferocity, the fervor that makes them capable of carrying out massacres and destroying cities. Built in 435, it was renovated and enlarged in 194 and again in 98, when a two-storey colonnaded portico was added to its façade.[6] It contains a large courtyard and a small temple dedicated to the goddess Flora, or the nymphs, and is adorned with paintings and statues. Parts are also given over to the registry office, the military district, and a guesthouse.

The next day, the dim light of the early morning illuminates an expanse of bodies lying on the ground in the internal courtyard of the Villa Publica. Thousands of men are deeply asleep amid luggage and food leftovers as three auxiliary cohorts arrive under Sertorius's command. The soldiers quickly surround the courtyard, trying not to make a sound. Then, at an agreed signal, they shoot arrows and throw javelins at the Bardiaei. Many of those targeted die immediately. The survivors wake up with a start and try to get to their feet, still half-asleep and confused, but are overwhelmed by the charging *equites*. When the massacre is over, 4,000 men are dead.

Meanwhile, away from Rome, the Mithridatic War has been continuing, with fighting in Asia Minor, islands in the southern Aegean Sea, and mainland Greece. The Pontic army, led by Archelaus, has invaded Greece. During the winter of 88/87, he attacked Delos, which had rebelled against Athens, killed 20,000 people there, many of whom were Italics, and sacked the city, taking the treasure from the Sanctuary of Apollo away with him.

Sulla's arrival in Greece turns the tide of the war.[7] While besieging Athens and the Piraeus, Sulla is joined by his wife, Caecilia Metella Dalmatica, and his daughter Cornelia (born from his first marriage with Julia Minor), who were fleeing from Rome. The siege of Athens begins in the summer of 87

---

6   E. Makin, "The Triumphal Route, with Particular Reference to the Flavian Triumph," *JRS* 11 (1921): 27. On the Villa Publica: S. Agache, "Villa Publica," in *Lexicon Topographicum Urbis Romae*, vol. 5, ed. E. M. Steinby (Rome: Quasar, 1999), 202–205; M. Gwyn Morgan, "Villa Publica and Magna Mater. Two Notes on Manubial Building at the Close of the Second Century B.C.," *Klio* 55 (1973): 231–245.

7   On the military campaigns in Greece during the First Mithridatic War: App. *Mithr.* 28–45, 49–50; Plut. *Sulla* 11–21.

amid assaults, sorties, bombardments, fires, and massacres, while, inside the city, people are dying of hunger and are reduced to eating anything, even human flesh.

On 1 March 86, a handful of legionaries, aided by the darkness of the night, scale the city walls, break the defenders' resistance, and open the gates wide to the rest of the army. Aristion, the Athenian philosopher who ruled as a tyrant over his fellow citizens after placing himself in the service of Mithridates VI, runs with his closest allies to barricade himself in the fortified citadel of the Acropolis after ordering everything that the enemy could use to build siege engines to be destroyed.[8] The legionaries besiege the Acropolis and succeed in cutting off the citadel's water supply. This obliges the besieged to give up.

Sulla appropriates the city's treasury (200 pounds of gold and 600 pounds of silver) by way of reparations and, as he's furious with the Athenians because of the insults they'd shouted at him and his wife during the siege, orders all the prisoners who had rebelled against Roman laws to be killed, though the lives of those who had never been subject to those laws are spared. Aristion is executed on the altar of Athena Polyades on the Acropolis, east of the ancient Temple of Athena.[9] Sulla allows himself to derogate further from the rule he had set by freeing some of those who had taken up arms against Rome, but he nevertheless deprived them and their children of Roman citizenship.

At this point, a group of senior officials and representatives of Athens' pro-Roman faction attempts to intercede for the city's safety. They beg Sulla not to let Athens end up like *Corinthus*, which had been razed to its foundations by Lucius Mummius Achaicus in 146. Sulla has always thought highly of Greek civilization and admired the centuries-old glory of Athens, even if that city was now a faint memory full of shadows. So, reluctantly, he pardons the city. But he abandons it to plunder to give his soldiers a chance to enrich themselves and to warn the other Greek cities not to follow Athens's lead. The looting is systematic. Part of the city is devastated despite Sulla's orders for damage limitation. In those hours, numerous Athenians commit suicide. The exact scale of the horrific tragedy that unfolded after the Roman conquest of Athens remains unknown, but it's estimated that one in two Athenians died.[10]

In the meantime, the theatre of war has moved further north. The vice-governor of Macedonia, Quintus Bruttius Sura, has engaged Metrophanes's fleet in battle with a small naval force, then raids the port of Skiathos and, after

---

8   App. *Mithr.* 38.

9   Paus. I.20.7. Plut. *Sulla* 23.2 reports that Aristion was killed on Sulla's orders.

10 App. *Mithr.* 38.

receiving reinforcements from Macedonia, attacks Archelaus in Boeotia (Battle of Chaeronea). While Bruttius Sura is engaged against the Pontics in Boeotia, the Maedi, a Thracian tribe, raids Macedonia, sacking the sanctuaries at *Dodona* and Delphi. In 85, Sulla defeats the Mithridatic armies, after which he marches against the Eneti, Dardani, Sinti, and Maedi, and devastates their villages as he waits for a response to the proposals for peace he has sent to Mithridates VI through Archelaus. These offers will be accepted in their entirety.

The Treaty of Dardanus (summer 85) ends the war. For Rome, it isn't a great victory. In practice, it has only restored the *status quo ante*, recovering the province of Asia, with Nicomedes IV and Ariobarzanes I returning to being king of *Bithynia* and king of *Cappadocia*, respectively.[11] But, given the starting point, these are notable concessions. The war broke out when Rome was already engaged in the Social War (a titanic struggle that threatened its very existence). To help their compatriots in Asia, who risked extermination, and to recover the territories stolen from them, the Romans had to draw a line under the conflict with the Italics as quickly as possible and, to do so, gave the enemy effectively what they asked for. Rome subsequently embarked on a new military undertaking even though the state was struggling with a severe economic and financial crisis. To finance this new war, the public treasury had to put a plot of land up for sale that had never been touched by real estate speculators before, due to the presence of a religious boundary. Going to war against Mithridates VI had been a real risk, involving fighting far from Italy against a very wealthy and powerful enemy. But Sulla's determination, valor, courage, and luck made the difference.

After the Treaty of Dardanus, Sulla must stay in Greece to flush out the last pockets of Pontic resistance and reaffirm Rome's supremacy over its overseas friends and allies. At this time, he accumulates considerable spoils of war and stockpiles books and works of art to give as gifts to his friends in Italy. In fact, since the Macedonian Wars, the Roman nobility has been collecting works by Greek artisans to decorate public buildings (as a manifestation of their own power and wealth) as well as private gardens and spaces. Sulla reserved Aristotle's priceless personal library for himself,[12] together with numerous

---

11 Flor. I.40.11–12. On the treaty's other clauses: App. *Mith*. 55, Plut. *Sulla* 22.5, 24.3.

12 Aristotle (384–322), one of the most universal, innovative, prolific, and influential minds of all time, was a student of Plato, who had founded a school of philosophy in Athens called the Academy. In turn, Aristotle founded the Lyceum, a peripatetic school of philosophy in Athens. His library was a personal collection of books and documents. After Plato's death, Aristotle took it with him on his travels. First, it went to *Scepsis* (Kurşunlutepe, Turkey), a settlement in the *Troad* in northwest Asia Minor, where the philosophers Choriscus and Erastus,

statues, paintings, and precious objects. However, not all the ships loaded with works of art that set sail from the ports of Attica for Rome reach their destination—some sink in the stormy seas, together with their crew and precious cargo.[13]

In Italy, preparations are being made ahead of Sulla's return. Everyone knows the civil war will resume as soon as Sulla sets foot on the peninsula again. In 85, Cinna, who has been consul since 87 and whose consular colleague is currently Cnaeus Papirius Carbo, decides to take the initiative and chooses Greece as the theatre of war. Italy has suffered a lot from the Social War, and he wants to spare it further suffering. In 84, an army musters in the port of *Ankon* (Ancona), ready to embark for Greece. But a military revolt breaks out after a first contingent, which left from the same port, is shipwrecked in a storm at sea, and Cinna falls victim to it. Carbo, re-elected to the consulship for 84, abandons the plan to fight in Greece and prepares to face Sulla on his return.

Shortly afterward, the political leadership of the *populares* passes from the deceased Cinna to Marius the Younger. This surprises everyone because Marius's son hadn't been considered among the likely contenders. The top-rated candidate had been Sertorius, already number two in the post-Marian regime, who was perceptive, aware, and always ready to support Cinna, repeatedly proving his friendship, understanding, and tact. This leaves Sertorius disappointed.

Sertorius and Marius the Younger haven't been fond of each other since the former criticized Marius for the excesses of the Terror. Proof of this comes when, immediately after assuming his new role, Marius the Younger urges Sertorius to take possession of his office of provincial governor of *Hispania Ulterior*, which he has held for some time and managed through a representative until now. The meaning behind the move is clear: Marius the Younger wants to distance himself from Sertorius and relegate him to the farthest province of the *imperium*. Sertorius obeys and sets off by land for *Carthago Nova*, accompanied by three cohorts, totaling around 1,800 men, plus non-combatants.

---

themselves followers of Plato, were attempting to implement their teacher's political ideals. Then it went to *Assos*, a coastal city in the *Troad*, where Aristotle, Choriscus, and Erastus founded a philosophical school with the help of the local tyrant, Hermias of *Atarneus*. On Aristotle's death, his library was inherited by Neleus, son of Choriscus. In turn, Neleus left the library as a legacy to his sons, who hid it in a cellar to prevent the Ptolomies of Alexandria and the Attalids of *Pergamon* from obtaining it (unfortunately, some of the books were damaged due to the humidity and worms). Finally, one of Neleus's descendants recovered it and gave it to a pseudo-academic from Athens, Apellicon of *Teos*, who brought it back to Athens.

13 On the shipwreck of Mahdia: A. J. Parker, *Ancient Shipwrecks of the Mediterranean and the Roman Provinces* (Oxford: Tempus Reparatum, 1992).

CHAPTER XIV

Sulla's Proscriptions

Sulla returns to Italy in 83 at the head of five legions, totaling 40,000 men. The consuls Lucius Cornelius Scipio Asiaticus and Caius Norbanus, meanwhile, have 15 generals and 45 legions (450 cohorts) at their disposal, totaling 100,000 men, if not 200,000.[1] Civil war breaks out when Sulla—who landed at *Brundisium* (Brindisi) and received reinforcements from Pompeius, Metellus Pius, and Crassus—arrives in Campania, taking the *Via Appia*.

In an early clash, Sulla overwhelms Norbanus in the foothills of Mount Tifata, near *Capua* (Santa Maria Capua Vetere). Norbanus flees to *Gallia Cisalpina*.

Next, Sulla puts Scipio Asiaticus to flight at *Teanum Sicidinum*. Scipio initiates peace talks, then changes his mind and breaks off negotiations. His troops, who have already begun fraternizing with the enemy, don't accept his decision, leading 40 cohorts to defect to Sulla's side. Scipio is taken prisoner but is later released. Subsequently, he tries to recruit new troops, but to no avail.

Sulla spends the winter of 83/82 in *Capua*. Then he gets back on his way and besieges several settlements in Campania, including *Nuvla* (which will resist until 80), and clashes with Marius the Younger at *Sacriportus* (lower *Latium*, about 40km south of Rome). Marius loses 28,000 men, whether killed (20,000), injured, or taken prisoner, and retreats to nearby *Praeneste*, where he is besieged by one of Sulla's legates, Quintus Lucretius Afella.

In addition to the defenders and the civilian population in *Praeneste*, also barricaded with Marius the Younger are numerous senators who opted to follow Marius's son into battle, plus various family members, friends, and clients. In obvious difficulty, Marius the Younger decides to order a massacre of the moderate senators who chose to remain in Rome. He obtains the help

---

1   Plut. *Sulla* 27.3; Vell. Pat. 2.24; T. Mommsen, *Storia di Roma antica*, vol. II, part I (Firenze: Sansoni, 1960), 385.

of the Lucanians and Samnites, historically Rome's enemies, against which Rome fought not only during the Samnite Wars (IV century) but also in the early phase of the Social War just a few years previously to carry out his order. The Samnites and the Lucanians are led by Pontius Telesinus and Marcus Lamponius, respectively.

The final battle takes place at the gates of Rome, right in front of the *Porta Collina*, which opens in the most vulnerable section of the Servian Walls. With the battle imminent, Telesinus rides past the front ranks to incite his soldiers to fight, shouting that "the Romans won't live to see another day" and that "the wolves who have tortured Italy's freedom won't be eradicated until the wood in which they live has been cut down." The "mother of all battles" between Rome and the Samnites is about to begin, a final showdown between two different and forever antagonistic civilizations. Furthermore, he wants to remind the troops about the ethnic contrast that has characterized various moments in their shared history.[2]

The Battle of the *Porta Collina* lasts a full day, all night, and part of the next day (1–2 November 82), resulting in the death of a vast number of combatants and the capture of 6,000 (or 8,000) Samnites and Lucanians. Among the fallen are the Marian leaders Caius Carrinas, Caius Martius Censorinus, and Lucius Iunius Brutus Damasippus, as well as Telesinus and Lamponius.[3] Telesinus is found mortally wounded, lying among the bodies of the dead and dying littered on the battlefield. Yet on his face isn't the expression of a dying man but that of a victor.[4]

On 3 November, hostilities cease around Rome but continue in *Praeneste* (Palestrina). Sulla decamps to *Antemnae* (Monte Antenne), just north of Rome, and orders the severed heads of Carrinas, Censorinus, Damasippus, Lamponius, and Telesinus to be delivered to Afella so that he can show them to those still holed up in *Praeneste*. The macabre demonstration demoralizes the besieged more than the hardships and deprivations they have already suffered. Before long, the besieged surrender unconditionally and leave the city moaning and crying, except for Marius the Younger and Telesinus's younger brother, who, accompanied by a slave, instead enter an underground tunnel with the hope of bypassing the enemy lines. But when they realize that all the exits are blocked and that they are trapped, Marius the Younger and Telesinus's brother cross

---

2   Vell. Pat. 2.27.1–2; Strab. 5.4.11.

3   For an account of the battle: Vell. Pat. 2.27. On the number of enemies captured and then executed: Plut. *Sulla* 30 (6,000) and App. *B. Civ.* 1.93 (8,000).

4   Santangelo, *Roma repubblicana*, 203–210, esp. 209.

swords, seeking death. The duel takes place in the flickering light of torches. Marius gets the better of his opponent before being killed by his slave, who then takes his own life.[5] But some tell this story differently. According to them, Marius the Younger tried to leave *Praeneste* by taking some underground tunnels which, built with great skill, led out to different parts of the countryside. But after emerging into the open air, he was killed by men stationed at the exit. Other versions say that Marius committed suicide or that he and Telesinus's brother each threw themselves on the other's sword.[6]

Sulla leaves *Praeneste* to be plundered, both to strip it of all wealth and ornaments and devastate what cannot be carried as well as to wreak havoc and destruction and terrorize the victims. Before long, the whole city is enveloped in thick black smoke from which only the tongues of the flames emerge. An immense fire lights up the night with sinister brilliance.

The prisoners are divided into three groups: Romans (senators and their relatives, friends, and clients), Samnites and Lucanians, and Praenestines. Sulla orders the 3,000 Samnites and Lucanians to be taken to Rome, exposed to public ridicule, and locked up and kept under watch in the Villa Publica. Then he summarily tries every Roman and Praenestine capable of bearing a weapon, judges them guilty, and sentences them to death. Among those about to die is a man with whom Sulla previously stayed as a guest. Sulla recognizes him and wants to let him live, but the man doesn't want to be indebted to someone who waged war on his homeland and voluntarily offers himself to the executioner.[7] In total, 12,000 people are executed in a single day. After their tortuous wait, some are killed with a gladius down through their collarbone, while others are pushed from a clifftop. Finally, a deadly silence envelops the site of the massacre.

Meanwhile, the bodies of Marius the Younger, Telesinus's brother, and the slave have been found. Marius the Younger is decapitated, and the severed head is delivered to Sulla, who first mocks it and then has it displayed to the public on the Orators' Tribune in the Roman Forum so that it can be recognized by his fellow citizens and serve as a warning to the defeated faction.

Later in November 82, Sulla summons what remains of the Senate, decimated after the execution of its Marian members. As the meeting cannot

---

5   Liv. *Per.* 88. Strabo (V.3.11) writes that "in addition to its natural strength, subterranean passages have been bored through [*Praeneste*] from all sides as far as the plains—some for water-supply, others for secret exits (it was in one of these that Marius was put to death when he was being besieged)." An ancient underground aqueduct still exists in Palestrina.

6   Vell. Pat. 2.27.

7   Plut., *Sulla* 32. Appian and other ancient authors agree.

be held in the *Curia*, the official seat of the Senate, because Sulla is proconsul and in command of an army and therefore cannot enter the city, it takes place in the Temple of Bellona on the *Campus Martius*, adjacent to the Villa Publica. In an imperious tone, Sulla demands that all the measures adopted against him during Cinna's consulship are revoked and that the Treaty of Dardanus and all the formal acts that he put in place first as consul and later as proconsul in Italy, Asia Minor, and Greece are ratified.

While Sulla demands the authorization to evaluate arbitrarily who among the persecutors should be acquitted and who should be punished to make the state safe,[8] the sounds of moans and screams come from the systematic killing of Lucanian and Samnite prisoners of war underway in the nearby Villa Publica.[9] The simultaneity is not a coincidence. Sulla evidently wants to intimidate the Senate to get what he wants. The senators, however, don't bat an eyelid. Many of them fought against the Lucanians and Samnites during the Social War and killed prisoners themselves to take revenge on them for the losses, suffering, and distress caused by the fighting, so their current suffering is far from bothersome.[10] In any case, as an aside to his speech, Sulla notes that it isn't worth worrying about the horrific soundtrack that accompanies his words since it's only a massacre of criminals.[11]

The Senate partially complies. It annuls all the measures adopted against Sulla under Cinna's regime and endorses the Treaty of Dardanus and all of Sulla's other acts with retroactive effect. However, it doesn't want to be an accomplice to the carnage but rather to let Sulla take personal responsibility for the bloodbath that even now is being carried out,[12] nor does it want to delegate the purge to Sulla and let his vengeance get out of hand by allowing him free rein to unleash all the hatred and resentment that has been building up in him for months.[13]

In the following days, Sulla heeds the exhortation of Caecilius Metellus and, it is said, the son of Quintus Lutatius Catulus, to purge only select political

---

8   See F. Hinard, *Silla* (Rome: Salerno Editrice, 1990), 172.

9   Sen. *Clem.* I.12.

10 Cf. F. Hinard, *Silla* (Rome: Salerno Editrice, 1990), 171. Hinard's thesis goes against the orthodoxy among the ancient authors, according to whom the massacre of the Samnites was deliberately staged by Sulla in conjunction with the meeting of the Senate so as to terrorize them into compliance.

11 Liv. *Per.* 88.2.; Val. Max. 9.2.1; Plut. *Sulla* 30.2–3; Flor. 2.9.2–4; Dio F109.5.

12 Cic. *Rosc. Am.* 153. For a reconstruction of the events of early November 82, see Plut. *Sulla* 31ff.; App. *B. Civ.*, 1.95.

13 For this interpretation: Hinard, *Silla*, 172.

opponents to avoid an indiscriminate massacre dictated only by personal grudges. He also accepts the suggestion of the centurion Lucius Fufidius to introduce a judicial procedure called proscriptions[14] that enables the proscriber to obtain compensation for the damage suffered, instill terror in their surviving enemies, and procure the necessary finances to satisfy their post-war needs.

At the end of November 82, Sulla delivers a speech from the Orators' Tribune in which he affirms that the return to normality cannot take place before punishment has been exacted on all those Roman citizens who, in the exercise of a military command, took up arms against the consuls after the truce of 83 (the one declared ahead of the negotiations with Scipio Asiaticus that were then abandoned) and allied themselves with the Lucanians and Samnites, mainly for having handed the latter—on a silver platter—the opportunity to attempt to fulfill their long-standing goal of destroying Rome. He says that the goddess Enyo appeared to him in a dream and authorized him to punish her enemies (Enyo is the Cappadocian equivalent of the Greek goddess Nemesis and the Roman goddess Bellona and is associated with the concept of just revenge). Finally, Sulla assures them that no reprisals will be taken against the civilian population and specifies that those guilty of common crimes will be sentenced separately.

The meaning of his announcement becomes crystal clear shortly afterward when Sulla issues an edict with which he regulates the proscriptions and has it posted not only in Rome but also in other Italian cities between 3–6 November 82. In it, it is stated that those responsible for the horrors committed in Rome in recent years, including because of the perpetrators' betrayal, and which are listed in an annex to the provision, can be killed by anyone who wants to; their goods will be confiscated and sold at auction, and their slaves will be freed (though their male children won't be able to pursue a career as a magistrate since they have just been deprived of the wealth necessary to finance an electoral campaign). Furthermore, anyone who helps a proscribed person in any way will share his fate; anyone who delivers the severed head of someone listed as proscribed to Sulla will receive a reward of two talents of silver, equivalent to 48,000 sesterces; anyone who provides the authorities

---

14 Oros. V.21.1. On the Sullan proscriptions: F. Hinard, *Les proscriptions de la Rome républicaine,* "Coll. de l'Ecole Française de Rome," 83 (Rome: Scuola Tipografica s. Pio X, 1985); F. Hinard, *La male mort. Exécutions et statut du corps au moment de la premiére proscription. Du Chatiment dans la cité* (Rome: Publications de l'École Française de Rome, 1984), 295–311; F. Hinard, *La Proscription de 82 et les Italiens. Les Bourgeoises municipales italiennes.* Actes du Colloque International du CNRS n. 609, Naples, 1983, (Naples: Publications du Centre Jean Bérard, Editions du CNRS, 1983), 325–331.

with information useful for the capture of a proscribed person will receive a lower reward (if a slave, they will be freed); and whoever has been rewarded will acquire a right of first refusal on the confiscated assets of his victims when these are auctioned off, on the proviso that he leaves something for the heirs of the deceased to live off.[15]

The annex to the proscription edict is a list of 80 names, which includes the names of those proscribed who have already died due to the edict's stipulations concerning their heirs. At the top of the list is Cinna, followed by Marius the Younger and Sertorius. Also proscribed are Lucius Cornelius Cinna, Cinna's son; the homonymous son of Lucius Cornelius Scipio Asiaticus, consul in 83; the *equites* Cnaeus Titinius and Caius Maecenas; Caius Marcius Censorinus, the killer of the consul Cnaeus Octavius, and his sons Caius and Lucius; Lucius Hirtuleius, Sertorius's deputy; and Lucius Insteius.

Sertorius, we recall, when Marius the Younger succeeded Cinna as the leader of the *populares*, assumed his office of governor of the Iberian provinces. When Sulla returned to Italy, Sertorius was attacked by the Sullan Caius Annius Luscus, an aristocrat of plebeian extraction, who had a force of 20,000 men. Sertorius found it impossible to resist and fled the field, seeking passage to *Mauretania*, the northwestern corner of Africa, with 3,000 men. But they couldn't disembark there because they were caught in a storm that took them off course and sent them crashing onto the Atlantic coast of southwestern *Hispania*. Sertorius briefly considered the idea of retiring to the *Insulae Fortunatae* (probably the Canary Islands) but abandoned it before finally landing in *Mauretania*, putting himself and his men at the service of some local warring chieftains. He would garner considerable success, become lord of Tangiers, then agree to lead the cause of the Lusitanians fighting against Rome and return to *Hispania*. At the head of an army that also included Hirtuleius and Insteius, he also assumed control of both *Hispania Ulterior* and *Hispania Citerior*, acting against the governor of the latter, Caius Valerius Flaccus, who had not recognized his authority. He then sent a part of his army to fortify

---

15 Sulla's edicts concerning the proscription haven't been preserved, but their content can be deduced from the edict relating to the later proscriptions carried out by the triumvirs Octavian, Mark Antony, and Marcus Aemilius Lepidus against their Pompeian opponents in 43 (see App. *B. Civ.*). Evidence for the rewards for killing the proscribed comes from the Heraclean Tablets (*Tab. Her.* 122). Unfortunately, we know only 75 of the total of 520 names. F. Hinard, *Les proscriptions de la Rome républicaine*, "Coll. de l'Ecole Française de Rome" 83 (Rome: Scuola Tipografica s. Pio X, 1985), 128–133. On the descendants of the proscribed: F. Hinard, "Sur les 'liberi proscriptorum'. Approches prosopographique et juridique d'un probléme politique," in *Mélanges Guarino, Napoli, 1889–1907* (1984); V. Vedaldi-Iasbez, "I figli dei proscritti sillani," *Labeo* 27 (1981): 163–213.

the passes through the Pyrenees. Sertorius later governed both provinces, endearing himself to both the Roman residents and the natives, the Hispani. To integrate the different components of the population, he established an interethnic senate and a school to train the children of Hispanic leaders.

Among the others proscribed are Cnaeus Papirius Carbo, consul in 85, 84, and 82; the consuls of 83, Lucius Cornelius Scipio Asiaticus and Caius Norbanus; the praetors of 83, Marcus Junius Brutus and Caius Burrienus; and the praetors of 82, Lucius Junius Brutus Damasippus, Marcus Perperna Veiento, Marcus Marius Gratidianus, Caius Carrinas, and Lucius Marcius Censorinus. The list continues with Marcus Iunius Brutus, tribune of the plebs in 83; and the poet and grammarian Quintus Valerius Soranus, tribune in 82. The latter was added to the list not just based on his Marian allegiance but also for sacrilege: he had revealed the secret name *amor* in one of his works, which is used to refer to Rome in the *evocatio*, thus giving Rome's enemies the opportunity to use it against the Romans.

Thus begins an orgy of blood that will make that of the Marian Terror pale in size, duration, and brutality. Those who are proscribed become the prey in a ruthless manhunt. Those who fall into the hands of the "bounty hunters" are led to the *Campus Martius*, where they are stripped naked, tied with their hands behind their backs, flogged with a rod, and executed by decapitation with an axe or by having their throats cut before Sulla, who presides over the torture and killing with one corner of his toga lifted over his head as a sign of mourning. The severed heads are then displayed on the Orators' Tribune in the Forum, placed or hung on the rostrums, or on or around the *Lacus Servilius*, a fountain found near the Tribune.[16] They will be left there until they have decomposed to the point of being unrecognizable. The headless bodies are mutilated further before being dragged with a hook through the entire city up to the *Pons Aemilius*, where they arrive in the form of a bloody, dusty pulp and are thrown into the Tiber, repeating the cycle of unbridled violence in Rome.

On 5 and 6 November, Sulla follows his first edict with two provisions of similar content, each of which has a list of 220 names of senators and *equites* attached. The total number of proscribed thus rises to 520.

The proscriptions are a celebration of the triumph not only of cruelty but also of abomination and profiteering. For many lower-class plebeians, they are the opportunity to take revenge on the rich, having them proscribed and

---

16 On the exhibition of severed heads at the lacus Servilius: Cic. *Rosc. Am.* 89; Sen. *De Prov.* III.7. Firm. *Mat. astron.* I.7.34.

obtaining their wealth. Sons denounce their fathers to cash in on a reward.[17] Anyone who wants a house, a villa, or even just a piece of furniture or an item of clothing works to have its owner added to the list of proscribed.[18] Nevertheless, there's no shortage of cases of generosity, impelled beyond concerns for personal safety. Some help a proscribed person who is neither a family member nor a relative. Nor is Rome the only city caught by the vortex of violence during the proscriptions.

The Sullan proscriptions will continue to have repercussions even after it has officially ended. In 80, the besieged city of *Nuvla* surrenders to the Sullans after a decade of resistance. Sulla grants them their lives on the proviso that they hand over any proscribed individuals in the city to him; when they emerge from the walls, a unit of cavalry slaughters them.

The effects of the proscriptions also have implications on the territories of the cities that gave refuge and protection to the proscribed in the form of land confiscation. This price was paid by all the major Etruscan cities, as well as some in lower *Latium* and Campania. Similarly, *Nuvla* was punished by being transformed into a military colony and its fertile lands being portioned out to Sulla's war veterans. A few years later (73), it was ravaged during Spartacus's revolt.

A further incident that deserves to be remembered here relates to *Norba*, the birthplace of the consul Norbanus, in the Monti Lepini mountains in *Latium*. Situated in an elevated position, it is an impregnable fortress, surrounded by polygonal, cyclopean walls, reinforced by massive square plan towers. *Norba* sided with Marius during the civil war, but it wouldn't accept defeat and resisted the Sullans. After a siege, it falls, following a betrayal, into the hands of Marcus Aemilius Lepidus. Upon his entry into the city, many citizens commit suicide en masse. Some hang themselves, others kill each other, and still others stab each other in the stomach. Others burn alive in their homes, which they set on fire themselves. The flames spread rapidly from district to district, fanned by a very strong wind. The entire city ends up melting amid the inferno to the extent that the victors cannot plunder any loot.

The activity of hunting the proscribed yields lavish rewards. The centurion Lucius Luscius delivers three heads of proscribed men to the public treasury

---

17 F. Hinard, *Prosopographie* II (1985), nn. 138 and 155, cites the cases of Caius Toranius, a former praetor, who was denounced by his son before being arrested and sentenced, and the praetor Lucius Villius Annalis, denounced by his son, who was running for office and will be rewarded for his betrayal by being elected to the aedileship. It seems, however, that these incidents took place during later proscriptions under Caesar and Octavian.

18 Sall. *Cat.* 51.33–34.

commissioner and collects a reward of 144,000 sesterces. He will invest this sum and, in 20 years' time, between interest and dividends, this will have increased to 10 million sesterces. Another man who gets rich by collecting bounties of proscribed men is the patrician Lucius Sergius Catilina, who deserves further attention as he will play a significant part in public life in Rome in the coming years.[19]

In 82, Catiline is 26/24 years old (he was born at the latest in 108 or 106). He was born in Rome from the marriage of Lucius Sergius Silus and Belliena. He has a sister, Sergia, and a younger brother, Quintus. His family, the Silii, is part of the *gens* Sergia, which claims descent from Sergestus, one of the groups of Trojan refugees led by Aeneas (he is mentioned as taking part in the boat race during Anchises's funeral games in Sicily).[20] They, like the *gens* Julia, are originally from *Alba Longa* and arrived in Rome as refugees in 673. One of the rural tribes—the Sergia—took their name from them.

The *Sergii* have often filled prominent positions in government. They have obtained the consulship many times, most recently in 380. The *Silii*, meanwhile, occupied positions of power particularly at the start of the II century and later. However, Lucius Sergius Silus, Catiline's father, wasn't a magistrate; he was poor (by the standards of the Roman aristocracy) and died without leaving any inheritance. Catiline, therefore, before becoming rich through hunting down the proscribed, was a fallen, penniless nobleman. He married Gratidia, a niece of Caius Marius, who died after giving him a son.

Catiline is tall with a lean, athletic physique, all muscles and sinew. He has dark eyes and a pale complexion. He wears his hair short, as is customary among Roman nobles. He is an individual strong in mind as well as body. He has stood out on several occasions for his exceptional resistance to hunger, cold, and lack of sleep and demonstrated valor, courage, and contempt for danger. Catiline is also bold, audacious, even reckless. Furthermore, he is versatile and flexible, insincere, and invidious, greedy for everything: riches, emotions, experiences. He is attracted by people of consequence, and he longs for it, desperate to be seen. He is at ease in any social environment, from high society to the lowest slums, and manages to command attention no matter what. He mostly has sex with women but also with the handsome young men who accompany him and from whom he chooses his lovers.

---

19 The primary sources for Lucius Sergius Catilina are Dio XXXVII; Cic. *Cat.*; Cic. *Cael.*; Cic. *Mur.*; Cic. *Sulla*; Sall.; App. *B. Civ.* II; Asc. 82ff.; Plut. *Caes. 7*, Cic. 10–22, Cic. *Sulla 32.* Sall. *Cat.*; Suet. *Iul.* 9, 14.

20 *Aen.* 5.121–122, 202–209, 270, 272.

In 89, aged around 19, he was military tribune under the command of Cnaeus Pompeius Strabo.[21] In those circumstances, he met Cnaeus Pompeius, later *magnus*, and Marcus Tullius Cicero, the future great judicial orator, writer, and consul of 63. He then followed Sulla to the East, following the example of other brilliant young officers: Cnaeus Cornelius Dolabella, Caius Antonius Hybrida, and Lucius Licinius Lucullus. He returned to Rome with Sulla in 84, and in 82, he distinguished himself at the Battle of the *Porta Collina*.

During the proscriptions, he commands a cavalry unit (a squadron of Gallic *auxilia*) and searches those proscribed everywhere, driven purely by the desire for profit. He kills with ferocity, including his brother Quintus, and he was responsible for the execution of his brother-in-law Quintus Caecilius. He killed the former before the news that he had been proscribed had even got out.[22] Caecilius, an *eques* and businessman, wasn't killed for political reasons but because his wife had asked her brother, Catiline, to help her get rid of him, paying him an advance on the agreed fee. Catiline paid Lucius Cornelius Chrysogonus, Sulla's secretary, to insert Caecilius into the proscription lists.[23] In the future (in the 60s), he will even kill the son he had with Gratidia so as not to obstruct his second marriage to Aurelia Orestilla, a beautiful, rich, and spirited woman with whom Catiline is deeply in love, although this is purely hearsay.

Another of Catiline's victims is Marcus Antonius Gratidianus, the adopted son of Marius's younger brother and the brother of Gratidia, Catiline's first wife. Gratidianus was tribune in 87, urban praetor in 86, and praetor again in 85. In the latter capacity, he proposed and obtained approval for a plebiscite to remove suberate coins from circulation, whose true purchasing power was at the heart of ongoing discussions. Gratidianus's monetary reform, since it safeguarded the value of coins, was in everyone's favor and won its promoter general approval.

But not all of Gratidianus's fellow citizens are pleased with his political activity, such as those penalized by the partial cancellation of debts ordered by the same law that introduced Gratidianus's monetary reform, which only

---

21 F. Hinard, "Solidarités familiales et ruptures à l'epoque des guerres civiles et de la proscription," in *Parenté et strategies familiales dans l'Antiquité romaine. Actes de la table ronde des 2–4 octobre 1986 (Paris, Maison des sciences de l'homme)* (Publications de l'Ecole française de Rome 129) (Rome: Ecole Française de Rome, 1990), 561, n. 40 ("En particulier Catilina s'était trouvé, en 89, dans le consilium de Pompeius Strabo"), citing N. Criniti, *L'epigrafe di Asculum di Gn. Pompeo Strabone* (Milan: Vita e pensiero, 1970), 160–162.

22 Plut. *Sulla* 32.2.

23 Whether Catiline carried out Caecilius's death sentence himself is unknown.

favored the debtors while harming the creditors. They now want to take revenge for their losses and see the proscriptions as a legal means for doing so at the urging of Quintus Lutatius Catulus Capitolinus, who hates Gratidianus for another, more personal reason: Catulus Capitolinus is the son of Quintus Lutatius Catulus, consul in 102, one of the victims of the Marian Terror.

In the days of the persecution of the Sullans, he not only lost his father but also had to leave Rome. Later, he joined Sulla and returned with him to Rome from the East. Catulus considers Gratidianus morally responsible for his father's death and has been waiting for six years to take revenge.[24]

It therefore happens that Gratidianus is proscribed not so much, or not only, because of his links with Marius's family but primarily because he is disliked by his fellow citizens, one of whom is Catulus Capitolinus. He asks Catiline to inflict an exemplary punishment on Gratidianus to which a political undertone could be attached, and Catiline sets out to hunt down the wanted man. Gratidianus is hiding in a sheepfold, lying under the belly of a sheep, but Catiline finds him, strips him, chains him, puts a rope around his neck, and drags him through the city streets, whipping him and exposing him to public ridicule. The citizens strike Gratidianus with sticks and rods, spit on him, and throw excrement at him amid laughter and uproar.

Catiline drags Gratidianus to the tomb of Catulus on the Janiculum. He ties him to a post, and, with the help of several other men, who are no less unsavory characters than him, breaks his arms and legs, his pelvis, and his spine, cuts off his hands and ears, tears out his tongue, and gouges out his eyes before grabbing his head by the hair with his left hand and slashing his throat with a knife. Finally, he beheads him.

Another of the proscribed men witnesses the horrific spectacle—Marcus Plaetorius, a compassionate, merciful man. He faints from shock and collapses. Catiline cuts off his hands, breaks his arms, gouges out his eyes, and beheads him,[25] perhaps not just because he has been proscribed but also to punish him for his humanity.[26]

Catiline then retraces his steps back across the *Pons Sublicius*, carrying Gratidianus's head under one arm, and places it at Sulla's feet while he is presiding over a meeting of the Senate in the Temple of Bellona on the Campus

---

24 On vengeance in Roman society: N. Tamassia, "La vendetta nell'antica società romana," *Atti del reale Istituto Veneto* 79 (1919): 1–37.

25 See Hinard, *Silla*, 182. On Plaetorius: Val. Max. IX.9.2.1*.

26 See Hinard, *Silla*, 182.

Martius. After that, he washes his blood-stained hands in the fountain of the nearby Temple of Apollo.

Catiline's notoriety is only just beginning. He will reach the peak of his criminal career in the late 60s when he plots a conspiracy to kill the consuls, sow terror, and seize power, although he fails in the attempt. He will fall in battle in 62 in the Apennines near Pistoia, together with many of his accomplices. He will go down in history as a controversial character. Some will consider him a villain and a political conspirator, others as the first revolutionary in the history of Rome.

Sulla's death

While the proscription is in progress, Sulla, according to the mandate he received upon his appointment to the dictatorship, reforms the State and its laws, ensuring that critical legislative interventions are promoted and brought to approval in a variety of areas: the composition and powers of the Senate, the formation of laws (jurisdiction and procedure), the judicial system, criminal legislation, and the administration of justice. However, in the long run, the Sullan regime reveals itself as largely corrupt and based on arbitrary, often violent authority, in contrast with normal political and civil life. The despotic exercise of authority reduces not only the freedom and personality of individuals but also the room for maneuver for great families.

After holding the office of dictator for two years, the nobles who have supported Sulla from the beginning—particularly Pompeius and the Metelli—begin to feel a growing dissatisfaction with him due to his excesses and his lackeys. Even the *equites* and the lower-class plebeians agree that Sulla is a tyrant and that the magistrates, officials, and businessmen who surround him take advantage of his benevolence to pursue very concrete personal interests, overriding the rights of others and acting against the general interest of the state.

The trial of Sextus Roscius, accused of parricide and defended by a young judicial orator, Marcus Tullius Cicero, is the occasion on which the nobles make Sulla understand that the time has come to step aside and return power to its natural custodians: the great families, chief among which are the Metelli. The dictator, however, is distracted by other interests and concerns, which prevail over considerations of the risks underlying the discontent that surrounds him. Among other things, the deterioration of his relations with Pompeius worries him. An "incident" occurs on 12–13 March 79 after Pompeius told Sulla that he is the rising star of Roman politics and that Sulla represents the past. It presents comical aspects (many spectators can barely refrain from laughing) but is really a political provocation intended to signify, in an indirect and allusive way, that Pompey has now become a character who requires more space than is normally attributed to a victorious commander. During the celebration of Pompeius's triumph, which he arrogantly claimed, overcoming Sulla's reluctance, while also giving himself the honorific name of *magnus*, Pompeius appears on a chariot pulled by elephants instead of the usual horses, and the beasts are so large that they cannot pass under the arch of the triumphal gate.[27]

In July 79, Sulla supports the election to the consulship for 78 of Quintus Lutatius Catulus Capitolinus, one of his most loyal supporters and the most prominent exponent of the *optimates* and expects Pompey to do the same. However, Pompey chooses to support another candidate: Marcus Aemilius Lepidus, a former comrade in arms. Sulla has a very low opinion of Lepidus and has warned Pompey against him. But Pompey is of a different mind about Lepidus, or—more probably—he intends to pit Lepidus against Sulla. The outcome of the elections demonstrates that Pompey's decision had as much influence on the electorate as Sulla's, as both Catulus Capitolinus and Lepidus are elected. The episode marks the definitive breakdown of relations between Sulla and Pompey. From now on, each will take his own path. But unlike Pompey's, the road that remains for Sulla to travel is no longer very long.

In 79, Sulla consecrates a tenth of his wealth to Hercules and puts on sumptuous banquets for the people. During the feasts, his wife, Metella Dalmatica, becomes seriously ill and dies within a few days. Shortly afterward, Sulla is struck by a second tragic loss when his son Lucius dies at just 17 from an illness. Having challenged death fearlessly on the battlefield so many times, Sulla now becomes discouraged. What depresses him above all is the loss of his much-beloved son. Sulla withdraws into himself and, after a period of profound distress, decides on a change in his life. In a public speech, he announces his resignation from the dictatorship and the consulship. It's a sensational *coup de théâtre*, in line with his passion for the theater.

Soon afterward, Sulla leaves Rome, although he will return from time to time to participate in Senate meetings. He retires to a villa in the countryside near *Cumae* (Cuma) in Campania, where he will live for the rest of his life, protected by his war veterans. He will spend his time writing his memoirs, hunting, and living a decadent lifestyle, though his excesses aren't good for his health (Sulla suffers from an intestinal ailment).[28]

---

27   E. Badian, "The Date of Pompey's First Triumph," *Hermes* 83 (1955): 107–118. Grimal, however, gives the date as 17 March 79. P. Grimal, *Cicerone* (Milan: Garzanti, 2011), 66.

28   For Sulla's disease: Plut. *Sulla* 36, 1–4. See also J. Carcopino, *Silla* (Milan: Bompiani, 2000), 156.

On 18 February 78, Sulla dreams of his son, Lucius. Standing beside him, the boy begs Sulla not to worry about anything anymore because he will soon join his family and live with them again.[29] When he wakes up, Sulla connects that dream to a prophecy given to him in *Melitene* in Mesopotamia (Malatya, Turkey) (where he was leading a military expedition) by a Chaldean soothsayer—according to which he will die at the height of his fame and fortune—and understands that his end is near.

Accordingly, he prepares to leave the scene in the best possible way. Sulla puts his affairs in order, finishes writing his memoirs, instructs his secretary regarding their publication, and makes his will. In declaring his last wishes, he orders that his tomb be a mound (for the Romans, this type of tomb is an instrument of self-celebration and serves to connect the deceased directly to the burials of the heroes of myth and legend) and orders that it be written on his tomb that "No one has done more good to friends and harm to enemies than he." Finally, he waits for death with a calm soul, though without neglecting his daily activities.[30]

Sulla is in Rome, where he has gone to take care of one last piece of business, when he feels ill after an outburst of anger provoked by the *duumvir* Granius, who was delaying the payment of a tax for the reconstruction of the Temple of Jupiter Optimus Maximus. Beside himself with fury, Sulla orders his bodyguards to kill Granius on the spot and is immediately obeyed. Feeling unwell, Sulla is helped to bed, but his condition worsens overnight.

In the morning, Sulla takes his last breath. It is 3 March 78.

Before his death, Silla ordered that his body should be cremated to prevent his remains from being mistreated (those of Marius were dug up from his "eternal home" and thrown into the Aniene). Before the cremation, however, one of his fingers is removed, which will be buried together with his ashes to respect the tradition of the *Cornelii*, who, unique among the Roman family clans, bury their dead rather than cremate them.[31]

---

29 Plut. *Sulla*, 37; E. Cavaignac, "Un songe de Sylla," *Aesculape* 31 (1959): 180ff.

30 For Sulla's last hours: App. *B. Civ.*, 105.

31 For Sulla's funeral: App. *B. Civ.*, I, 105–6.

Conclusions

The great turning point in the internal politics of the *res publica* came in 133 with a new regulation concerning the use of *ager publicus* for economic valorization. The intervention was proposed and brought to approval by a tribune of plebs of aristocratic extraction, Tiberius Sempronius Gracchus.

It aimed, firstly, to defuse the ticking social bomb of Rome's demographic congestion, fueled by the continuous immigration of many small agricultural entrepreneurs and workers who had lost their businesses and jobs due to the unsustainable competition from wealthy landowners. The latter were able to produce more and at lower costs thanks to the massive use of large numbers of slaves, mostly prisoners of war. Hordes of people, expelled from the countryside, moved to the city with their families in the hope of finding a job, but were disappointed and ended up merely swelling the mass of society's outcasts, who lived by their wits. The phenomenon knew no limits and worried the authorities as it presaged public order disturbances and threats to security.

The reform's strategic objective was the revitalization of small peasant property ownership. To achieve this, it set a maximum limit on the square meters of state land that could be owned, ordered the confiscation of any excess, and its redistribution. It was expected that both the most disadvantaged parts of society and, secondly, the army would benefit. The reform would, in fact, have had the effect of reconstituting that reservoir of recruits formed by the peasantry before the crisis. The army could thus have returned to drawing on that reservoir to fill the gaps that had opened in the ranks of the legions due to Rome's continuous wars, most recently its very costly wars in Spain.

However, the formation of the reform law and then its application were bitterly opposed by the *optimates*, who reflected the economic interests of the senatorial (noble) families and the senatorial and consular (aristocratic) families, most of whose assets were based on land ownership. All of these saw the reform as a threat to their quasi-monopoly over the use of the *ager publicus*.

The story had a tragic outcome. Gracchus was unjustly accused of wanting to overthrow the *res publica*, and, accused of aspiring to tyranny and trying to make himself king, he was beaten to death during a public meeting that turned into a gigantic brawl in which 300 other Roman citizens also died. Subsequently, Gracchus's friends were persecuted by the public authorities on charges of complicity in an attempted coup (which had never occurred) and executed in one of the first documented examples of the political use of justice.

Subsequently, the phrase "daggers in the Forum" was coined to summarize this political process. The arrival of "daggers in the Forum" heralded a tormented political period that, in the space of about a century, would lead to the overthrow of the *res publica*—a mixture of monarchy, oligarchy, and democracy—with a different form of government. In practice, it caused the transition from the "rule of a few" to the "rule of one" (the *princeps*, the *augustus*), the final outcome of which is known today as the Principate. Everything that happened on the political level in Rome in the last three decades of the II century and the first seven decades of the I century was, in some way, a consequence of the changes that occurred in the political game in 133 due to the entry of "daggers in the Forum." More specifically, the result was an interminable factional struggle—*populares* against *optimates*—intertwined with the eternal social conflict between the patriciate and the plebs.

The deterioration of internal relations within Roman society reached a new peak in 122 following the tragic death of Tiberius Sempronius Gracchus's younger brother, Caius, also a tribune of the plebs whose reforms were bitterly opposed by the *optimates*. Caius's reforms were more "revolutionary" than Tiberius's agrarian reform—one sought the downsizing of the Senate—and history repeated itself. Like Tiberius, Caius was accused of wanting to overthrow the *res publica* and make himself king. And again, a political meeting ended in a mass brawl, as a result of which Caius met a violent death.

The killings of the Gracchi brothers were followed by the mysterious death of the twice consul Scipio Aemilianus, the destroyer of *Carthago* and *Numantia*, in 129; Caius Marius's tribuneship of the plebs in 119, sparking the personal conflict between Marius and the Metelli, a family of wealthy entrepreneurs and landowners; the Jugurthine War from 111 to 105, which brought Lucius Cornelius Sulla to prominence; Marius's exploitation of the political activity of Lucius Cornelius Saturninus, a tribune of the plebs; and the political eclipse of Marius, overshadowed by the political adventurism of Saturninus, who had escaped the control of the *equites* group. In the end, Saturninus fell victim to a lynching organized by his political opponents.

In 91, the tribune of the plebs Marcus Livius Drusus was killed in his home after having proposed the mass naturalization, by law, of Rome's Italic allies both to fulfill their pressing request and to avert the risk of an armed uprising.

Shortly afterward, a massacre in Asculum put an end to any prospect of a peaceful resolution to the crisis. The *socii*, united in a political confederation, went to war against Rome, sparking the Social War. The conflict lasted three years, during which time Rome risked losing the war, and it only ended after innumerable pitched battles, ambushes, sieges, and massacres, resulting in 300,000 victims and endless destruction. Ultimately, Rome won, but it lost at the same time because, eventually, it granted the vanquished what they had asked for anyway.

Having emerged, very weakened, from the most useless of wars, Rome had to engage in a new war, this time to be fought far from Italy in Anatolia and Greece. This was the First Mithridatic War (89–85), named after Mithridates VI Eupator, king of Pontus. Mithridates VI was one of Rome's most dangerous and irreducible enemies during three very bloody wars. The first war began with the invasion of *Pontus* by the Romans and a successful counteroffensive by the Pontics. One of the conflict's most tragic events was the pogrom unleashed by Mithridates VI against the Roman citizens residing in the province of Asia and their slaves, resulting in the death of 150,000 people in a single day, of whom 80,000 were Roman citizens.

Another catastrophe of that war was the landing of the Pontic army in Delos, a sacred city on the Cycladic island of the same name, which led to the killing of tens of thousands of people and rampant looting. Yet another was Sulla's capture of Athens after a siege. The city of the Acropolis wasn't destroyed, despite having resisted Sulla's demands to surrender, but it was abandoned to plunder and stripped of great treasures, including countless statues, architectural elements, paintings, and other cultural assets (including the Library of Aristotle), which were sent back to Italy to decorate the houses and villas of rich Romans.

The first of the crises in which Rome was subsequently involved originated in 88, born from the personal conflict between Marius and Sulla, itself caused by a maneuver by Marius who, using Publius Sulpicius Rufus, a tribune of the plebs, removed Sulla from his command of the Mithridatic War. The dispute degenerated into a factional struggle and resulted in a civil war, the first in the history of the Roman state. This saw Sulla's legions marching on Rome, taking it by storm and fighting in the streets and squares against the militia recruited by Marius. The conflict was unprecedented. The civil war deeply shocked the Romans, who saw it as absolute evil because, in excluding every form of good, it prompted a complete reversal of values.

The conflict resumed in 83 upon Sulla's return from the Mithridatic War. In the meantime, Marius died of illness (in 86) after having taken Rome after a siege and spreading terror there. Marius's political legacy was picked up first by Lucius Cornelius Cinna and then by his son, Caius Marius the Younger. The fighting inflamed Italy, Sicily, Sardinia, the Iberian Peninsula, and North Africa and only ended in 82 with Sulla's definitive victory at the Battle of the *Porta Collina*, achieved not only over the Marians but also over their allies, the Samnites and Lucanians, Rome's bitter enemies.

Immediately afterward, Sulla was legally made dictator by the people gathered in assembly in a climate of intimidation and fear (82). He took revenge on his political opponents and personal enemies for the personal wrongs he had suffered through a system of legalized killings now known as proscriptions, which was advantageous not only for Sulla and the Sullans but also for the Roman state because it involved the confiscation and auctioning of the assets of the proscribed, with a share of the proceeds paid to the public treasury.

Sulla's dictatorship only lasted a few years, but it had a profound impact on Roman society and its systems. When, in 79, Sulla realized that his political decline had begun and could not be stopped, he left the scene with a dramatic *coup de théâtre*. Suddenly and unexpectedly, he resigned from his dictatorship and retired to private life. Sulla spent his last days in a country villa in the company of his family and close friends before dying on 3 March 78.

Before long, the *populares* began to chip away at Sulla's legislation, partially repealing it. In the following years, the characters who will dominate the political scene of the last generation of the *res publica* come to the fore: Marcus Tullius Cicero, Cnaeus Pompeius Magnus, Lucius Licinius Crassus, Caius Julius Caesar, Marcus Porcius Cato Uticensis, Lucius Sergius Catilina, Publius Claudius Pulcher, etc.

Marius and Sulla were the leading protagonists of Rome's political life in their time. Initially, they collaborated on a military level, but Marius's tendency to appropriate the merits of others drove a wedge between them. The two broke off their friendship, and Sulla took different and antithetical political positions to Marius. Marius was the leader of the *populares*, while Sulla was strongly supported by the Senate, or rather, the *optimates*.

Marius and Sulla were different people in terms of their origin, character, and way of doing things. Marius came from the lower-class plebeians. He was a poorly educated man and was schooled by the army, which he joined at a very young age. He was rude, impulsive, impetuous, and homophobic. Conversely, Sulla was born into a family of fallen aristocrats. He was educated and cultured, loved literature and the theatre, and was rational and endowed with great self-control, though he could become angry suddenly and unexpectedly. Sulla was also bisexual. He married five times and had six children, but the true great love of his life was a Greek named Metrobius. Sulla met him when he was a young actor and fell in love with him, and their relationship lasted until the end of Sulla's life. When Sulla was dying, it wasn't his wife at his bedside but Metrobius.

In some ways, however, Marius and Sulla were very alike. They were relentlessly ambitious, driven by boundless self-centeredness, and lucky. Furthermore, they shared a passion for eating and drinking in company, among friends, and a trust in divination. Both were predicted to have great success in life. A Syrian fortune teller prophesied that Marius would be consul seven times but would be surpassed in fame by his nephew, Caius Julius Caesar, while a Chaldean soothsayer predicted that Sulla would become the most powerful man in the world but would die when he was at the height of his glory.

In both cases, the prophecy came true.

Chronology

133	Tiberius Sempronius Gracchus serves as tribune of the plebs, proposes an agrarian reform bill, and is killed in a massacre on the Capitoline. Attalus III, king of *Pergamum*, bequeaths his kingdom to the Roman people. Publius Cornelius Scipio Aemilianus conquers *Numantia* (end of the Numantine War).
132	Aristonicus's revolt in Asia Minor.
129	The Asian territories inherited from Attalus III are organized into a province. Scipio Aemilianus dies in mysterious circumstances.
126–125	Tension rises between Rome and its Italic allies. Consulship of Marcus Fulvius Flaccus, a draft law of consular initiative that meets the request for the mass naturalization of *socii* is proposed. Revolt and destruction of *Fregellae*.
123–121	Caius Sempronius Gracchus, tribune of the plebs, launches legislative proposals to relaunch the colonization and refoundation of *Carthago*, downsize the Senate, and valorize the *equites*. A massacre on the Aventine results in the death of Gracchus.
120	Mithridates VI Eupator becomes king of *Pontus*.
119	Tribuneship of Caius Marius.
111–105	War against Jugurtha, king of *Numidia*.
109	Consulship of Quintus Caecilius Metellus.
107	First consulate of Gaius Marius.

105	Consulship of Publius Rutilius Rufus. Rome suffers a disastrous defeat at the Battle of *Arausio* against the Cimbri, Teutons and Ambrones.
104–100	Marius serves successive consulships.
103	First tribuneship of Lucius Appuleius Saturninus.
100	Saturninus proposes an agricultural bill while serving as tribune.
91	Assassination of Marcus Livius Drusus, a tribune of the plebs.
91–88	The Social War.
88	Sulla's first consulship Sulla takes Rome by force and banishes Marius from the city.
88–85	First Mithridatic War. Siege of Athens, followed by immense massacre and looting.
86	First consulship of Lucius Cornelius Cinna. Seventh consulship of Caius Marius. Marius takes Rome after a siege and sows a reign of terror. Marius dies of illness.
85	Treaty of Dardanus between Sulla and Mithridates VI.
83	Sulla returns to Italy. Civil war breaks out.
82	The Battle of the *Porta Collina*.
81	Sulla's dictatorship and proscription of political opponents.
80	Sulla's second consulship.
79	Sulla spontaneously resigns from the dictatorship and retires to private life in Campania.
78	Sulla dies of illness. The consul Marcus Aemilius Lepidus attempts a coup, which fails.

References

Agache, S. "Villa Publica." In *Lexicon Topographicum Urbis Romae*, vol. 5, Rome: Quasar, 1999.

Alexander, M. C. *Trials in the Late Roman Republic, 149 BC to 50 BC*. Toronto, Buffalo, London: University of Toronto Press, 1990.

Badian, E. "The pig and the priest." In *Ad fontes! Festschrift für Gerhard Dobesch zum fünfundsechzigsten Geburtstag am 15. September 2004*. Vienna: De Gruyter, 2004.

Badian, E. "Tiberius Gracchus and the beginning of the Roman revolution." *ANRW* I/I (1972).

Badian, E. *Foreign Clientelae*. Clarendon: Oxford.

Badian, E. "Caepio and Norbanus." *Historia* 6, no. 3 (1957).

Badian, E. "From the Gracchi to Sulla (1940–59)." *Historia* 11 (1962).

Balbo, M. *Riformare la res publica. Retroterra sociale e significato politico del tribunato di Tiberio Gracco*. Bari: Edipuglia, 2013.

Barrandon, N. *Les massacres de la République romaine*. Paris, Fayard, 2018.

Bartoli, D. *Le Morali*. Rome: Stamperia del Varese, 1684.

Bauman, R. A. "The hostis declarations of 88 and 87 B.C." *Athenaeum* 51 (1973).

Bennett, H. *Cinna and his Times: A Critical and Interpretative Study of Roman History During the Period 87–84 B.C.* Menasha, WI: George Banta, 1923.

Bocchiola, M., and Sartori, M. *Teutoburgo. La selva che inghiottì le legioni di Augusto*. Milan: Mondadori, 2014.

Bulst, C. M. "Cinnanum Tempus: A Reassessment of the 'Dominatio Cannae.'" *Historia* 13, no. 3 (1964).

Canali, L. *Annibale e la "fobia" romana di Freud*. Roma: Carocci, 2008.

Canfora, L. "Cesare scrittore." In *Giulio Cesare. L'uomo, le imprese, il mito. Catalogo della mostra (Roma, 23 ottobre 2008–3 maggio 2009)*. Milan: Silvana Editore, 2008.

Carandini, A. *Angoli di Roma. Guida inconsueta alla città antica*. Roma: Laterza, 2016.

Carcopino, J. *Silla*. Milan: Bompiani, 1977.

Carney, T. F. "A biography of Marius." *JRS* 54, no. 1–2 (1964).

Cavaggioni, F. *L. Apuleio Saturnino. Tribunus plebis seditiosus*. Venezia: Istituto Veneto di Scienze, Lettere ed Arti, 1998.

Clark, A. J. "Nasica and Fides." *CQ* 57 (2007).

Criniti, N. "Ludovico Antonio Muratori e i Bardiaei." *Aevum* 53, no. 1 (1979).

Criniti, N. *L'epigrafe di Asculum di Gn. Pompeo Strabone*. Milan: Vita e Pensiero, 1970.

Coarelli, F. "La statue de Cornélie, mère des Gracques et la crise politique à Rome au temps de Saturninus." In *"Revixit ars". Arte e ideologia a Roma. Dai modelli ellenistici alla tradizione repubblicana*. Rome: Quasar, 1996.

Dumézil, G. *La religione arcaica romana. Miti, leggende, realtà*, 3rd ed. Milan: Rizzoli, 2011.

Earl, D. C. "Tiberius Gracchus's Last Assembly." *Athenaeum* 43 (1965).

Earl, D. C. *Tiberius Gracchus: A Study in Politics*. Brussels-Berchem: Latomus, 1963.

Everitt, A. *Roma. Nascita di una grande potenza.* Milan: Hoepli, 2013.

Floris, P. 2009, *Lucius Equitius Insitivus Gracchus.* Cagliari: Edizioni AV, 2009.

Flower, H. I. *The Art of Forgetting: Disgrace and Oblivion in Roman Political Culture (Studies in the History of Greece and Rome).* Chapel Hill, NC: The University of North Carolina Press, 2006.

Gabba, E. "Rome and Italy: The Social War." In *Cambridge Ancient History*, vol. IX: *The Last Age of the Roman Republic, 146–43 B.C.*, 2nd ed. Cambridge: Cambridge University Press, 1994.

Gabba, E. *"Mario e Silla."* ANRW (1972).

Gilbert, C. D. "Marius and Fortuna." *CQ* 23 (1973).

Golden, G. K. *Crisis Management during the Roma n Republic: The Role of Political Institutions in Emergencies.* Cambridge: Cambridge University Press, 2013.

Grimal, P. *La civiltà dell'antica Roma.* Roma: Newton Compton, 2012.

Gruen, E. S. *Roman Politics and the Criminal Courts, 149–78 B.C.* Cambridge, MA: Harvard University Press, 1968.

Guarino, A. *La coerenza di Publio Mucio.* Napoli: Iovene, 1981.

Gwyn Morgan, M. "Villa Publica and Magna Mater. Two Notes on Manubial Building at the Close of the Second Century B.C." *Klio* 55 (1973).

Hallett, J. P. "Matriot Games? Cornelia, Mother of the Gracchi, and the Forging of Family-Oriented Political Values." In *Women's Influence on Classical Civilization.* London-New York, 2004.

Hallett, J. P. "Women Writing in Rome and Cornelia, Mother of the Gracchi." In *Women Writing Latin from Roman Antiquity to Early Modern Europe.* New York-London: Routledge, 2002.

Harris, W. V. "A Revisionist View of Roman Money." *JRS* 96 (2006).

Hemelrijk, E. A. *Matrona Docta: Educated Women in the Roman Élite from Cornelia to Julia Domna.* London-New York: Routledge, 1999.

Hinard, F. *Silla.* Rome: Salerno Editrice, 1990.

Hinard, F. "Solidarités familiales et ruptures à l'époque des guerres civiles et de la proscription." In *Parenté et strategies familiales dans l'Antiquité romaine. Actes de la table ronde des 2–4 octobre 1986 (Paris, Maison des sciences de l'homme)*, Publications de l'Ecole française de Rome 129. Rome: Ecole Française de Rome, 1990.

Hinard, F. "Les proscriptions de la Rome républicain." In *Collection de l'Ecole Française de Rome 83.* Rome: Scuola Tipografica s. Pio X, 1985.

Hinard, F. *La male mort. Exécutions et statut du corps au moment de la première proscription. Du châtiment dans la cité.* Rome: Publications de l'École Française de Rome, 1984.

Hinard, F. *La Proscription de 82 et les Italiens. Les Bourgeoises municipales italiennes.* Naples: Publications du Centre Jean Bérard, Editions du CNRS, 1983.

Hinard, F. *Prosopographie* II (1985).

Ibba, A. *L'Africa mediterranea in età romana (202 av. C.-442 d. C.).* Rome: Carocci, 2012.

Keaveney, A. *Lucullus: a Life.* London-New York: Routledge, 1992.

Keaveney, A. "Sulla, Sulpicius and Caesar Strabo." *Latomus* 38 (1979).

La Rocca, E. and Sortorella, S., eds. "La processione trionfale come spettacolo per il popolo romano." In *Trionfi romani. Catalogo della mostra (Roma, 5 marzo-14 settembre 2008).* Milan: Mondadori Electa, 2008.

Lewis, R. G. "P. Sulpicius law to recall the exiles, 88 BC." *CQ* 48 (1998).

Lewis, R. G. "Some Mothers." *Athenaeum* 66 (1989).

Linderski, J. "The pontiff and the tribune: the death of Tiberius Gracchus." *Athenaeum* 90 (2002).

Lintott, A. W. "The tribunate of P. Sulpicius Rufus." *CQ* 21 (1971).

Lintott, A. W. *Violence in Republican Rome.* Oxford: Oxford University Press, 1968.

Marco, F. & Pina Polo, F. "Mario Gratidiano, los compita y la religiosidad popular a fines de la república." *Klio* 82 (2000).

McDonnell, M. *Roman Manliness: Virtus and the Roman Republic.* Cambridge: Cambridge University Press, 2006.

Millar, F. *The Crowd in Rome in the Late Republic.* Ann Arbor: University of Michigan Press, 1998.

Mommsen, T. *Storia di Roma antica.* Firenze: Sansoni, 1960.

Makin, E. "The Triumphal Route, with Particular Reference to the Flavian Triumph." *JRS* 11 (1921).

Nicolet, C. *Rome et la conquête du monde méditerranéen.* Paris: Presses Universitaires de France, 2001.

Nippel, W. "Emergency Powers in the Roman Republic." In *La théorie politico-constitutionelle du gouvernement d'exception.* Paris: CREA/École Polytechnique, 2000.

Nippel, W. *Aufruhr und 'Polizei' in Der romischer Republik.* Stuttgart: Klett-Cotta, 1988.

Nippel, W. *Caio Mario come uomo politico.* Pavia: Amministrazione dell'Athenaeum, 1934.

Passerini, A. "Epigrafia Mariana." *Athenaeum* 17 (1939).

Pina Polo, F. *The tyranny of the* Gracchi *and the concordia of the* Optimates: *an ideological construct.* Roma: L'Erma di Bretschneider, 2017.

Powell, J. G. F. "The tribune Sulpicius." *Historia* 39 (1990).

Roller, M. B. "Demolished Houses, Monumentality and Memory in Roman Culture." *CA* 29 (2010).

Rosenstein, N. S. *Imperatores Victi: Military Defeat and Aristocratic Competition in the Middle and Late Republic.* Berkeley: University of California Press, 1990.

Ruck, B. "Das Denkmal Der Cornelia in Rom." *MDAIR* 111 (2004).

Santalucia, B. *Diritto e processo penale nell'antica Roma.* Milan: Giuffrè, 1998.

Santangelo, F. "*Pax deorum* and Pontiffs." In *Priests and State in the Roman World.* Stuttgart, 2011.

Santangelo, F. *Roma repubblicana. Una storia in quaranta vite.* Rome: Carocci, 2019.

Santangelo, F. "A survey of recent scholarship on the age of the Gracchi (1985–2005)." *Topoi* 15, no. 2 (2007).

Scullard, H. H. *From the Gracchi to Nero: A History of Rome from 133 BC to AD 68,* 5th ed. London: Routledge, 1982.

Scullard, H. H. *Storia del mondo romano: Dalle riforme dei Gracchi alla morte di Nerone.* Milan: Rizzoli, 1992.

Seager, R., ed. *The Crisis of the Roman Republic.* Cambridge: Heffer, 1969.

Sini, F. *Bellum Nefandum. Virgilio e il problema del "diritto internazionale antico* (Sassari: Dessì, 1991.

Stanley Spaeth, B. "The Goddess Ceres and the Death of Tiberius Gracchus." *Historia* 39 (1990).

Tamassia, N. "La vendetta nell'antica società romana." Atti del Reale Istituto Veneto 79 (1919).

Tantillo, I. "Gli uomini e le risorse." In *Roma Antica.* Roma: Laterza, 2014.

Thein, G. "The via Latina, the via Labicana and the Location of Ad Pictas." *PBSR* 73 (2005).

Treggiari, S. *Servilia and Her Family.* Oxford: Oxford University Press, 2019.

Valgiglio, E. "Sulla legislazione di P. Sulpicio Rufo (88 a.C.)." *RSCI* 15 (1967).

Vedaldi Iasbez, V. "I figli dei proscritti sillani." *Labeo* 27 (1981).

Warner, R. *Il giovane Cesare.* Roma: Castelvecchi, 2012.

Further Reading

(In chronological order, starting from the most recent publication)

Aristonicus of *Pergamon*

Daubner, F. *Bellum Asiaticum. Der Krieg der Römer gegen Aristonikos von Pergamon und die Einrichtung der Provinz Asia*, 2., ed. riv. München: Herbert Utz Verlag, 2006.

Jones, C. "Events surrounding the bequest of Pergamon to Rome and the Revolt of Aristonicos: new inscriptions from Metropolis." *Journal of Roman Archaeology* 17 (2004): 469–485.

Potter, D. "Where did Aristonicus Revolt Begin?" *Zeitschrift für Papyrologie und Epigraphik—ZPE* 74 (1988): 293–295.

Delplace, C. "Le contenu social et économique du soulèvement d'Aristonicos: opposition entre riches et pauvres?" *Athenaeum* 56 (1978): 21–28.

Hopp, J., *Untersuchungen zur Geschichte der letzten Attaliden*. München: C. H. Beck, 1977.

Carrata, F. T. *La rivolta di Aristonico e le origini della provincia romana d'Asia*. Torino: Giappichelli, 1968.

Africa, T. W. "Aristonicus, Blossius, and the City of the Sun." *International Review of Social History* 6 (1) (1961): 110–124.

Vavrinek, V. *La révolte de Aristonicos*. Rozpravy Ceskoslovenské Akademie, 1957, VED 67.

Wilken, U. In *Real Encyclopädie der classichen Altertumswissenschaft, II*.

Rostovtzeff, M. *Social and economic History of the Hellenistic World, II*. Oxford: Oxford University Press, 1941.

Broughton, T. R. S. "Stratoniceia and Aristonicus." *CPh* 29 (1934): 252–254.

Blossius, Gaius (Blossius of Cumae)

La Greca, F. "Blossio di Cuma." *Studi di Storia e di Geostoria Antica, Quaderni del Dipartimento di Scienze dell'Antichità* 23. Napoli: Università degli Studi di Salerno, 2000, 59–123.

La Greca, F. "Blossio di Cuma: stoicismo e politica nella Roma dei Gracchi." *Quaderni del Dipartimento di Scienze dell'Educazione* 5. Napoli: Università di Salerno, 1995, 141–177.

Garbarino, G. *Roma e la filosofia greca alla fine del II sec. a. C.* Torino, 1971. I, 112 ff.; II, 445–458.

Dudley, D. R. "Blossius of *Cumae*." *JRS* 31 (1941): 94–99.

Catilina, Lucius Sergius

Canfora, L. *Catilina. Una rivoluzione mancata*. Bari-Roma: Laterza, 2023.

Levick, B. *Catilina*. Bologna: Il Mulino, 2015.

Marshall, B. A. "Catilina and the Execution of M. Marius Gratidianus." *CQ* 35 (1985): 124–133.

Cato, Marcus Porcius

Catone, Marco Porcio. *Le opere*. Torino: UTET, 2013.
Astin, A. E. *Cato the Censor*. Oxford: Oxford University Press, 1978.

Catulus, Quintus Lutatius

Bardon, H. "Q. Lutatius Catulus et sono cercle litteraire." *LEC* 18 (1950): 145–64 (=*Litt. inconnue*, I, 1952: 115–132).

Caesar, Caius Julius

Goldsworthy, A. K. *Caesar: Life of a Colossus*. New Haven: Yale University Press, 2012.
Warner, R. *Il giovane Cesare*. Castelvecchi: Roma, 2012.
Zecchini, G. "Cesare e il 'mos maiorum.'" *Historia* 151 (2001).
Gelzer, M. *Caesar: Der Politiker und Staatsmann*. Stuttgart: Franz Steiner Verlag, 2008.
Gentili, G., ed. *Giulio Cesare. L'uomo. Le imprese. Il mito*. Milan: Silvana Editoriale, 2008.
Agazzi, R. *Giulio Cesare stratega in Gallia*. Pavia: Iuculano, 2006.
Goldsworthy, H. *Caesar. Life of a Colossus*. New Haven: Yale University Press, 2006.
Fraschetti, A. *Giulio Cesare*. Bari-Roma: Laterza, 2005.
Meier, C. *Caesar*. Munich: Siedler Verlag, 2004.
Meier, C. *Caesar: A Biography*. New York: Basic Books, 1997.
Frediani, A. *Le grandi battaglie di Giulio Cesare*. Roma: Newton & Compton, 2003.
Ridley, R. T. "The Dictator's Mistake: Caesar's Escape from Sulla." *Historia* 49 (2000): 211–229.
Horst, E. *Cesare*. Milan: RCS Libri, 2000.
Canfora, L. *Giulio Cesare. Il dittatore democratico*. Bari-Roma: Laterza, 1999.
Gelzer, M. *Caesar: Politician and Statesman*. Cambridge, MA: Harvard University Press, 1968.
Halpern, S. "Caesar and the Aurelii Cottage." Dissertation, University of Pennsylvania, 1964.
Taylor, R. "Caesar's Early Career." *CPh* 36 (1941): 113–32.

Caesar Strabo, Cnaeus

Funaioli, G. v. "Cesare Strabone, Gaio Giulio (C. Iulius Caesar Strabo, anche detto Sesquicolo e Vopisco)." *Enciclopedia Italiana*, Treccani, 1931.

Cicero, Marcus Tullius

Grimal, P. *Cicerone*. Milan: Garzanti, 2011.
Narducci, E. *Cicerone. La parola e la politica*. Roma-Bari: Laterza, 2009.
Cicero, Marcus Tullius. *Defense Speeches*. Translated by Berry, D. H. New York: Oxford University Press, 2009.
Fezzi, L. Il "'*Commentariolum petitionis*': sguardi dalle democrazie contemporanee." *Historia* 56 (2007): 14–26.
Treggiari, S. *Terentia, Tullia, Publilia: The women of Cicero's Family*. London: Routledge, 2007.

Cicero, Marcus Tullius. *Letters to Atticus*, 4 vols, translated by Shackleton Bailey, D. R. Cambridge, MA: Harvard University Press, Loeb Classical Library Series, 1999.

Cicero, Marcus Tullius. *Selected Letters*. Translated by Shackleton Bailey, D. R. Harmondsworth: Penguin, 1995.

Crawford, J. W. *M. Tullius Cicero: The Lost and Unpublished Orations*. Gottingen: Vandenhoeck & Ruprecht GmbH & Co KG, 1984.

Zetzel, J. E. G. "Cicero and the Scipionic Circle." *HSCPh* 76 (1972): 173 ff.

Ward, A. M. "The Early Relationship between Cicero and Pompey until 80 B.C." *Phoenix* 24 (1970): 119–129.

Shackleton Bailey, D. R. *Cicero's Letters to Atticus*, III–V. Cambridge: Cambridge University Press, 1966–1968.

Cinna, Lucius Cornelius

Sartori, F. "Actes du colloque 1971 sur l'esclavage. Besançon 10–11 mai 1971." In *Cinna e gli schiavi*. Besançon: Presses Universitaires de Franche-Comté, 1973. 151–152.

Bulst, C. M. "Cinnanum tempus: a reassessment of the domination Cinnae." *Historia* XIII (1960): 307–337.

Bennet, H. "Cinna and his Times." Dissertation, Menasha: University of Chicago, 1923.

Cornelia Africana Minor

Hallett, J. P. "Matriot Games? Cornelia, Mother of the Gracchi, and the Forging of Family-Oriented Political Values." In *Women's Influence on Classical Civilization*. London & New York: Routledge, 2004.

Ruck, B. "Das Denkmal Der Cornelia in Rom." *MDAIR* 111 (2004): 477–494.

Hallett, J. P. *Women Writing in Rome and Cornelia, Mother of the Gracchi*. In *Women Writing Latin from Roman Antiquity to Early Modern Europe*, I. New York & London: Taylor & Francis, 2002.

Suerbaum, W. "Cornelia die Mutter der Gracchen." *Die archaische Literatur von den Anfängen bis Sullas Tod* (=Handbuch der lateinischen Literatur der Antike, Band 1). München: C. H. Beck, 2002.

Hemelrijk, E. *Matrona Docta: Educated Women in the Roman Elite from Cornelia to Julia Domna*. New York: Oxford University Press, 1999.

Coarelli, F. "Le statue de Cornélie, mère des Gracques et la crise politique à Rome au temps de Saturninus." *Revixit ars—Arte e ideologia a Roma. Dai modelli ellenistici alla tradizione repubblicana* (1996): 280–299. Before in H. Zehnacker (ed.), *Le dernier siècle de la République romaine et l'époque augustéenne. Journées d'étude, Strasbourg, 15–16 février 1978*, vol. I de Contributions et travaux de l'Institut d'Histoire Romaine. Strasbourg, 1978: 13–28.

Gunther, L. M. "Cornelia und Ptolemaios VIII. Zur Historizitat des Heiratsantrages (Plu. TG 1, 3)." *Historia* 39 (1990): 124–128.

Barnard, S. "Cornelia and the Women of her Family." *Latomus* 49 (1990): 383–392.

Kajava, M. "Cornelia Africani f. Gracchorum." *Arctos* 23 (1989): 119–131.

Horsfall, N. "The 'Letter of Cornelia': Yet More Problems." *Athenaeum* n.s. 65 (1987): 231–234.

Briscoe, J. "Supporters and Opponents of Tiberius Gracchus." *JRS* 64 (1974): 175 ff.

Crassus, Marcus Licinius

Schettino, M. T. *Marcus Licinius Crassus. Pratique et conception du pouvoir.* Roma: L'Erma di Bretschneider, 2023.

Traina, G. *La resa di Roma. 9 giugno 53 a.C., battaglia di Carre.* Roma-Bari: Laterza, 2010.

Traina, G., "Note in margine alla battaglia di Carre," in Dabrowa, E., ed., *Orbis Parthicus. Studies in Memory of Professor Jozef Wolski. Electrum,* vol. 15. Krakow: Jagiellonian U. P., 2009: 235–247.

Sampson, G. *The Defeat of Rome. Crassus, Carrhae, and the Invasion of the East.* Barnsley: Pen & Sword, 2008.

Fawcett, B. "The Battle of Carrhae." In *How to lose a Battle. Foolish Plans and Great Military Blunders.* New York, London, Toronto, Sydney: Harper Collins, 2006.

Mattern-Parkes, S. P. "The Defeat of Crassus and the Just War." *CW* 96 (2003): 387–396.

Antonelli, G. *Crasso, il banchiere di Roma.* Roma: Newton Compton, 1995.

Angeli Bertinelli, M. G. *Plutarco. Le vite di Nicia e Crasso.* Milan: Mondadori, Fondazione Lorenzo Valla, 1993. Esp. xxviii–xlvi, lviii–lxvi, 317–425.

Brizzi, G. "Studi militari romani." In *Note Sulla battaglia di Carre.* Bologna: Patron, 1983.

Rawson, E. "Crassorum funera." *Latomus* 41 (1982): 540–549.

Marshall, B. A. *Crassus. A Political Biography.* Amsterdam: Hakkert, 1976.

Adcock, F. E. *Marcus Crassus, Millionaire.* Cambridge: Heffer, 1966.

Garzetti, "M. Licinio Crasso," *Athenaeum* (1941–44): n.s. 29, 3–37; 30, 12–40; 32, 1–61.

Regling, K. "Crassus' Partherkrieg." *Klio* 7 (1907): 357–394.

Drusus, Marcus Livius

Boren, H. C. "Livius Drusus t. p. 122 and his Anti Gracchan Program." *CJ* (1956): 27 ff.

Equitius, Lucius

Beness, J. L. and Gillard, T. W. "The Death of Lucius Equitius on 10 December 100 B.C." *CQ* n.s. XL, 1 (1990): 269–272.

Twyman, B. L. "The Day Equitius Died." *Athenaeum* n.s. LXVII, III—IV (1989): 493–509.

Münzer, F. *RE* VI/1 (1907), c. 322, n. 3, s.v. *Equitius.*

Flaccus, Marcus Fulvius

Reiter, W. "M. Fulvius Flaccus and the Gracchan Coalition." *Athenaeum* LXV, I (1978): 125–144.

Hall, U. "Notes on M. Fulvius Gracchus." *Athenaeum* LXV (1977): 280–288.

Glaucia, Caius Servilius

Ferrary, J.-L. "Recherches sur la législation de Saturninus et de Glaucia [II. La loi de iudiciis repetundarum de C. Servilius Glaucia]." *MEFRA* 91, 1 (1979): 85–134.

Robinson, F. W. "Marius, Saturninus und Glaucia: beiträge zur geschichte der jahre 106–100 v. Chr." *J. Savants,* 11, 4 (1913).

Gracchi

Barca, N. *I Gracchi: Quando la politica finisce in tragedia*. Roma: L'Erma di Bretschneider, 2019.

Pina Polo, F. "The 'tyranny' of the Gracchi and the concordia of the *optimates*; an ideological construct." In *Costruire la memoria: uso e abuso della storia fra tarda repubblica e primo principato, Venezia, 14–15 Gennaio 2016*. Roma: L'Erma di Bretschneider, 2017.

Hermon, E. "Le Mythe des Gracques dans la législation agraire du ier siècle av. J.-C." *Athenaeum* n.s. 80 (2001): 97–131.

Horvath, R. *The Origins of the Gracchan Revolution*. In C. Deroux (ed.), SLLRH, *VII*, Collection Latomus 227 (1994): 87–116.

Perelli, L. *I Gracchi*. Roma: 1993.

Stockton, D. L. *From the Gracchi to Sulla: Sources for Roman History, 133–80 B.C.* London: London Association of Classical Teachers, 1991.

Gabba, E. "Il tentativo dei Gracchi." In *Storia di Roma. II. L'impero mediterraneo. I. La repubblica imperiale*. Torino: Einaudi, 1990.

Perelli, L. "Questioni graccane," *RFIC* 118 (1990): 237–252.

Gabba, E. *"Il tentativo dei Gracchi."* In *Storia di Roma*, 2. Torino: Einaudi, 1990.

Schiavone, A. *Giuristi e nobili nella repubblica romana*. Bari-Roma: Laterza,1987.

Greenidge, A. H. J. and Clay, A. M. *Sources for Roman History, 133–70 B.C.*, 2d ed. Oxford: Clarendon Press, 1986.

Scullard, H. H. *From the Gracchi to Nero: A History of Rome from 133 B.C. to A.D. 68*. London: Routledge, 1982.

Rossi, R. F. *Dai Gracchi a Silla*. Bologna: Cappelli, 1980.

Stockton, D. L. *The Gracchi*. Oxford: Oxford University Press, 1979.

Brendan Nagle, D. "The Failure of the Roman Political Process." *Athenaeum* LVIII (1970): 372–394.

Gabba, E. *"I Gracchi."* In *I protagonisti della storia universale*, II. Milan: CEI, 1968.

Boren, H. C. *The Gracchi*. New York: Twayne, 1968.

Nicolet, C. *Les Gracques ou Crise agraire et révolution à Rome*. Paris: Julliard, 1967.

Carcopino, J. *Autour des Gracques*. Paris: Les Belles Lettres, 1967.

Cardinali, G. *Studi Graccani*. Roma: L'Erma di Bretschneider, 1965.

Becker, J. B. "The Influence of Roman Stoicism upon the Gracchi's Economic Land Reforms." *La Parola al Passato* (1964): 125–134.

Taylor, L. R. "Forerunners of the Gracchi." *JRS* (1962): 19–27.

Boren, H. C. "The Urban Side of the Gracchan Economic Crisis." *AHR* (1958): 890–902.

Fraccaro, P. "Oratori e orazioni dell'età dei Gracchi, I—II (1912)." *Studi stor.*, I—II (Pisa-Pavia: Spoerri, 1912–1913).

Gracchus, Caius Sempronius

Mantovani, D. "Gaio Gracco e i DIKASTAI di Plut. C. Gr. 3.7," *Athenaeum* 82 (1994): 13–29.

Fraccaro, P. 1925, *"Ricerche su Gaio Gracco."* *Opuscula*, II (1957): 19–51.

Corradi, G. *"Caio Gracco e le sue leggi."* *Studi italiani di Filologia classica* (1927): 235–297.

Gracchus, Tiberius Sempronius

La Greca, F. *Tiberio Gracco e Blossio di Cuma. Filosofia e politica a Roma nel secolo degli Scipioni.* Ogliastro Cilento: LICOSIA, 2016.

Ossier, J. F. "Greek Cultural Influence and the Revolutionary Policies of Tiberius Gracchus." *Studia Historica. Historia Antigua* 22 (2004): 63–69.

La Greca, F. "I beneficiari della legge agraria di Tiberio Gracco e le assegnazioni in Lucania." *RSS* 46 (2000): 1–42.

Spaeth, B. S. "The Goddess Ceres and the Death of Tiberius Gracchus." *Historia* 39 (1990): 182–195.

Gabba, E. *Il tentativo dei Gracchi, in AA. VV., Storia di Roma,* II, 1 (Torino: Einaudi, 1990): 671–689.

Bleicken, J. "Überlegungen zum Volkstribunat des Tiberius Sempronius Gracchus." *Hist Z* (1988): 265–293.

Moir, K. M. "Pliny HN 7.57 and the Marriage of Tiberius Gracchus." *CQ* 33 (1983): 136–45.

Richardson, J. S. "The Ownership of Roman Land: Tiberius Gracchus and the Italians." *JRS* 70 (1980): 1–11.

Shochat, Y. *Recruitment and the Program of Tiberius Gracchus* (Collection Latomus, vol. 169). Brussels: Latomus, 1980.

Guarino, A. "L'abrogazione di Ottavio." *AAN* LXXXI (1980): 236–266.

Shochat, Y. "The *lex agraria* of 133 B.C. and the Italian Allies, in B.C." *Athenaeum* LVIII (1979): 372–394, and LIX (1971): 111–128.

Bernstein, A. H. *Tiberius Sempronius Gracchus.* Ithaca: Cornell University Press, 1978.

Sordi, M. "La tradizione storiografica su Tiberio Sempronio Gracco e la propaganda contemporanea." In *Sesta Miscellanea Greca e Romana* (Roma, 1978): 299–330.

Bernstein, A. H. *Tiberius Sempronius Gracchus: Tradition and Apostasy.* Ithaca: Cornell University Press, 1978.

Morgan, M. G. and Walsh, J. A. "Ti. Gracchus (TR. PL. 133 B.C.), The Numantine Affair, and the Deposition of M. Octavius." *CPh* 3 (1978): 200–210.

Briscoe, J. "Supporters and Opponents of Tiberius Gracchus." *JRS* 64 (1974): 125–135.

Badian, E. "Tiberius Gracchus and the Beginning of the Roman revolution." *ANRW* 1.1. (Politische Geschichte) (1972).

Earl, D. C. "Tiberius Gracchus' Last Assembly." *Athenaeum* 43 (1965): 95–105.

Earl, D. C. *Tiberius Gracchus: A Study in Politics* (Collection Latomus, Vol. LXVI). Brussels-Berchem: Latomus, 1963.

Last, H. 1932, "Tiberius Gracchus." In *The Cambridge Ancient History, IX* (Cambridge: Cambridge University Press, 1932): 1–39.

Lepidus, Marcus Aemilius

Labruna, L. *Il console "sovversivo."* Napoli: Liguori, 1976.

Criniti, N., Aimilius, M., "Q. f. M. n. Lepidus, 'Ut ignis in Stipula'" *MIL* 30 (1969): 4.

Lucullus, Lucius Licinius

Keaveney, A. *Lucullus: a Life.* London-New York: Routledge, 1992.

Antonelli, G. *Lucullo.* Rome: Newton Compton, 1989.

Ooteghem, J. (Van), *Lucius Licinius Lucullus.* Brussels: Palais Des Académies, 1959.

Marius, Caius

Santangelo, F. *Gaio Mario*. Napoli: Jouvence, 2021.

Santangelo, F. "Marius and Sulla." In *Oxford Bibliographies in Classics* (Oxford & New York: Oxford University Press, 2019).

Barca, N. *Gaio Mario. Alle origini della crisi di Roma*. Roma: L'Erma di Bretschneider, 2017.

Peruffo, A. *Le battaglie dei Cimbri e dei Teutoni (113–101 a.C.). Roma e la prima invasione barbarica*. Roma: Arbor Sapientiae Editore, 2017.

Labitzke, M. *Marius. Der verleumdete Retter Roms*. Munster: LIT Verlag, 2013.

Vassalli, S. *Terre selvagge*. Milan: Rizzoli, 2014.

Evans, R. "The military reputation of Gaius Marius." In *Questioning Reputations* (Pretoria: University of South Africa, 2004): 11–35.

Goldsworthy, H. *In the Name of Rome*. London: Phoenix, 2003.

Ballesteros-Pastor, L. "Marius' words to Mithridates Eupator (Plut., Marius, 31.3)." *Historia* XLVIII (1999): 506–508.

Werner, V. *Quantum bello optimus, tantum pace pessimus: Studien zum Mariusbild in der antiken Geschichtsschreibung*. Habelt, 1995.

Evans, R. J. *Gaius Marius. A Political Biography*. Pretoria: University of South Africa, 1994.

Sordi, M. "L'ultimo Mario e la sua immagine." In *L'immagine dell'uomo politico: vita pubblica e morale nell'antichità*, Contributi dell'Istituto di Storia antica 17 (Milan, 1991): 151–58, esp. 155.

Corbellini, C. "La presunta guerra tra Mario e Cinna e l'episodio dei Bardiei." *Aevum* 50 (1976): 154–156.

Sordi, M. "La legatio in Cappadocia di C. Mario nel 99–98." *RIL* 107 (1973): 375.

Andreotti, R. *Cajo Mario*. Milan: Tipografia Eugubina, Celuc, 1971.

Luce, T. J. "Marius and the Mithridatic Command." *Historia* 19 (1970): 161–94.

Carney, T. F. *A Biography of C. Marius*. Chicago: Argonaut Publishers, 1970.

Kikdahl, P. A. *Caius Marius*. New York: Twayne Publishers, 1968.

Badian, E. "Marius and the Nobles." *DUJ* XXXVI (1964): 141–54.

Oetheghem, J. (Van), *Caius Marius*. Bruxelles: Académie Royale de Belgique, 1964.

Carney, T. F. "The Flight and Exile of Marius." *Greece and Rome* VIII (1961): 98–121.

Badian, E. *Foreign Clientelae, 264–70 B.C.* Oxford: Clarendon, 1958.

Schur, W. "Das Zeitalter des Marius und Sulla." *Klio*, Beiheft XLVI (1942): 145.

Weynand, K. "Marius," C., *RE*, Supplement-band 6 (Stuttgart: J. B. Metzler, 1935): col. 1363–1425.

Momigliano, A. "Sullo svolgimento della battaglia dei Campi Raudii." *RFIC*, n. s., XIII, fasc. 3 (1935): 367–369.

Passerini, A. *Caio Mario come uomo politico*. Pavia: Amministrazione dell'*Atenaeum*, 1934. Reprinted in 1971 with the title: *Studi su Caio Mario*.

Clerc, M. *La Bataille d'Aix: études critiques sur la campagne de Caius Marius en Provence*. Marseille: Fontemoing, 1906.

Dervieu, C. *Campagne de C. Marius contre les Teutons*. Paris: L. Baudoin, 1891.

Memmius, Caius

Korolenkov, A. "The Murder of Gaius Memmius." *Politica Antica* X (2020): 37–44.

Metelli

Tatum, W. J. "Metellus Numidicus on Gaius Marius in his Exilic Epistolography." *SCI* XXXVII (2018): 99–109.

Simmons, D. W. "From Obscurity to Fame and Back Again: The Caecilii Metelli in the Roman Republic." MA thesis, Brigham Young University, 2011.

Morgan, M. G. "Lucius Cotta and Metellus: Roman campaigns in Illyria during the late second century." *Athenaeum* 59 (1971): 271–301.

Morgan, M. G. "The Roman Conquest of the Balearic Isles." *California Studies in Antiquity* 2 (1969): 217–231.

Ooteghem, J. Van, "Les Caecilii Metelli de la Règublique." *Mémoires de l'Académie Royale Belgique* T. 59 fasc. 1, Palais des Académies, Brussels (1967).

Gruen, E. S. "The Exile of Metellus Numidicus." *Latomus* 24 (1965): 576–580.

Morgan, M. G. "The Rise and Fall of the Caecilii Metelli, 284–46 B.C." PhD dissertation, University of Exeter, 1961.

Mithridates VI

Mayor, A. *Il re Veleno*. Milan: Einaudi, 2010.

Mayor, A. *Mithridathes*. Princeton: Princeton University Press, 2010.

Højte J. M., ed. *Mithridates VI and the Pontic Kingdom*. Aarhus: University of Aarhus Press, 2009.

Matyszak, P. *Mithridates the Great, Rome's Indomitable Enemy*. London: Pen & Sword, 2008.

Ramsey, J. T. "Mithridates, the Banner of Ch'ih-yu, and the Comet Coin." *HSCPh* 99 (1999): 197–253.

Ballesteros Pastor, L. *Mitridates Eupator, rey del Ponto*. Granada: Universidad de Granada, 1996.

Griffin, J. P. "Mithridates VI of Pontus, the First Experimental Toxicologist." *Adverse Drug Reactions & Acute Poisoning Reviews*, 14 (1995): 1–6.

Hind, J. G. F. "Mithridates." In *Cambridge Ancient History, IX, Last Age of the Roman Republic, 146–43 B.C.* (Cambridge: Cambridge University Press, 1994): 129–164.

McGing, B.C. *The Foreign Policy of Mithridates VI Eupator, King of Pontus*. Leiden: Brill, 1986.

Bengtson, H. Mithridates, *Herrschergestalten des Hellenismus*. München: Beck, 1975.

Duggan, A. *King of Pontus: The Story of Mithridates Eupator*. New York: Coward-McCann, 1959.

Duggan, A., *He Died Old: Mithridates Eupator, King of Pontus*. London: Faber & Faber, 1958.

Mastrocinque, A. (ed.), Appiano, *Le Guerre Mitridatiche*. Milan: Mondadori, 1999.

Norbanus Balbus, Caius

Ryan, F. X. "The Quaestorship of Norbanus." *Classica et Mediaevalia* 46 (1995): 145–150.

Badian, E. "The Silence of Norbanus. A note on provincial questors under the Republic." *AJPh.*, Vol. 104, n. 2 (1983): 156–171.

Badian, E. "Caepio and Norbanus: Notes on the Decade 100–90 B.C." *Historia* 6 (1957): 318–346.

Pompeius Magnus, Cnaeus

Hillman, T. P. "Pompeius' *imperium* in the War with Lepidus." *Klio*, Vol. 80, Issue 1 (1998): 91–110.

Haley, S. P. "The Five Wives of Pompey the Great." *Greece & Rome*, Vol. 32, Issue 1 (1985): 49–59.

Spann, P. O. "M. Perperna and Pompey's Spanish Expedition." *HAnt* 7 (1977): 45 ff.

Gruen, E. S. "Pompey and the Pisones." *CSCA* 1 (1968): 155–170.

Anderson, W. S. *Pompey, His Friends, and the Literature of the First Century B.C.* Berkeley: University of California Press, 1963.

Badian, E. "The Date of Pompey's First Triumph." *Hermes* 83 (1955): 107–118.

Pompeius Strabo, Cnaeus

Hillman, T. P. "The Serpent under the Flower. Pompeius Strabo and Q. Sertorius, 89–87 B.C." *SLLRH* VIII (1997): 85–115.

Mattingly, H. B. "The 'consilium' of Cn. Pompeius Strabo in 89 B.C." *Athenaeum* III (1975): 262–266.

Posidonius

Kidd, I. G. "Posidonius as Philosopher-Historian." *Philosophia togata*, vol. I: *Essays on Philosophy and Roman Society*, eds. Griffin, M. and Barnes, J. (Oxford: Oxford University Press, 1989).

Strasburger, H. "Poseidonios on Problems of the Roman-Empire." *JRS* 55, no. 1–2 (1965).

Rufus, Publius Rutilius

Gioachin, L. *M. Emilio Scauro et P. Rutilio Rufo: due autobiografie,* thesis, Università degli Studi di Padova, 2013.

Broughton, T. R. S. *Candidates Defeated in Roman Elections: Some Ancient Roman "Also-Rans."* Philadelphia: University of Pennsylvania Press, 1991. 47, nrs. 8, 16, 32.

Saturnius, Lucius Appuleius

Manuwald, G. *Fragmentary Republican Latin. Oratory.* Part. I, Loeb Classical Library 540, no. 64A. Cambridge, Mass. & London: Harvard University Press, 2019. 377–381.

Cavaggioni, F. *L. Apuleio Saturnino. Tribunus plebis seditiosus.* Venezia: Istituto Veneto di Scienze, Lettere ed Arti, 1998.

Beness, J. L. "The Urban Unpopularity of Lucius Appuleius Saturninus." *Antichton* 25 (1991): 33–62.

Badian, E. "The Death of Saturninus: Studies in Chronology and Prosopography" *Chiron* XIV (1984): 101–147.

Schneider, H. "Die politische Rolle der plebs urbana während der tribunate des L. Appuleius Saturninus." *AncSoc* 12/3 (1982–1983): 193–221.

Crawford, M. H. "Saturninus and the Italians." *CPh* 64 (1969): 37–38.

Seager, R. "The Date of Saturninus' Murder." *CR* n.s. XVII, I (1967): 9–10.

Scaurus, Marcus Aemilius

Candau, J. M. "Republican Rome." In *Political Autobiographies* (2011). 121–150; 133–139.

Lepore, A. *Marco Emilio Scauro princeps senatus.* Marina di Minturno: Caramanica Editore, 2005.

Tansey, P. "The Death of M. Aemilius Scaurus (cos. 115 B.C.)." *Historia* 52 (2003): 378–383.

Suerbaum, W. "M. Aemilius Scaurus." In *Die archaische Literatur. Von den Anfängen bis Sullas Tod* (*Handbuch der lateinischen Literarur der Antike, Band 1*). München: C. H. Beck, 2002.

Lewis, R. G. "Scope for Scaurus." *Athenaeum* 89 (2001): 345–354.

Bates, R. L. "Rex in Senatu: a political biography of M. Aemilius Scaurus." *PAPHS* 130 (1986): 251–288.

Flammini, G. "Marco Emilio Scauro e i suoi frammenti." *AFLN* 10 (1977): 37–56.

Hands, A. R. "Sallust and Dissimulatio." *JRS* 49 (1959): 56–60.

Fraccaro, P. "Athanaeum." *Opuscula*, vol. 3, parte II (Pavia, 1957).

Munzer, F. *Römische Adelsparteien und Adelsfamilien, J. B. Metzler, Stuttgart*. [translation: Roman Aristocratic Parties and Families.] Baltimore: The John Hopkins University Press, 1920.

Pais, E. "M. Emilio Scauro, i suoi processi e la sua autobiografia." In *Dalle guerre puniche a Cesare Augusto*, vol. 1. Torino, 1918. 91–167.

Bloch, G. "M. Aemilius Scaurus. Étude sur l'histoire des partis au VIle siècle de Rome." *Mélanges d'histoire ancienne* (1909).

Sertorius, Quintus

Konrad, C. F. *Plutarch's Sertorius: A Historical Commentary*. Chapel Hill: University of North Caroline Press, 1994.

Matyszak, P. *Sertorius and the Struggle for Spain*. Barnsley: Pen & Sword, 2013.

Katz, B. R. "Sertorius, Caesar, and Sallust." *AAntHung* 29 (1981): 285–313.

Murphy, W. J. "Quintus Sertorius: the reluctant rebel." MA thesis, Michigan State University, 1973.

Spann, P. O. *Quintus Sertorius and the Legacy of Sulla*. Fayetteville: University of Arkansas Press, 1987.

Scipio, Publius Cornelius Aemilianus

Beness, J. "Scipio Aemilianus and the Crisis of 129 B.C." *Historia* 54 (2005): 37–48.

Werner, R. "Die Gracchische Reformen und der Tod des Scipio Aemilianus." In *Beitrage zur Alten Geschichte und deren Nachelen, Festschrift Althein*, I. Berlin, 1969. 413–440.

Astin, A. E. *Scipio Aemilianus*. Oxford: Clarendon Press, 1967.

Renard, M. "L'Assassinat de Scipion," *RUB* XXXVII (1941): 483–498.

Martin Brown, R. "The Circle of Scipio—A Study of the Scipionic Circle," *CR* XLVIII (1934): 246.

Sulla Felix, Lucius Cornelius

Barca, N. *Sangue chiama sangue: terrore e atrocità nella Roma di Mario e Silla*. Roma: L'Erma di Bretschneider, 2016.

Brizzi, G. *Sylla*. Paris: Pluvia Nocturna, 2011. (Orig: *Silla*, 2004, preface of F. Hinard (Roma: RAI—ERI, 2011).

Christ, K. *Sulla, Eine römische Karriere*. München: C. H. Beck, 2011.

Fündling, J. *Sulla*. Darmstadt: WBG, 2010.

Santangelo, F. *Sulla, the Elites and the Empire: A Study of Roman Policies in Italy and the Greek East*. Leiden & Boston, MA: Brill, 2007.

Carcopino, J. *Silla o la monarchia mancata*. Milan: Bompiani, 2005. Appendix II, 175–187.

Keaveney, A. *Sulla: the last republican.* London & New York: Routledge, 2005.

Carcopino, J. *Silla.* Milan: Bompiani, 2000.

Letzner, W. *Lucius Cornelius Sulla: Versuch einer Biographie.* Münster: Lit, 2000.

Mastrocinque, A. "Studi sulle Guerre Mitridatiche." *Historia Einzelschriften* 124 (1999): 29–46.

Behr, H. *Die Selbstdarstellung Sullas: Ein aristokratischer Politiker zwischen persönlichem Führungsanspruch und Standessolidarität.* Frankfurt am Main: P. Lang, 1992.

Corey Brennan, T. "Sulla's Career in the Nineties: Some Reconsiderations." *Chiron* 22 (1992): 103–158.

Arnaud, Sylla, P. "Tigrane et le Parthes. Un nouveau document pour la datation de la propréture de Sylla: Sidoine Apollinaire, Paneg. Aviti, v 79–82." *REA* 93 (1991): 55–64.

Keaveney, A. *Sulla the last republican.* London: Croom Helm, 1986.

Hinard, F. *Silla.* Roma: Salerno Editrice, 1990 (orig. *Sylla.* Paris: Fayard, 1985).

Keaveney, A. "Sulla, Sulpicius and Caesar Strabo." *Latomus* 38 (1979): 451 ff.

Sumner, G. V. "Sulla's career in the nineties." *Athenaeum* 56 (1978): 395–396.

Sherwin-White, A. N. "Ariobarzanes, Mithridates, and Sulla." *CQ* n.s. 27 (1977): 173–183.

Garton, G. "Sulla and the Theatre." *The Phoenix,* (summer 1964): 137–156.

Carney, T. F. "The Death of Sulla." *Acta Classica* 4 (1961): 64–79.

E. Cavaignac. "Un songe de Sylla." *Aesculape* 31 (1959): 180 ff.

Volkmann, H. *Sullas Marsch auf Rom. Der Verfall der Römischen Republik.* Munich: WBG, 1958.

Valgiglio, E. *Vita di Silla, Vita di Silla.* Turin: S. Lattes e C., 1954.

Carcopino, J. *Sylla ou la monarchie manquée.* Paris: L'Artisan du Livre, 1947.

Lanzani, C. "Silla e Pompeo. La spedizione di Sicilia e d'Africa." *Historia* (1933): 343–362.

Baker, G. P. *Sulla the fortunate: the great dictator: being an essay on politics in the form of a historical biography.* London: J. Murray, 1927.

Daudet, L. *Sylla et son destin: récit de jadis et de toujours.* Paris: E. Flammarion, 1922.

Plutarch. *Lives, Volume IV: Alcibiades and Coriolanus. Lysander and Sulla.* Translated by Bernadotte Perrin. Cambridge, MA: Harvard University Press, 1916.

Spartacus

Le Bohec, Y. *Spartaco, signore della guerra.* Rome: Carocci, 2018.

Brizzi, G. *Ribelli contro Roma. Gli schiavi, Spartaco, l'altra Italia.* Bologna: Il Mulino, 2017.

Strauss, B. *La Guerra di Spartaco.* Rome & Bari: Laterza, 2009.

Sulpicius Rufus, Publius

Powell, J. "The Tribune Sulpicius." *Historia* XXXIX (1990): 446–460.

Terentius

Piazzi L., and Pepe, L., "Terenzio Commedie." In *I Classici Collezione.* Milan: Mondadori, 2007.

Indexes

Personal Names

Aeneas, 94, 147, 148, 171
Anchises, 147, 148, 171
Andriscus, 11
Apollo, xx, 81
Appius Claudius Caecus, 61, 94
Appius Claudius Pulcher, 6, 14, 15, 16, 31, 32, 48, 120, 128, 135, 138
Appius (or Aulus) Nonius, 85, 86, 89
Apollonius Molon, 155
Arcathias (or Ariarathes IX), 110
Archelaus, 110, 158, 160
Ariobarzanes I, 160, 198
Aristion, 110, 159
Aristonicus of *Pergamon*, 183, 188
Aristotle, 160, 161, 179
Aulus Postumius Albinus, 88
Aurelia Cotta, 147, 149
Aurelia Orestilla, 172
Arvina, 127, 128
Asinius (Herius Asinius), 100, 104
Athena Polyades, 159
Attalus III, 10, 28, 183
Attius Clausus, 7
Bacchus, 38
Belliena, 171
Bellona, 119, 167
Bocchus, 71, 72
Caecilia Metella, daughter of Metellus Macedonicus, 11, 118
Caecilia Metella Calva, 11, 118
Caecilia Metella Dalmatica, 158
Caecilii Metelli, 12, 48, 71, 111, 118, 121, 174, 178, 195
Caesar Strabo (*see also* Caius Julius Caesar Strabo Vopiscus), 112, 137, 151, 186, 198
Caius Annius Luscus, 168
Caius Aurelius Cotta, 101

Caius Atilius Serranus, 142
Caius Caelius, 136
Caius Blossius of *Cumae*, 6, 19, 31, 189
Caius Burrienus, 169
Caius Caecilius Metellus Caprarius, 11, 45, 82
Caius Carrinas, 164, 169
Caius Claudius Pulcher(?), 94
Caius Cassius Longinus, 96
Caius Fannius, 51
Caius Flavius Fimbria, 68, 136, 152, 157
Caius Julius Caesar, vi
Caius Julius Caesar Octavianus, xlvii
Caius Julius Caesar Strabo Vopiscus, 112, 137, 151, 186, 198
Caius Laelius Sapiens, 30, 42, 44, 45
Caius Licinius Stolo, 16
Caius Livius Drusus, 49
Caius Maecenas, 168
Caius Marcius Censorinus, 138, 139, 164, 168, 169
Caius Marius, xvii, xix, 69, 93, 104–105, 110, 123, 149, 171, 178, 183–184, 194
Caius Marius the Younger, 105, 123, 125, 161, 163–166, 168, 180
Caius Memmius, 68, 69, 88–89, 194
Caius Milonius, 128–129, 133, 138
Caius Mummius, 121
Caius Nemetorius, 142
Caius Norbanus Balbus, 73, 112, 123, 195
Caius Octavius, 12, 112–113, 125, 127–128, 130, 133, 134, 136–139, 168
Caius Paulus Mutilus, 99, 100, 102–103, 107, 135–136, 142
Caius Pontidius, 100
Caius Saufeius, 90
Caius Sempronius Gracchus, xviii, xix, xxxiv, xlvii, 14, 23, 31–32, 43, 48, 67, 79, 85, 94, 183
Caius Sergius Orata, 128

Caius Servilius Augur, 87–88, 118
Caius Servilius Glaucia, xix, 84–85, 88–89, 90–91, 191
Caius Servilius Vatia, 11
Caius Titus Didius, xvi, 74, 81, 127
Caius Toranius, 170
Caius Valerius Flaccus, 168
Caius Vidacilius, 100, 104–105
Catulus Caesar (Quintus Lutatius Catulus Caesar), 84
Ceres, 29, 187, 193
Cnaeus Pompeius Strabo, xviii, 95, 101–102, 106, 172
Cnaeus Domitius Ahenobarbus, 50, 87, 97, 152
Cnaeus Mallius Maximus, 75–77, 81
Cnaeus Octavius, 112, 125, 127, 130, 168
Cnaeus Papirius Carbo, xvii, 17, 51, 75, 123, 161, 169
Caius Papirius Carbo Arvina, 62, 127
Cnaeus Pompeius (*Pompeius Magnus*), 102, 135, 156, 172
Cnaeus Pompeius Strabo, xviii, 95, 101–102, 106, 132, 172, 180
Cnaeus Titinius, 168
Concordia, goddess, 61, 63
Copillus, 76
Cornelia Africana Minor, 2, 3, 4, 52, 60, 73, 156, 190
Decimus Junius Brutus Callaicus, 55
Decimus Julius Silanus, 95
Drausus, 48
Drusus (Marcus Livius Drusus), xvii, 48–50, 94–98, 100, 135, 178
Enyo, 167
Erastus, 160–161
Fides, goddess, 22, 185
Flora, goddess, 158
Gracchi, brothers, xviii, xix, xxxiv, xlvii, 2, 4, 13, 16, 27, 29, 43, 53, 59–63, 72, 74, 91, 156, 178, 185–188, 190–192
Granius, 176
Gratidia, 128–172
Herius Asinius (Asinius), 100, 104
Homonoia, 61
Hermias, 161
Jugurtha, 71–72, 75, 103, 124, 183
Julia Major, 70, 130, 149, 151
Julia Minor, 149

Juno, xliii, xliv
Juno Sospita, 12
Julius Obsequens, 19
Junia Prima, 95
Junia Secunda, 95
Junia Tertia, or Tertulla, 96
Lares Compitales, divinities, xv, 63
Livia Drusa, 94, 95, 105
Lucius Acilius Glabrio, 102
Lucius Aelius Stilo Praeconinus, 101
Lucius Aemilius Paulus, 1
Lucius Aemilius Paullus Macedonicus, 4
Lucius Aemilius Scaurus, 95
Lucius Antistius Reginus, 74
Lucius Appuleius Saturninus, xvi, xxxiv, 61, 69, 72–78, 80–89, 90–91, 93, 95, 111–112, 125, 156, 178, 184, 185, 190–191, 196
Lucius Aurelius Cotta, 71, 74, 81
Lucius Basilius, 121–122
Lucius Caecilius Metellus Calvus, 11
Lucius Caecilius Metellus Dalmaticus, 11, 71, 118
Lucius Caecilius Metellus Diadematus, 11, 45
Lucius Cluentius, 107
Lucius Cornelius Scipio Barbatus, 46
Lucius Cornelius Cinna, 105, 112, 125, 127, 168, 180, 184
Lucius Cornelius Chrysogonus, 143, 172
Lucius Cornelius Merula, 114, 137, 144
Lucius Cornelius Scipio Asiaticus, 3, 102, 163, 167, 168–169
Lucius Cornelius Sulla, xvi, xix, xxxiv, xl, xlii, xlvi, 71, 72, 76, 90–91, 95, 101, 104, 105, 107, 110–112, 114, 115–125, 127–128, 130, 134, 138, 141, 143, 150, 156–159, 160–161, 163–169, 170–172, 173–176, 178–179, 180–181, 184–187, 189, 191–192, 194, 197–198
Lucius Cotta, 195
Lucius Decimius, 123
Lucius Equitius, 73, 74, 90, 186, 191
Lucius Hirtuleius, 168
Lucius Insteius, 168
Lucius Julius Caesar, xviii, 100, 102, 137, 151
Lucius Junius Brutus, 121
Lucius Junius Brutus Damasippus, 164, 169
Lucius Licinius Lucullus, 12, 87–88, 117–118, 120, 172, 186, 193

Lucius Marcius Philippus, l, 94, 96–97, 138
Lucius Mummius Achaicus, 101, 159
Lucius Opimius, 51, 78, 79
Lucius Porcius Cato, 105
Lucius Postumius, 107
Lucius Rufus, 22
Lucius Septimuleius, 59
Lucius Sergius Catilina, 171–172, 180, 188
Lucius Sergius Silus, 171
Lucius Sextius Lateranus, 16
Lucius Valerius Flaccus, son of Marcus, 55
Lucius Valerius Flaccus, consul in 131 BC,
   censor in 97 BC, 85, 93
Lucius Valerius Flaccus, son of the
   homonymous consul of 131 BC, consul in
   turn in 86 BC, 85
Lucius Villius Annalis, 170
Mamercus Aemilius Lepidus Livianus, 98,
   135, 143–144
Manius Aquillius, 86
Marcus Aemilius Lepidus, 96, 168, 170, 175,
   184
Marcus Aemilius Scaurus, 68, 101, 143, 197
Marcus Antonius Orator, 88, 96, 101, 113,
   128, 145
Marcus Antonius Gnipho, 150
Marcus Antonius Gratidianus, 172
Marcus Baebius, 74–74, 142
Marcus Claudius Marcellus, l, 102
Marcus Fulvius Flaccus, 20, 25, 43, 47, 79,
   184
Marcus Junius Brutus, 7, 95, 121, 123, 131,
   169
Marcus Lamponius, 100, 164
Marcus Laetorius, 123
Marcus Licinius Crassus, 63, 191
Marcus Livius Drusus (see also Drusus), xvii,
   48–50, 94–98, 100, 135, 178, 184, 191
Marcus Livius Drusus Claudianus, 94
Marcus Marius Gratidianus, 128, 169
Marcus Minucius Rufus, 13, 15, 51–52
Marcus Octavius, 12–13, 21, 30, 193
Marcus Perperna, 101, 138, 169, 196
Marcus Plautius Hypsaeus, 47, 79
Marcus Perperna Veiento, 169
Marcus Plautius Silvanus, xvii, 135
Marcus Pletorius, 142
Marcus Porcius Cato the Censor, or the Elder,
   3, 150, 189

Marcus Porcius Cato Salonianus, 95, 105
Marcus Porcius Cato Uticensis, 3, 95, 180
Marcus Popillius Laenas, 30
Marcus Terentius Varro, 99
Marcus Terentius Varro Lucullus, 118, 148,
   157
Marcus Tullius Cicero, l, 69, 73, 82, 150,
   156–157, 172, 174, 180, 189–190
Marcus Vergilius, 128–129, 138
Marcus Valerius Corvinus, 84
Marius Egnatius, 103
Martha, 130
Metella Dalmatica (Caecilia Metella
   Dalmatica), 158
Metelli, see Caecilii Metelli
Metellus Macedonicus, 10–11, 14, 45
Metrobius, 181
Metrophanes, 110
Mithridates II of Parthia, 104
Mithridates VI of Pontus (Mithridates VI
   Eupator Dionysus), xix, 82–83, 95, 108–
   110, 130, 159–160, 179, 183–184, 195
Neleus, 161
Nemesis, goddess, 167
Nicomedes IV, 160
Numa Pompilius, xxviii, 8, 153
Octavian (Caius Publius Caesar Octavianus),
   xlvii
Oxyntas, 103
Perseus, 11
Philocrates, 58–59
Polybius, 156
Pomponius, 58
Pontius Telesinus, 164
Posidonius, 155, 196
Postumius, commander, 103
Postumius, foreteller, 107, 119
Ptolemy VIII Euergetes II Tryphon, 3
Publius Albinovanus, 123
Publius Claudius Pulcher, 180
Publius Cornelius Cethegus, 123–124
Publius Cornelius Scipio, son of Scipio
   Africanus Major, 41, 183
Publius Cornelius Scipio Aemilianus, xxxiii,
   4, 5, 14–15, 30, 41–46, 49, 62, 74, 156,
   178, 183, 197
Publius Cornelius Scipio Africanus Major, 3, 4
Publius Cornelius Scipio Nasica Serapio, 11,
   20, 21–23, 25–29, 31, 185

Publius Lentulus, 142

Publius Mucius Scaevola Augur, 6–7, 13, 20–21, 23, 25–27, 30–31, 123, 157

Publius Rupilius, 30

Publius Rutilius Rufus, 184, 101

Publius Servilius, *praetor pellegrinus*, 121

Publius Servilius Vatia Isauricus, 95, 135

Publius Mettius, 89

Publius Satyreius, 22

Publius Sulpicius Rufus, xix, 109, 112–116, 118, 120–121, 123–124, 134, 179, 186–187, 198

Publius Terentius Afer, 5, 198

Publius Vettius Scato, 100, 102, 104

Quintus Antyllius, 53–54

Quintus Bruttius Sura, 159–160

Quintus Caecilius, brother-in-law of Catiline, 172

Quintus Caecilius Metellus Balearicus, 11–12, 45

Quintus Caecilius Metellus Numidicus, 11, 71–74, 80, 82, 86, 88, 111, 118, 195

Quintus Caecilius Metellus Pius, 86, 90, 111, 128, 135–138, 153, 163

Quintus Cornelius Lentulus, 69

Quintus Fabius Maximus Allobrogicus, 45, 51

Quintus Granius and his brother Cnaeus, 123

Quintus Lucretius Afella, 163–164

Quintus Lutatius Catulus, 83–84, 94, 104, 137, 143, 149, 150, 166, 173, 189

Quintus Lutatius Catulus Capitolinus, 173, 175

Quintus Lutatius Catulus Caesar, 84

Quintus Mucius Scaevola Pontifex, xvii, 6, 93–94, 96, 114, 153, 157

Quintus Mummius, 13, 18–20

Quintus Pompeius (consul of 141), 102

Quintus Pompeius Rufus (consul of 88), 110–111, 134

Quintus Pompeius Rufus, son of the consul with the same name, 115, 135

Quintus Poppaedius Silo, 97–100, 104–105, 135

Quintus Rubrius Varro, 123

Quintus Sertorius, 75–76, 127–131, 133, 138, 146, 157, 161, 168–169, 196–197

Quintus Servilius Caepio, xix, 75, 86, 94–95, 98, 100, 112

Quintus Varius Severus Hybrida Sucronensis, xx, 95, 98, 101, 106, 139, 152, 172

Quintus Valerius Soranus, 169

Romulus, xxiv, xxvii, xliv, xlvi, 13, 48, 148

Rubrius, tribune of the plebs, xviii, 18, 49

Sempronia, sister of Tiberius and Caius Gracchus, xxxiv, 3, 43, 45, 60–61, 74

Servilia Caepio, 87, 94, 95, 187

Servius Tullius, xl, 13

Sextus Julius Caesar, 84, 95, 100, 149, 151

Sextus Lucilius, 124, 141

Sextus Roscius Amerinus, 174

Sempronius Asellio, 18

Sergestus, 171

Servilius Augur (Caius Servilius Augur), 87–88, 118

Spartacus, 198

Spurius Postumius Albinus, 89

Tarquinius Priscus, 8

Tarquinius Superbus, xxvii, xliv

Tiberius Sempronius Gracchus, xviii, xix, xxxiv, xlvii, 2–4, 6, 15, 17–19, 26–27, 28, 31, 47–48, 52, 55, 60, 73–74, 80, 85, 128, 177–178, 183, 185–187, 190, 193

Titus Annius Luscus Rufus, 14

Titus Didius (Caius Titus Didius), xvi, 74, 81, 127

Titus Labienus, 90

Titus Lafrenius, 100, 104, 105

Titus Pomponius Atticus, 157

Tryphon, royal name of King Salvus, 67

Tullius Hostilius, xlii

Valerius, military commander, 132

Valerius Maximus, author, 73, 86

Place Names in Rome

Antemnae, hill, 164

Apollo's temple, 174

Area Capitolina, xli, xliii, xliv, 18–20, 53, 56, 90

Area Volcani, 61

Arx, one of the two summits of the Capitoline Hill, xliii, 61

Aventine, hill, xxxiv, xxxix, xl, 7, 47, 56–59, 60, 62, 66, 79, 115, 183

Bellona, temple, 90, 158, 166, 173

Caelian, hill xxxix, 7

Campus Martius, xli, 11, 67, 84, 89–90, 97, 111, 123, 131–133, 146, 149, 158, 166, 169

Campus Esquilinus, cemetery, xl

Capitoline, hill, xxxix, xl, xli, xliii, 27, 31, 56, 59, 61, 115, 183

Capitoline Triad, temple, xliii

Capitolium, one of the two summits of the Capitoline Hill, xliii,

Ceres, Libera et Liberus, temple, 56

Circus Flaminius, 11, 158

Circus Maximus, xl, 115

Clivus Capitolinus, street, 54, 90

Clivus Publicius, 58

Concordia, temple, xliii

Curia Hostilia, official seat of the Senate, xiii, xli, xlii, 54–55, 80, 90–91, 166

Diana, temple, 58

Dioscuri, temple, xlii, xliii

Emporium, river port, 56, 66

Esquiline, hill, xxxix, xli, 121

Fagutal, a part of the Esquiline Hill, xl

Fides, temple, xliii, 20, 22

Forum Boarium, xl, 56, 57, 66

Fulvia-Aemilia, basilica, xlii

Horrea Sulpicia, 66

Janiculum, hill, xxxix, 58, 131, 133, 137–138, 173

Juno Moneta, temple, xliii

Jupiter Feretrius, temple, xliii

Jupiter Optimus Maximus, temple, xliii, xliv, 19, 22, 53, 82, 90, 144, 176

Iacus Servilius, a fountain near the Tribune of the Orators, 169

Mars Ultor, temple, xliii

Opimia, basilica, xlii

Palatine, hill, xxxix, xl, xli, 51, 57, 115, 148, 150

Palatium, one of the two summits of Capitoline Hill, 42, 56, 142–143

Pons Aemilius, 66, 169

Pons Sublicius, 58, 173

Porcia, basilica, xli, xlii

Porta Capena, gate, 45–46, 115, 122

Porta Collina, gate, xxxix, 122, 132, 138, 157, 164, 172, 180, 184

Porta Esquilina, gate, xxxix, 122

Porta Trigemina, 52, 58

Porticus Aemilia, 66

Porticus Metelli, 11, 61

Quirinal, hill, xxxix, xl, xli, 136

Roma Quadrata, xxvii, xliv, 48, 148

Sacra Via, street, xlii, xliii, 114

Saturn, temple, xliii

Scalae Gemoniae, 61

Sempronia, basilica, xlii, 3, 54, 90

Servian Walls, xxxix, xliii, 58, 65, 122, 164

Subura, neighborhood, xl

Sulla's *curia*, xiii

Testaccio, 66

Tiber, river, xxvi, 23, 59, 65–66, 124, 131, 133, 148, 156–157, 169

Tiber Island, 66

Tiberinus, river port, 66

Tomb of the Scipios, 46

Trans Tiberim (Trastevere), suburb, 65

Vatican Plain, 131

Velabrum, valley and neighborhood, xl

Velian, hill, xli

Venus Libitina, temple, xl

Vesta, sanctuary, xliii

Via Appia, 115–116, 163

Vicus Tuscus, street, xl

Villa Publica, 117, 158, 165–166, 186

Viminal, hill and urban district, xl, xli, xxxix, 136

Vinarius, river port, 66

Geographical Names

Abella (ancient town near Nola, Campania), 136

Abellinum (city of Avellino, Campania), 136

Abruzzo (a particular area in central Italy), 97

Acerrae (Acerra, Campania), 97

ad Pictas (Valle Fredda, near Labico, Lazio), 121, 187

Aeclanum (Mirabella Eclano, near Avellino, Campania), 107

Aenaria (submerged site in the sea of Ischia, Campania), 123–124

Aesernia (Isernia, Campania), 102–104, 128, 135

Ager Romanus (a particular zone in Lazio), 116

Agrigentum (Agrigento, Sicilia), 88

Alba Fucens (archaeological site in Lazio),101, 129

Alba Longa (site of uncertain location, in any case in Lazio, near Rome; perhaps Castel Gandolfo), 7, 147–149, 171

Alban Hills (a particular zone in Lazio), 37, 148

Alexandria, battle, xlvii

Alsium (Aliso, Lazio), 131

Apulia (ancient name of modern Puglia), 39–40, 105, 107

Aquae Sextiae (Aix-en-Provence, France), 83, 130

Aquileia (Friuli Venezia Giulia, northern Italy), 134, 136

Arausium (Orange, France), battlefield, 75–77, 81, 87, 95

Argentario, monte (a promontory in Lazio), 129

Ariminum (Rimini, Emilia Romagna, northern Italy), 48, 136

Armenia, country in the West Asia, 104

Assos, ancient coastal city in the Troad (Turkey), 161

Athens (Greece), xliii, 109–110, 159–161, 179, 184

Asculum Picenum (Ascoli Piceno, Marche), 100

Basilicata (a particular area in southern Italy), 40, 88, 107

Beneventum (Benevento, Campania), 106

Bithynia, a Roman province in Anatolia (Turkey), 109, 160

Bovianum (Bojano near Campobasso, Molise, southern Italy), 106

Brundisium (Brindisi, Puglia), 163

Calabria (a particular area in southern Italy), 39

Cameria, or *Camerta* (Cameria, Lazio), 79

Campania (a particular area in southern Italy), xxvi, 60, 65, 87, 100, 102–103, 106–107, 156, 163, 170, 175, 184

Cannae (Canne, Puglia), 103, 185

Canusium (Canosa, Puglia), 103

Capo Miseno (a promontory in Campania), 60, 156

Cappadocia, a Roman province in Anatolia (Turkey), 104, 109, 119, 160, 194

Capua (Santa Maria Capua Vetere, Campania), 102, 120, 136, 163

Caralis (Cagliari, Sardinia), 129

Carthago (Carthage, Tunisia), xviii, xxxiii, 3–4, 49–50, 124, 178, 183

Carthago Nova (Cartagena, Spain), 161

Cercina (Kerkennah Islands, Tunisia), 91, 124–125, 129

Chaeronea, battle of—(Greece), 160

Commagene, ancient kingdom in Anatolia (Turkey), 130

Corfinium (Corfinio, Abruzzo, Italy), 99

Corsica, island (France), 78, 129

Cilicia, Roman province in Anatolia (Turkey), 88, 104, 109

Cirta (Costantina, Algeria), 124

Corinthus (Latin name of the modern Corinth, Peloponnesus, Greece), 101, 159

Cumae (Cuma, Campania), 6, 31, 175, 188

Delphi, ancient sanctuary (Phocis, Greece), 81, 160

Delos, island (Cyclades, Greece), 109–110, 158, 179

Dodona, ancient sanctuary (Dodoni, Epirus, Greece), 160

Etruria (ancient name of Toscana), 6, 98, 106, 130–131

Euphrates, river (Turkey–Syria–Iraq), 104

Fanum Fortunae (Fano, Marche), 48, 136

Firmum Picenum (Fermo, Marche), 73

Fregellae (archaeological site in Lazio), 78, 183

Fucino, lake (Umbria), 100

Gallaecia (a particular area of Spain), xiv, 55

Gallia Cisalpina (Roman name of northern Italy), xvii, xviii, 47, 76, 78, 84, 86, 106, 108, 110, 127–128, 132, 134–136, 138, 163

Gallia Narbonensis (ancient name of a Roman province in France), 75, 84

Gallia Transalpina (Roman name of France, Belgium, and the Netherlands), 75–76, 130–131

Gerunium (ancient town in Campania), 106

Gole della Melfa (a particular zone of Lazio), 136

Grumentum (Grumento Nova-Potenza, Basilicata, southern Italy), 103

Heraclea (Scanzano Jonico, Basilicata, southern Italy), 88

Herculaneum (Ercolano, Campania), 103

Hispania (ancient name of Spain and Portugal), 4–5, 14, 127, 131, 168

Hispania Citerior (a Roman province in Spain), 3, 10, 30, 75, 87, 168

Hispania Ulterior (a Roman province in Spain), xiv, 3, 75, 161, 168

Inregillum, or *Regillum* (unknown site, probably in Lazio), 7

Insulae Fortunatae (Canary Islands, Spain), 168

Ischia (island, Gulf of Naples, Campania), 60, 123

Italia propria (Italian peninsula below the ideal line between the mouth of Magra River in Toscana and that of the Aesinus River in the Marche), xv, xvii, 108

Italica (or *Corfinium*, now Corfinio, Marche), 99, 106

Judea, kingdom of, 130

Lake Fucino, battle of (Umbria), 104

Lake Lucrine (Campania), 128

Latium (Roman name of Lazio), xlii, 7–8, 12, 40, 48, 70, 124, 128, 136, 147–148, 163, 170

Lavinium (Pratica di Mare, near Pomezia, Lazio), 124, 138, 148

Lazio (a particular area of central Italy), 40

Leucopetra, battle (Greece), 101

Lilybaeum, city (Marsala, Sicily), 129

Liris River (Lazio), 104

Lusitania (ancient name of Portugal), 55

Magna Graecia (ancient name of a particular area in southern Italy), xv, xxi, 38, 40

Magnesia, battle of—, 3

Magra, river (Toscana), xv

Mahdia, shipwreck, 161

Marche (a particular area of central Italy), xv, 40, 48, 73, 95

Massilia (Marseille, France), xv, 40, 48, 73, 95

Mauretania (ancient name of Mauritania), 63, 168, 71

Megàle Hellàs (*see also Magna Graecia*), xxi

Melitene (Malatya, Turkey), 176

Milonia (Ortona dei Marsi, Abruzzo), 97

Minervum (ancient town in Campania), 103

Montecristo (an island in the Tyrrhenian Sea and part of the Tuscan Archipelago in Italy), 129

Mytilene/Lesbos, island (Greece), 110

Nabataean Kingdom (Giordania), 130

Neapolis (Napoli, Campania), 107

Narenta river (Croatia, and Bosnia and Herzegovina), 131

Norba (Norma, Lazio), 170

Nuceria Alfaterna (Nocera, Campania), 103

Numantia (ancient city-fortress (Spain), xxxiv, 5, 30, 178, 183

Nuvla (Nola, Campania), 103, 107–108, 110, 115, 117, 119, 128–129, 135–136, 163, 170

Ostia, seaport (Ostia, Lazio), xxvi, 52, 65–66, 124, 131–133

Palmyra (Syria), 130

Pireaus, seaport (Greece), 158

Pisaurum (Pesaro, Marche), 48, 136

Pithekoussai, island (Ischia, Gulf of Naples, Campania), 123

Placentia (Piacenza, Emilia-Romagna), 134, 136

Politorium (an ancient city of uncertain location in Lazio), 7

Pompeii (Pompei, Campania), 95, 103

Pontus, kingdom of (Turkey), 82, 108–109, 179, 184, 195

Po Valley (a particular area in northern Italy), 83

Praeneste (Palestrina, Lazio), 12, 18, 48, 60, 163–165

Procida, island (Gulf of Naples, Campania), 60

Protopachium, battle (ancient fortress, Turkey), 109

Puglia (a particular area of southern Italy), 39, 103

Puteolis (Pozzuoli, Campania), xxvi, 65–66, 123

Raudine Plain, battle (unknown site in the Po Valley), 79, 83–84, 104

Rhone Valley (France), 75

Rusicade, ancient seaport (Algeria), 124

Sacriportus (Segni, Lazio), 163

Salapia (archaeological site in Puglia), 103

Salernum (Salerno, Campania), 103

Sardinia, island (Italy), 18, 60, 65, 129, 180

Scepsis (Kurşuntepe, Turkey), 160

Sicily, island (Italy), xix, xxi, 29, 52, 65, 67–68, 78, 83, 87, 118, 123–124, 129, 148, 171, 180

Silan Forest (Sila, Calabria), 39

Sinope (Sinop, Turkey), 109

Syracusae (Siracusa, Sicily), 67
Talamo (Talamone, Toscana), 129–130
Teanum Sicidinum (Teano, Campania), 104, 163
Tifata, mount (near Capua, Campania), 163
Tolenus, river, battle (Toleno, Lazio), 104
Toleria (Valmontone, Lazio), 116
Tolosa (Toulouse, France), 75–76, 78, 81–82, 100
Tusculum (Tuscolo, Lazio), 116
Triokala (Caltabellotta, Sicily), 88
Umbria (a particular area in central Italy), 40, 75, 98, 132
Venusia (Venosa, Puglia), 103, 107, 135
Venafrum (Venafro, Campania), 102
Via Aemilia (ancient road in northern Italy), 136
Via Aurelia (ancient road in central Italy), 131
Via Flaminia (ancient road in central Italy), 136
Via Latina (ancient road in central-southern Italy), 116, 120–121, 128, 187
Via Tiburtina Valeria (ancient road in central Italy), 97

Roman Laws

lex Acilia de repetundis (or *lex Acilia repetundarum*), xvi, 85
lex Appuleia de maiestate minuta, xvi, 77–78
lex Appuleia de quaestio extraordinaria istituenda, xvi, 77
lex Caecilia Didia de modo legum promulgandarum, xvi, 116, 138
lex curiata de imperio, xvi, xlvii
lex Domitia de sacerdotiis, xvi, 152–153
lex Genucia de magistratibus, xvii, 16
lex Julia de civitate latinis et sociis danda, xvii, 105, 107
lex Licinia Mucia de civibus redigundis, xvii, 93
lex Livia iudiciaria, xvii, 94
lex Maria de suffragiis ferendis, xvii, 71
lex Plautia-Papiria de civitate sociis danda, xvii, 107
lex Pompeia de Transpadanis, xviii, 132
lex provinciae Asiae, xviii, 111
lex Rubria de colonia Carthaginem deducenda, xviii, 49, 52
lex Sempronia agraria, xviii
lex Sempronia de potestate tribunicia M. Octavio abroganda, xviii, 13
lex Sempronia (*C. Gracchi*) *de provincia Asia a censoribus locanda*, xviii
lex Sempronia frumentaria, xix, 52, 67, 86
lex Sempronia iudiciaria, xvii
lex Sempronia Ti. Gracchi agrarian secunda, xix
lex Servilia Caepio de repetundis, xix, 85
lex Servilia Glaucia de repetundis, xix, 85
lex Sulpicia de bello mithridatico C. Mario decernendo, xix, 116, 118, 128
lex Valeria de sacrando cum bonis capite eius qui regni occupandi consilium inisset, xix, 26, 27
lex Varia de maiestate, xx, 101, 112, 114, 137, 139
lex Villia annalis, xx, 15–17, 85